IMMERSIVE GAMEPLAY

IMMERSIVE GAMEPLAY

Essays on Participatory Media and Role-Playing

Edited by Evan Torner *and*
William J. White

Foreword by Zach Waggoner

McFarland & Company, Inc., Publishers
Jefferson, North Carolina, and London

This edition corrects the order of names of the authors of the essay "Role-Playing Communities, Cultures of Play and the Discourse of Immersion" (page 71).

LIBRARY OF CONGRESS CATALOGUING-IN-PUBLICATION DATA

Immersive gameplay : essays on participatory media and role-playing /
   edited by Evan Torner and William J. White ; foreword by Zach
   Waggoner.
      p.   cm.
   Includes bibliographical references and index.

   ISBN 978-0-7864-6834-8
   softcover: acid free paper ∞

   1. Fantasy games — Social aspects.   2. Role playing — Social
aspects.   3. Mass media — Social aspects.   I. Torner, Evan.
II. White, William J., 1966–
GV1202.F35166 2012
793.92 — dc23   2012018314

BRITISH LIBRARY CATALOGUING DATA ARE AVAILABLE

Cover images © 2012 Dark Geometry Studios

Manufactured in the United States of America

*McFarland & Company, Inc., Publishers
   Box 611, Jefferson, North Carolina 28640
   www.mcfarlandpub.com*

To Kat, to my parents, and to the
far-flung indie game community.
—E.T.

To my brother Mel, in honor
of years of gaming together.
—W.J.W.

Acknowledgments

The editors would like to thank the Northeast Modern Language Association (NeMLA) for accepting the panel at which much of the work contained in these pages was originally presented, as well as for providing a travel stipend for our colleague Markus Montola. The opportunity for trans–Atlantic collaboration and collegiality that was thereby enabled was instrumental in bringing this project to fruition.

The editors additionally owe a debt of gratitude to Zach Waggoner for his participation in the project; he responded to our entreaties with verve and intelligence. Finally, Evan Torner is grateful to the Department of German and Scandinavian Studies at the University of Massachusetts Amherst for partially subsidizing his travel to the aforementioned NeMLA conference.

Table of Contents

Foreword by Zach Waggoner

Immersion. I remember the first time I encountered this word in an academic context. I was conducting research for my dissertation on identity construction in video-role-playing games. The text? Janet Murray's *Hamlet on the Holodeck: The Future of Narrative in Cyberspace*. Over the years, I've reread and discussed her text with students in my videogame theory courses many times; I remain astonished by how prescient, how remarkably **present** Murray's ruminations are today for new media scholars, fifteen years after the fact. Murray's definition of immersion in that text remains branded in my subconscious:

> Immersion is a metaphorical term, derived from the physical experience of being submerged in water. We seek the same feeling from a psychologically immersive experience that we do from a plunge in the ocean or swimming pool: the sensation of being surrounded by a completely other reality, [...] that takes over all of our attention, our whole perceptual apparatus. We enjoy the movement out of our familiar world, the feeling of alertness that comes from being in this new place, and the delight that comes from learning to move within it. In a participatory medium, immersion implies learning to swim, to do the things that the new environment makes possible [pages 98–99].

For a young videogame theorist like myself, the concept of immersion was fascinating. Of course, I wasn't the only person who became enamored with the term. In the first decade of the 21st century, "immersion" became a trendy buzzword, used by scholars, journalists, and the masses alike to superficially and generically explain the ever-growing appeal of videogames and other new media. As a result, "immersion" lost its theoretical and terminological potency. It sunk into the abyss of over-used jargon.

Immersive Gameplay helps dredge it back up. The essays here contribute to the reclamation of "immersion" in scholarly inquiry, delving into topics from larping to the archetypes of reality television. As a scholar who fixates primarily on videogame theoretical terminology, I was pleased to encounter terms and concepts ("agentic imagination" and "bleed," to name but two) that resonate with my own digital media studies. Of course, my realization is part of the point of *Immersive Gameplay*: the studies of play, of games, and of "immersion" are conversations that require a wide range of perspectives, from digital to tabletop to pop culture performativity. In *Hamlet on the Holodeck*, Murray proved she knew this fact. In *Immersive Gameplay*, Evan Torner and William J. White demonstrate they know it too. But don't take my word for it. Go ahead: dive in. Immerse yourself.

Zachary Waggoner has a Ph.D. in rhetoric and composition from Arizona State University, where he teaches classes in videogame theory, writing and rhetoric. He is the associate director of ASU's writing programs, the largest such program in the United States.

Introduction

EVAN TORNER and WILLIAM J. WHITE

Gamespace and Immersion

This book is driven by a theoretical commitment to *immersion* as a fundamental concept for making sense of mediated (popular) culture in contemporary society. It may fairly be said that immersion is to the 21st century entertainment industry what *illusion* was to that of the 20th century.[1] No longer constrained by the traditional divisions of work and life within industrial modernity, post-industrial society turns to technologically mediated gameplay in order to construct alternate (and hitherto unanticipated) blendings of living and working.

Theorists such as Bertolt Brecht and Theodor Adorno have leveled worthy critiques at cultural industries that under the guise of "entertainment" serve as distraction and act to alienate labor. But rather than adopt such a position — one which has historically both grounded anti-establishment critiques as well as served the interests of a high cultural elite in condemning mass culture — the authors of this volume all assert that immersive media establish their own unique terms of engagement and must be taken seriously if the rapid shift toward a participatory digital media culture is to be understood. Live-action role-playing (LARP),[2] digital games, and reality television all demand a research apparatus that portrays the immersive emotional experiences they offer in all their complexity. The immersed subject, a person ensconced within a "gamespace" or artificial (virtual) reality, is thus the focus of our overall study.

"Gamespace" itself is a daunting concept that should give the reader pause. In what ways do games serve as the dominant hegemonic force, shaping our discourse and the very topoi of which we speak? Much like, Michel Foucault's totalizing concept of the *panopticon* or Gilles Deleuze and Félix Guattari's equally totalizing *rhizome*, Australian scholar McKenzie Wark has used the term gamespace to signify the topological merger of reality and fantasy.

Such a merger operates via the construction of all-encompassing information flows that simultaneously constitute the objects of experience and render them susceptible to manipulation, modification, and repetition. One plays a quick round of *Battleheart* on a tablet computer, only to exit out to do one's homework for the score-like reward of a grade, so that then one can make progress toward one's chosen career with its own systems of punishment and reward.[3] In his research on *World of Warcraft*, for example, Scott Rettberg finds a similarly all-encompassing corporate ideology motivating play:

> While it's certainly true that some students are failing out of college, some marriages are falling apart, and some bodies are slipping into flabby obesity as a direct result of *World of Warcraft* addiction, in a larger sense the game is training a generation of good corporate citizens not only to consume well and to pay their dues, but also to climb the corporate ladder, to lead projects, to achieve sales goals, to earn and save, to work hard for better possessions, to play the markets, to win respect from their peers and their customers, to direct and encourage and cajole their underlings to outperform, and to become better employees and perhaps, eventually, effective future CEOs. Playing *World of Warcraft* serves as a form of corporate training.[4]

With the dissolution of a privileged "realspace" outside of it—when the real takes on the semblance of a game, in other words—those trapped in gamespace find themselves exiting the magic circle of one game to land in another, a frame within a frame within a frame. And it is game all the way down.

Immersive gameplay is not so much a means of escaping reality, but of escaping the interminable frames that place every aspect of human experience—growing up, education, physical activity, war, lifepaths—under the unblinking gaze of the panoptic metrics that delineate losers from winners. The individual agency enacted in the choice of new or reconfigured magic circles, from those that physically protect us to those that deliberately do us emotional harm, expresses the very essence of play itself within such a world. As Jean-Paul Sartre once said, play "strips the real of its reality ... [and] releases subjectivity."[5] The jury remains out as to whether or not the current gamelike systems governing our social order are, indeed, exerting otherwise absolute control over subjectivity itself.

On its most fundamental level, gamespace has at least given rise to a variety of new cultural practices—reality television shows, motion-control video games, larp, augmented reality gaming (ARG) and other pervasive games—that either promise immersion or render immersive experience as mediated spectacle. Examples abound: real children living in a *Lord of the Flies* simulation for a reality TV show called *Kid Nation*; Danes who played a larp called *The White Road* (2006) dressed as hobos and living as such for several days; Londoners and other participants around the world using their Nokia cell phones to locate books destined for a school in Zambia in the

Conspiracy for Good (2010), and everyday New Zealanders collaborating with Weta Workshop (famous for special effects on *Lord of the Rings* and *Avatar*) to stage vast pseudo-medieval battles, to name but a few. The immersive experience is thus both a design goal as well as a potentially marketable product.

Of course, we should remain ever suspicious of the word "immersion." There are many definitions and, as White, Harviainen and Boss argue in this volume, each one projects a specific goal in game design or media philosophy. Matthijs Holter states that any definition of "immersion seems to be characterized by its subjective nature."[6] For example, Jane McGonigal sees it as a kind of willing escape, regardless of whether or not it has a goal.[7] Henry Jenkins defines it in *Convergence Culture* as "a strong fantasy identification or emotional connection with a fictional environment, often described in terms of 'escapism' or a sense of 'being there.'"[8] Staffan Björk and Jussi Holopainen see it as being "deeply focused on the interaction [players] are having within the game."[9] In short, immersion in media is personal, escapist, emotional, about presence and concerned with interaction with participants and an environment. Immersion is a subjective experience and different for all involved: competitive gamers immerse themselves in tournaments, simulationists prefer photorealistic environments, and narrativists become deeply involved only when they perceive the arc of a story during play. More cannot be said in general without marginalizing productive conversation about the term.

At this stage in the scholarship, inductive reasoning from an interdisciplinary viewpoint may serve us better in identifying immersive media than a top-down approach from any one discipline. After all, how else might we qualify the body of diverse works that *Wired* editor Frank Rose analyzes in his recent book *The Art of Immersion* including the film *Batman: Dark Knight* (2008), the computer game *Myst* (1993), the novel *Pattern Recognition* (2003), and the Disney World corporate theme park? The playing field is indeed vast, and the points of entry many.

It might very well be the case that "immersive gameplay" as an organizing principle is what contributor Emily Care Boss elsewhere justifiably calls a "tar baby": a concept that provokes and aggravates polemic posturing rather than producing academically viable discourse.[10] Her position should resonate among the majority of game scholars[11] writing today, or at least among those who read them. For is a player immersed when they "feel" they're a character, or when an environment creates a sense of verisimilitude with the natural world, or when they reveal an emotional truth about themselves through a symbolic game? Naturally, such a concept shares much in common then with other hotly contested media studies topics such as genre, modernism and gender. Taking a cue from Judith Butler on the latter, however, immersive play could very well be seen as socially *performative*, even when it impacts major cognitive functions. There is a phenomenology of an immersed subject; certain cues that tell us someone is really "getting into the game" or "hooked on the show." Some media and games highlight the specific way in which their aesthetic and narrative propositions divorce viewers/players (or "viewers" as Kristen Daly calls them)[12] from reality, while others, such as *Pong*, unobtrusively absorb countless hours of human productivity without calling attention to themselves.

Thus every assertion of "immersion" as an academic concept implies consent to multiple cultural and media-specific truths held by the author. So when an author in this volume invokes the term — and many do — it is actually in our best interest that his or her definition remain his or her own. Only at the intersection of different definitions of immersion can one then negotiate, as if by discursive Venn diagram, a consensual understanding of the term. "Intersections" may very well have been an appropriate book title, given the diversity of disciplines and scholarly perspectives found in this volume on topics related to role-playing and transmedial realities. As it turns out, not just psychological, but also semiotic and sociological readings of immersive play yield insights when placed in direct disciplinary dialogue with each other. Using parallel intellectual tool kits, the authors observe and comment upon the systems that produce immersion, customary behaviors associated with immersive play/labor, as well as the phenomenology of immersive play itself: what immersion *looks* and *feels* like.

Foundations

This volume thus proceeds from the idea that immersive play is historically, socially, and aesthetically specific. A brief glance at our table of contents reveals it is also primarily occupied with the medium of the live-action and tabletop role-playing game. Why this emphasis on a 40-year-old analog, social participatory art form over the reward systems and identity interplay on cultural juggernauts such as *World of Warcraft* or even *Angry Birds*? Several reasons come to mind. The first and foremost would be that *World of Warcraft* scholarship is blossoming, such that surrogate identities and avatars have been definitively examined by scholars such as Zach Waggoner, Tanya Krzywinska, Martti Lahti, Jesper Juul and a burgeoning field of others. But the dynamics of role-playing beyond identity studies — that is the comparative study of role-playing design agendas — remains fairly underexplored. Indeed, contributors to this volume refer to influential theorists like Carl Jung, Johan Huizinga, Bernard Suits, Katie Salen, and Eric Zimmerman, but use them to tackle older-yet-unresolved issues that earlier, non-digital iterations of role-playing games raise that are thoroughly in dialogue with any new media.

Another justification of our emphasis can be credited to Pat Harrigan and Noah Wardrip-Fruin's seminal *First Person, Second Person, Third Person* (MIT Press: 2006, 2007, 2009) series of co-edited volumes, which set the bar for what interdisciplinary new media research ought to look like. In this series, Harrigan and Wardrip-Fruin sought "a wide-ranging overview of how fictions are constructed and maintained in different forms of media at the start of the twenty-first century."[13] Often when a sweeping statement like that is uttered, however, the "different forms of media" in praxis take on one of two stereotypical guises. The first would be class-inflected studies of film, books, and possibly television, with the word "media" expressing repressive tolerance[14] for the occasional meditations on a Pasolini film appearing in volumes on Chaucer and so forth, but would certainly be hard pressed to include Twitter feeds, tabloid magazines, drinking games or *Vampire: The Masquerade* as topics of scholarly inquiry. The second takes the opposite tack, focusing purely on digital mass media and the teleology of their historical development.[15] Both of these positions — one of upper middle-class privileged consumption, the other of *nouveau riche* technophilia — sometimes obscure the media consumed outside of a fairly limited cultural sphere, mostly ignore international developments to privilege Anglo-European media experiences, and certainly scoff at small-scale participatory media such as role-playing games and board games. Rather than seeing these media as merely auxiliary formations, Harrigan and Wardrip-Fruin laudably choose instead to place them at the center of new, participatory media discourse. As video game guru Ken Rolston's article says in his contribution to their *Third Person* book: "Deep study and practical experience with larp design, presentation, and gaming experience is profoundly recommended for those who want to develop vast narratives in computer games."[16] Our world's narratives increasingly become explainable through game logic, and new media scholars can only profit in noting exchanges between small-scale, laboratory-like social games and massive-scale Internet experiences like those discussed by McGonigal, Jenkins and Rettberg.[17]

A point of distinction within this American volume is the presence of many Finnish scholars. In the history of role-playing studies, one would find this by no means coincidental. Though the United States saw the role-playing hobby begin there in the early 1970s, its global impact was most noticeably felt by a country moving into the Internet-connected world with a strong tradition of organized young adults and non-commercial game activity.[18] Qualitatively different gaming cultures emerged, as we see it, to the long-term benefit of all worldwide gaming communities. Nordic countries have steadily embraced all forms of gaming over the last two decades, from experimental live-action role-playing[19] to massively multi-player video games. Finland's academic tradition now reflects this societal trend, as it is home to some of the world's leading game studies institutes, such as the Game Research Laboratory at the University of Tampere, the Helsinki Institute of Information Technology (HIIT) and others. Our authors Montola, Holopainen, and J. Tuomas Harviainen have emerged from this landscape as leading theorists of immersive and pervasive gaming, largely thanks to the annual Nordic larp convention *Knutepunkt* ("meeting point"),[20] which has been extant since 1997 and annually publishes a multicontributor scholarly volume on role-playing games. Their emergent notion of "bleed," that is the porousness between player and character, has recently taken American academic larp discussions by storm. To say that this volume is more or less framed by the Nordic discourse of gaming and the media would be an understatement.

Equal parts social science and humanities, this book also reflects several American trends in studies of ludic interactions. One would be so-called "Forge theory," a role-playing episteme that came from the eponymous Internet discussion board[21] in the late 1990s. The theory establishes that players come to any game with specific, oft-unarticulated expectations for play ("creative agendas"), and will suffer from a loss of "immersion" when these are not met. As Emily Care Boss summarizes it, "player preferences matter and ... procedures applied will affect both a player's enjoyment of a game and how the game functions."[22] Largely created as an engine for coherent game design, this simple premise has supported a community of gamer-author-theorists such as Ron Edwards or Vincent Baker who have redefined the gamespace of the conventional tabletop RPG by taking procedures and game rules as serious reward systems in sculpting narrative and creativity. Another theorist whose work dominates this volume is sociologist Gary Alan Fine, whose 1979 role-playing game study *Shared Fantasy* still informs most contemporary game studies texts to date. Fine's framing of gameplay as a serious practice inscribed with social meaning underlies most texts in the volume. Finally, sociologist Erving Goffman continues to hold sway over the authors, as his seminal 1959 work *The Presentation of Self in Everyday Life* refracts across virtually every essay: the variable performance of what we call a "Self" and the way in which dynamic systems such as games pleasurably or painfully stimulate it.

Contributions[23]

To highlight the dialogic nature of this project, the diverse articles collected here have been divided into three overarching parts, with each part reflecting a specific media conversation. The first part, entitled "Mind Breaches

Role-Playing," examines how roles played in games influence psychological states and *vice versa*. Markus Montola and Jussi Holopainen's essay "First Person Audience and the Art of Painful Role-Playing" looks at experiences playing the controversial larp *Gang Rape* (2008) in terms of the surprising egalitarianism of shared psychological stress. They find that role-playing games specifically designed to elicit negative emotional experiences are actually considered rewarding by their participants. Sarah Lynne Bowman's "Jungian Theory and Immersion in Role-Playing Games" explores mainstream games such as *Dungeons and Dragons* and *World of Darkness* as means of individuating Jungian archetypes and Campbellian heroic journeys. She contends that the explanatory power of Jungian archetypes may be used to debunk the "escapist" moniker stamped on so many game-related activities. The final essay in this part, Nathan Hook's "Circles and Frames: The Games Social Scientists Play," argues that Solomon Asch's 1951 Conformity Experiment and Philip Zimbardo's 1971 Prison Experiment among others, when read as games, interrogate the boundary between the so-called "magic circle" and "protective frame" of play. His essay implies that there is but a thin line between psychology experiments and live-action games, and between player and character in such situations.

Part 2, "Role-Playing Breaches Reality," investigates how immersive fictions are caught in the interstices of society and culture. "Role-Playing Communities, Cultures of Play and the Discourse of Immersion" by William J. White, J. Tuomas Harviainen and Emily Care Boss provides a breakthrough analysis of Nordic and American interpretations of role-playing immersion, contrasting emotionally resonant and creative play/design philosophies. They advocate for a bottom-up definition of immersion, based on communities' play experiences rather than any sweeping philosophical distinctions as found with, for example, Jenkins or McGonigal. In "Gary Alan Fine Revisited: RPG Research in the 21st Century," sociologist Katherine Castiello Jones examines Fine's *Shared Fantasy* study on the basis of contemporary cultural sociology, arguing for a conditional reading of his influential findings. She levels a critique at scholars who do not historicize Fine while also expanding on several underappreciated aspects of his work, such as comparisons of gaming with broader leisure cultures. Todd Nicholas Fuist elaborates on social science methodology in studying gaming with "The Agentic Imagination: Tabletop Role-Playing Games as a Cultural Tool." Fuist offers the notion of "agentic imagination" to explain the social interactions that pivotally shape narrative and identity within tabletop role-playing games. The piece serves as a fitting conclusion to the RPG-focused portion of the book, combining ethnographic data with speculations about broader implications of role-playing research on the gaming hobby.

The third and largest part, "Reality Breaches Media," looks at uses and abuses of socially constructed game mechanics within the media of television and video games. Thanks to Sheila Murphy's research, which draws a genealogy between those very two media, Evan Torner's essay "*Kid Nation*: Television, Systemic Violence and Game Design" shows television's reliance on game mechanics through an analysis of the 2007 CBS reality show *Kid Nation*. These game mechanics often compete with the voyeuristic fantasy presumably offered by the show and wind up producing instead an incoherent, ideologically charged end product. Erik Dulick takes on reality shows' often highly scripted emotional arcs in "*Survivor* Meets the Hero's Journey: Connecting Mythic Structures to Reality Television." Dulick uses today's intellectual descendants of Jung and Joseph Campbell, namely writing gurus Stuart Voytilla and Christopher Vogler, to expose cliché formulas of character formation within television series design. Producers do not so much play with reality as they do the symbols that are most legible to their target demographic. The final two essays view the topic of immersion through the lens of new media, specifically gazing at the vanishing border between user behavior and semi-fictional game premises. Eric Newsom tackles the act of murdering your friends on Internet-enabled devices in "A Game About Killing: Role-Playing in the Liminal Spaces of Social Network Games." There he investigates the popular game *Spymaster* (2010) as a hybrid of virtual game relations and real social relations. Newsom's conclusion of the dissolution of the player-character boundary echo game design goals discussed in the first chapter. M.-Niclas Heckner concludes the volume with a piece entitled "Deleting Memory Space: The Gaming of History and the Absence of the Holocaust," in which he discusses the game *Wolfenstein* (2009) in terms of affect-laden generic and aesthetic cues that situate the player between the pleasures of fiction and the possibility of vicariously experiencing the emotional realities of another time period. Whatever constitutes an immersive experience, according to Heckner, those set in the past lay claim on our historical memory through a series of ahistorical symbols and tropes.

Taken together, these essays form the intellectual corpus of a younger generation of scholars grappling with game-like media that unequivocally demand emotional and social engagement. Whether through a reality television show or a pervasive cell phone game, gamespaces are being crafted to intervene and re-frame the seemingly endless gameplay that many of our lives have become. They immerse us in potential selves, social environments, reward systems and emotional dilemmas so as to let us play our way through an ideological standpoint. The challenge faced by many modern gamers today is to recognize that standpoint for what it is: the dynamization of human experience within a closed playing field in the service of a usually specific cultural belief system; often the one of neo-liberal capital, as Rettberg pointed out. Yet the authors in this volume have taken on this challenge and — achievement unlocked — have maintained the primacy of the social and the psychological with an eye on the virtual and the vast.

Notes

1. And there is, we would argue, a mild moral panic afoot about this very fact. For a good example thereof, see Hedges, *Empires*.

2. As per conventions in Nordic role-playing scholarship, such as in Stenros and Montola's *Nordic Larp*, the acronym LARP is written in lower-case letters.

3. This experience of framed human alienation is perhaps best articulated by Erich Fromm in his 1955 book *The Sane Society*, which argues that advanced capitalism elicits a populace's consent through the increased routinization and quantification of human relations.

4. Rettberg, *Corporate Ideology* 20.

5. Sartre, "Consciousness" 310.

6. Holter, "Stop Saying Immersion" 20.

7. McGonigal, *Reality Is Broken* 6.

8. Jenkins, *Convergence Culture* 295.

9. Björk and Holopainen, *Patterns* 205.

10. Boss, "Thoughts."

11. To name a few: Barry Atkins (2003), Katie Salen and Eric Zimmerman (2004), Esther MacCallum-Stewart and Justin Parsler (2008) and Gordon Calleja (2011). Of these studies, Calleja goes so far as to develop a taxonomy of different immersions: immersion as absorption and immersion of transportation. Calleja's study also incorporates previous discourses of mediated immersion (such as presence theory) into a cohesive literature review of the topic.

12. Daly, *Cinema* 82. We can also opt for game designer Stephen Dinehart's "viewer/user/player" (VUP) definition in his 2006 USC thesis *Journey of Jin & Transmedial Play*.

13. Harrigan & Wardrip-Fruin, *Third Person* 1.

14. See Marcuse, "Repressive Tolerance."

15. See for example Hassan and Thomas, *New Media*.

16. Rolston, "My Story" 119.

17. In this vein, it will be interesting to see if Voorhees, Call and Whitlock's forthcoming book *Dungeons, Dragons and Digital Denizens: Digital Role-playing Games* on digital role-playing games prioritizes recent role-playing theory or will refer simply to new media and cultural studies paradigms to explain role-playing processes.

18. Stenros and Montola, *Nordic Larp* 15.

19. Culminating in the games *The Journey* and *GR*, both discussed in Montola and Holopainen's contribution to this volume.

20. For more information: http://en.wikipedia.org/wiki/Knutepunkt.

21. For more information: http://www.indie-rpgs.com.

22. Boss, "Key Concepts" 233.

23. Many of the contributions emerged from a panel titled "Immersions: Breaching Reality through Play" organized at the 2011 Northeast Modern Language Association (NeMLA) conference in New Brunswick, New Jersey. We would like to thank the conference for serving as a starting point for this publication.

Part 1. Mind Breaches Role-Playing

First Person Audience and the Art of Painful Role-Playing

Markus Montola and Jussi Holopainen

The Nordic role-playing community has produced a number of games that are not considered fun or entertaining.[1] Instead, role-playing has been used to convey and produce nuanced and serious experiences, in a manner resembling theater and performance art.[2]

As fun is sometimes considered a core element of play, Montola[3] conducted a study in order to understand reasons behind playing games that are not fun. He interviewed players of two games, *Gang Rape* (Wrigstad, 2007) and *The Journey* (Axelzon, 2010),[4] finding out that these games were regarded as painful but rewarding aesthetic experiences. Most players reported being stressed, horrified, and repulsed during the game, but afterwards were satisfied that they had participated in a meaningful and worthwhile activity. In this essay, we revisit those interviews, looking deeper into the psychological and aesthetic mechanisms of such games, analyzing *Gang Rape* in detail.

The way in which Nordic role-players choose to experience "negative" emotions as a part of their artistically meaningful role-playing produces what Aaron Smuts[5] calls the *paradox of painful art*. Based on the *paradox of tragedy*[6] and the *paradox of horror*,[7] Smuts formulates the following paradox:

1. People do not seek out situations that cause painful experiences.
2. People have painful experiences when encountering certain kinds of art.
3. People still seek out these art experiences even though they know they will be painful.

He proposes that the paradox can be solved through satisfactory answers to following questions:

1. The Hedonic Question: Do people seek out painful art in order to derive more pleasure than pain from the experience?

2. The Difference Question: Why do people seek apparently painful experience more often in response to art than in real life?

3. The Motivational Question: Why do people desire painful art experiences if they find them painful?[8]

In order to give indications on how to tackle the paradox we will follow Smuts' account of the *rich experience theory* together with some explanations of art experiences based on evolutionary psychology. According to the rich experience theory people seek out novel experiences, whether pleasurable or painful, in order to get "relief from boredom." We will use *Gang Rape* and *The Journey* player interviews as indications of empirical support for the rich experience theory of painful art.

Gang Rape is an extreme example, to be sure, but the design and play of painful role-playing games has been well-established within the Nordic larp[9] scene. These games have involved such settings, themes, and motifs as refugee centers,[10] nuclear war,[11] totalitarianism,[12] military occupation[13] and mental illness.[14] Understanding *Gang Rape* thus sheds light on a larger subculture of serious recreational play as well as exploring the paradox of painful art at greater length. As serious recreational play, Nordic-style role-playing differs from typical serious play in the sense that it is a grassroots scene where players organize games for their own community.

We begin with a detailed description of *Gang Rape* followed by a discussion of play as art. The essay continues with a summary of the findings of earlier player interviews.[15] Finally, we analyze the aesthetics and design of the game from a social psychological perspective, revisiting the paradox of painful art.

Gang Rape

As a game product, *Gang Rape* is a small booklet containing the rules of the game along with some background. The rules describe a *freeform roleplaying scenario* examining gang rape as a brutal form of violence.

Nordic freeform role-playing is a flexible form of role-playing, mixing and matching expressive techniques of tabletop role-playing games and larp. The players combine performance and pretend play in order to portray fictional people in a fictional situation. Even though the freeform role-playing is entirely recreational, it can be compared with psychodrama[16] in the sense that it employs a wide assortment of expressive techniques, including soliloquies and role reversals. It takes just a moment for the players to create the interior of a car out of four chairs, but it allows them to play out a road trip in a very intuitive way.[17]

The play proceeds through three scenes, lasting maybe half an hour each:

- The *first scene* portrays how the rape came to happen. The players decide where and how the rape happens; who is the Victim and who are the perpetrators. For instance, the scene might portray a bachelor party that goes horribly wrong. The first scene is played out like improvisational theater.
- The *second scene* begins as the situation turns into a rape. The players sit down, and narrate the act of gang rape. Rapists take turns with the Victim one by one, describing their actions verbally for a few minutes. They narrate everything physical and biological that happens in the diegetic world, even narrating how the Victim's body responds to their actions. Then, the Victim replies, narrating her emotions, feelings and thoughts, and also how the Rapist reacts mentally to the situation. Then the next Rapist takes over.
- The *third scene* is the aftermath. The Victim narrates what happens after the rape, and may require Rapists to larp a brief aftermath scene. She gets to frame and define the situation, including how the Rapists feel about the event.

A number of psychodrama-style techniques are employed to exacerbate the experience. These include:

- *Familiarity* and *Paper-Thin Characters*. The players get to choose the setting and define their player characters. However, all these things must be familiar to the players — the setting cannot be a prison, unless everyone has been to one. The characters are defined very briefly, but they are left very superficial. Use of cliché stereotypes such as "The Sadist" is discouraged. A typical character might be defined just as "Peter, an athlete who used to date the Victim."
- *Eye Contact* and *Unfaltering Narration*. As the rape is narrated, the Rapists must maintain eye contact with the Victim. Additionally, there must be no stammering, repetition or hesitation when the players narrate the rape.
- *No Secrets, No Game Master*. In order to establish an informed consent, the rules state that all participants must read through the scenario before the play commences. There is no game master, but the rules dictate the precise procedures of play.

Gang Rape follows the design ideal of *bleed games*,[18] where the aim is to produce play where players experience strong feelings and emotions generated by fictional events. This is in contrast to a traditional philosophy of role-playing, where the aim is to mentally separate characters and players. Bleed designs aim to simultaneously maintain a sense of alibi and weaken the protective frame of play,[19] in order to explore powerful emotions. According to Montola,[20] the bleed rhetoric is also sometimes applied to gameplay that produces strong feelings, even though they do *not* correspond with characters' diegetic feelings — for example when a player feels guilt over the actions of a remorseless character. This has been called *indirect bleed*.

As a critical game, *Gang Rape* is a political comment on the difficulty of showing evidence of gang rape in the Swedish legal system, and a demonstration of the human capacity to fantasize about brutal things. The rules dictate that it must be played with a serious mindset.

Gang Rape was published in the Fastaval 2008 convention in Aarhus, Denmark, as a part of the five-game collection *Teknisk Uheld*.[21] The idea was that players had to play four of the games, and *Gang Rape* was intended to be the hardest one. The other games had themes ranging from abuse to alcoholism, but out of the more than ten groups that played *Teknisk Uheld*, only one played *Gang Rape*. Afterward, *Gang Rape* has usually been played as a stand-alone game.

PLAYER INTERVIEWS

The interviews used in this essay have been presented earlier in Montola.[22] As there are only a couple of dozen people who have played *Gang Rape*, data for this study was collected from a variety of sources. Ten players, including the designer, were interviewed. Half of the interviews were conducted in-person, while the rest were based on an email questionnaire and follow-up questions. The questions were the same in both formats, but the live interviews were conducted in a semi-structured fashion. The author of *Gang Rape* was interviewed both as a designer and as a player, but his player interview is not cited.

Five players of another harsh freeform game, *The Journey*, were also interviewed and those interviews are also used as background for this essay. *The Journey* is a grim post-holocaust game based on Cormac McCarthy's *The Road*, which uses gamemaster power to force player characters to commit numerous horrible actions.

One of the central problems of researching role-playing games is *ephemerality*: role-playing games, as processes, cannot be accessed after they end, and many types of role-playing games are not repeatable.[23] While many authors have combined ethnography or autoethnography with transcript analyses,[24] it would have been against the spirit of the rules of *Gang Rape* to record it. The rules state that "Having a game master is not allowed — every player must be either the victim or one of the rapists." According to the author of the game, the rationale of that rule is that everyone in the situation must be equally committed to it. However, as the game is repeatable, it was possible to obtain informants from several runs of the game, mitigating the problems that improvisation and player differences pose to the study. *Gang Rape* is a particularly suitable object for study, as a repeatable, small, short and tightly focused game.

Interviewees were contacted during Knutepunkt 2009, Norway; Fastaval 2010, Denmark; and Knutpunkt 2010, Sweden. Every player that could be reached was interviewed. The sample consisted of two female Victims, one male Victim[25] and seven male Rapists. Altogether, they had participated in four instances of *Gang Rape*. Four players were Swedish, three Danish and the rest from three other countries. The age of the interviewees was 19 to 42. They were experienced role-players, often with 10 to 20 years of experience.

Gang Rape was not staged for this study; all informants had played it prior to being contacted. The reader should take note that the interview material is entirely qualitative in nature, and even though it covers approximately 20 percent to 30 percent of all *Gang Rape* players to date, this study should be considered exploratory in nature.

PAINFUL PLAY

The central findings of the *Gang Rape* interviews — together with the interviews of *The Journey*—have already been reported in Montola.[26] A summary of the earlier findings is necessary for further analysis.

There is no doubt that *Gang Rape* can be a painful experience. Several players cried while playing, and almost all of them felt a strong need to debrief the experience with other players. Some of the email interviewees expressed that it was taxing to revisit the experience by writing answers, while many in-person interviewees considered the interviews a valuable opportunity to debrief the game again with a neutral outsider. Both Rapists and Victims found the experience rough.

> Every time we talk about it — just like we are doing now — I just start feeling very unpleasant and uncomfortable in my body. And I think that's because the game has been great and has been doing what it was designed to do, and I didn't want to be reminded of that constantly.[27]

However, the majority of the interviewees were satisfied with their experiences. Many players found themselves thinking about sexual violence, and even though they tended to be critical of *Gang Rape* as a simulation, they felt that it gave them insights into sexuality, violence and the culture surrounding rape.

I cannot read through a newspaper without reacting to news about someone being raped, and actually searching for those news [articles] to some extent, and that aspect has to be counted for one of the strong pros with this game, to see things freshly and not looking the other way anymore.[28]

Many players experienced physiological stress reactions from playing the game, including sweating, shakes, nausea and restlessness. The participants who chose to play the game did so because they wanted intense role-playing experiences. Female players chose to play Victims and male players Rapists, often because they felt that those roles were the hardest for them, respectively. As the game has a reputation for harshness, a few players expressed disappointment over the fact that the game had touched them less than they had expected.

I had witnessed how other participants of the game experienced shakings and all sort of nerve malfunctions, resulting of tension and anxiety, and waited to find the equivalents of these phenomena on myself, but could not notice any.[29]

As the game is emotionally tough, the players need to support each other to get through the game. After going through the experience and the subsequent debriefing, many players felt intimacy and connectedness. This happened both between Rapists and between Rapists and Victims.

During the game, we said things we would most likely not even say to someone we know very well. I definitely felt some kind of connection between us after the game. I felt a lot closer to them so that it did not feel weird or unusual at all when, for instance, one the players put his arm around my shoulder while we both were talking to someone else.[30]

Even though gang rape is a controversial topic for a game, the players had nothing to complain regarding the ethics of the game. The Victim players especially considered it a valuable piece of artistic merit, feeling that it conveyed an important political message. None of the interviewees regretted playing *Gang Rape*.

As the previous study discussed *what* kind of experiences role-playing can create, this essay focuses on some *hows* and *whys*. Based on the earlier interviews, we can propose an informed analysis of the aesthetics of *Gang Rape*.

Play as Art and Performance

We are using the paradox of painful art as one way to approach *Gang Rape*. Indeed, our stance is that designing and playing some games *can* be considered art.

The debate of what is art or a work of art has been central to much philosophy of art throughout history. Different forms of performance elude simple categorization, and Richard Schechner,[31] for example argues that performance itself is an inclusive concept. Theater, rituals, sports, play, happenings, and political demonstrations are nodes in the performance concept network.

There are many complementary and often contradictory definitions presented in the existing literature from Greek philosophy to the most contemporary discussions. The debate is still on but the most promising ones are the cluster theories of art. Out of the several cluster theories available, such as those of E.J. Bond,[32] Berys Gaut,[33] and Julius Moravcsik,[34] we consider the one proposed by Denis Dutton[35] perhaps the most elaborate one. The common theme in the theories is that art can be characterized by satisfying a set of features in any number of ways. Unlike the other proposed sets, Dutton's is based on a naturalistic understanding of art as a natural and universal disposition based on the evolved psychological and social conditions shared by all humans.

Dutton's feature list[36] includes direct pleasure, display of skill or virtuosity, style novelty and creativity, criticism, representation, "special" focus, expressive individuality, emotional saturation, intellectual challenge, traditions and institutions, and imaginative experience. A work of art does not have to necessarily satisfy all these features. However, lacking a significant amount of the features would raise doubts whether the object could be called art or not. A famous painting displayed in a well-known museum, such as Rembrandt's *Night Watch* at Amsterdam Rijksmuseum, satisfies all the required features, while a dinner at a three-star Michelin restaurant might be a borderline case of art, and an ordinary six-pack of Budweiser in a corner-shop is not art as such. *Gang Rape* easily meets most of the criteria. For example, there is certainly emotional saturation and imaginative experiences in *Gang Rape*, while criticism and traditions and institutions are currently being formed for larps in general. Grant Tavinor[37] has used cluster theories of art in a similar way to argue that at least some videogames are art.

Building on authors such as Gaut and Tavinor, Jaakko Stenros[38] traces the historical and structural relationships between role-playing, games, and art,[39] contextualizing role-playing in the fields of theater, performance art, and games. Situating larps as one node in the network with connections to, for example, theater, performance art, and games would be more illustrative than just trying to classify role-playing into rigid, pre-existing forms of performance.

The nature of *Gang Rape* as art can be looked at two different levels: first, the game as a piece of art characterized by a set of rules, and second, the game as an activity and a performance. The distinction is similar to looking at a theater piece as a written play and a theater piece as a performance by actors. The rules of *Gang Rape* give instructions for the players to be able to perform a game of *Gang Rape* in a similar way as the stage directions and the text inform how to perform a theater piece. The difference is that while theater is performed for an external audience, *Gang Rape* is aimed at the performers themselves.

Understanding Gang Rape

The central concept of understanding the relationship of role-playing games and their audiences is that role-playing is aimed for the players themselves, who constitute a *first person audience*.[40] Even though films and books sometimes place the audience in the first-person perspective, role-playing games are even more powerful in the way they can make players to feel committed to fictional characters. The first person audience in role-playing, as opposed to literature, shows itself in at least two respects:

- *Real Decisions.* As role-players are in charge of their characters' decisions, they feel a very intimate commitment to them. In a situation where a fictional character makes a mistake, it is the difference between "my mistake" and "my character's mistake." Depending on the playing style, players may seek to detach themselves from their characters, or to try to maximize their perception of engagement and character immersion. In some games, some decisions are given and players may not influence them; for instance, *Gang Rape* is a deterministic game in the sense that it invariably portrays a rape.[41]

- *Inner Play.* Much of what happens in a role-playing situation happens only in the mind of each player. Characters' intentions, plans, regrets and such are not necessarily ever communicated to other players. This makes role-playing, daydreaming and make-believe unique forms of expression: As the creator is the only audience of this part of play, inner play actually skips the whole semiotic process of coding and representation.

The larp *The Executive Game*[42] is a perfect example of first person audience, where the players portrayed mobsters playing poker. The players were asked to pretend that gambling chips really represented real money, but as gamblers, they were also expected to conceal their emotions regarding the poker chips. You are the only audience of your pretence, when you decide whether call or fold.

The aesthetic of first person audience can make a role-playing experience very personal, and close to real life — it is not an accident that the vast majority of role-players refer to their characters in first-person singular. Thus, there is reason to believe that emotions elicited by role-playing experiences may be even stronger in some sense than those elicited by other fictional experiences, matching the audiovisual power of film and the immediate interactivity of video games. According to Jenefer Robinson,[43] the reality status of fictional events affects the intensity of emotional responses: the closer the event feels to be to reality, the stronger the response. Heidi Hopeametsä[44] has also observed that role-played situations have a potential to elicit very real and strong emotions.

Even though film and literature have long traditions of first-person narrators, diegetic filming, the idea of first person audience goes a step deeper, which is central to understanding the psychology of *Gang Rape*. Schechner[45] notes that actors in theater or performance art have *double-consciousness* during acting. They are simultaneously both themselves and the characters they portrait. The actors have to constantly monitor their own actions, gestures and so on in order to perform for both themselves and the real audience. The similar happens in larps, even though the audience consists of other players.

THIN ALIBI

Games serve as empowering mechanisms, a game that allows people to engage with strange or taboo activities[46] play is an *alibi*. Poremba uses the example of the game *Twister* that serves as an alibi for getting close to other players. The idea of an alibi is based on the idea that play is enclosed within a *magic circle* that separates play and ordinary life.[47] The people within the magic circle are subject to different rules than people outside it, thus it is acceptable for boxers to punch each other within the ring — boxing is an alibi for punching. Apter argues that play is based on a *protective frame*,[48] which shields the players from actual harm during play. Thus, boxers use gloves, and gang rape is enacted by narration and eye contact instead of physical violence in *Gang Rape*.

While playing *Gang Rape* is only made possible through the alibi it presents, and through the fact that it is enclosed within the protective magic circle, it features a number of design decisions that serve to make that protection appear to be as weak as possible.

- *Thin Characters*. The game features no fleshed-out character descriptions. The players are expected to quickly come up with thin, superficial characters. This is done in order to avoid giving each player too powerful an alibi; the artistic goal is to force the players to play "close to home" during the game.

As the characters are very superficial, they resemble Goffman's *roles*[49] as much as full role-playing *characters*. "Peter, the college athlete who used to date the Victim" is not entirely dissimilar to the roles professionals take in their work, whether they are doctors or strippers. Compare Steve-as-doctor and Steve-as-Peter-the-Rapist, where the personality of Peter is left shallow enough to be almost completely meaningless. The fiction of Peter gives Steve an alibi, the opportunity to portray Steve-as-Rapist in the game. Instead of creating fiction about imaginary people, the thin characters allow players to invest themselves into play, reflecting how they would personally react to what happens in the play.

> I have made the conscious choice, not to [provide players with ready character descriptions]. Partially because it *controls too much in this kind of game*, but also because I don't want to provide any more *absolution for the players' actions* than I already have.

- *Unfaltering Narration.* The players are not to take pauses or falter in the second scene. Like thin characters, the goal is to force players into investing themselves into play. Instead of censoring themselves or creating fiction, they are encouraged to say whatever comes to their mind. This also creates a sense of peer pressure, competition and performance anxiety.

- *No Game Master.* Even though *Gang Rape* proceeds strictly based on the instructions given in the booklet, there is no game master present. This helps create an atmosphere of trust and intimacy, but also removes the possibility of shifting responsibility of the fictional events to an authority figure. However, implicit authority is still present in the form of clear rules and implicit peer pressure, and that urges the players on. Quitting the game would be particularly hard for the Victim, as the performance cannot proceed without her.

- *Full Understanding.* All players must read the entire booklet before commencing play, and there are no secrets in the scenario. This requirement means that all players must be consent to step into the roles of Rapists and Victims — and it also establishes that they were willing to do so without external pressure, *before* stepping into the magic circle of play. Willing participation in a game titled *Gang Rape* carries a risk of certain stigma, making the experience more powerful.

Much of the painfulness of *Gang Rape* can be explained with the concept of *cognitive dissonance*; a "feeling of discomfort [...] caused by performing an action that is discrepant from one's customary, typically positive self-conception."[50] Cognitive dissonance causes discomfort, but also stress and physiological stress reactions,[51] all of which were strongly present in the *Gang Rape* interviews.

Especially on the Rapists, the pain elicited by *Gang Rape* is about the balance of the social alibi of playfulness, and the cognitive dissonance of engaging in a make-believe rape that is clearly painful to the player of the Victim. The clever design provides a clear alibi, making it possible to play the game in the first place, but leaves it thin enough not to entirely mitigate the cognitive dissonance.

INDIVIDUATION AND HUMANIZATION

Looking into reasons why people commit abuses and brutalities, Philip Zimbardo[52] lists factors such as *deindividuation* and *dehumanization*. Deindividuation[53] is a mental state where a person identifies with a group, seeing himself as a part of a group rather than as an individual. Dehumanization, on the other hand, is a larger process where people are made to see the target as non-human, e.g., as animals, which influences how people treat both individuals and ethnic groups.[54] In short; when an individual immerses in a group, he feels less responsible for his actions, and when he considers the victim as non-human, it eases and lowers the empathy felt towards her, alleviating the cognitive dissonance.

Looking at these psychological mechanisms, it is interesting to notice how *Gang Rape* is designed to *not* simulate the psychological characteristics of a gang rape. Many Rapist players comment that having to look the Victim into the eyes is the hardest thing in the game, but some also noted that it establishes a connection between the two players:

> Having to keep eye contact was extremely scary but I think it was also a very safe thing. Noticing the reactions of the other player (not character!!!) added significantly to my own emotions.[55]

The design — looking into the eyes, concentrating on the facial expressions and reactions — humanizes the Victim in the eyes of the Rapist. In *Gang Rape*, the eye contact also individuates the Rapist, who is singled out by the Victim's gaze. Both of these mechanisms are opposed to the psychological characteristics of actual gang rape, which is thought to depend on mechanisms such as dehumanization and deindividuation. The way the game design suppresses these central enabling factors of real-life brutalities allows it to be an emotionally straining experience — even though it is entirely pretend play.

VOLUNTARY VICTIM

Another aspect where *Gang Rape* is not a simulation is the role of the Victim. During the rape, the Victim player is constrained by rules. The point is to move the focus away from her attempts to resist the Rapists, and give her something else to do instead:

> *The woman must be still and passive* in the primary scene. She may give inner monologues, add details about the rapist's behaviour and importantly tell the rapist *what he feels like* in this situation. The reason for restraining the woman is that there is very little relevant input that she can [give]. Playing a screaming or crying or futilely kicking person in a number of consecutive scenes won't bring the game anywhere.[56]

Essentially, the Victim character is stripped of power, but her player is given some narrative agency instead.[57] While the character is powerless against the Rapists, the player gets to strike back at their players. She both represents the suffering character to the Rapist players, in first-person, while driving in the gruesome details of rape.

This solution creates a special dynamic for the player of the Victim — while the Rapist players inflict suffering on her with their naturalistic portrayal of sexual violence, it is her job to boost their guilt trip through emotional narration.

Player reactions to this double role varied. Victim-10 found this a strong, empowering mechanism, which allowed her to avoid much of the emotional pressure of rape, essentially creating a detaching structure working against the stated game design goals. Victim-8 considered it her job to *help* the Rapists feel as bad as possible during the game, vocally echoing the common players sentiment that *Gang Rape* is about creating the most intense possible experience together. Finally, Victim-9 was probably least distracted by the game master function, commenting that even though it was extremely difficult and challenging, the game was sexually arousing at times. She felt "excited, happy, overwhelmed and still a little shocked" afterward.

The players of games such as *Gang Rape* often underline the importance of debriefing, where the players process difficult experiences together.[58] The interviewees[59] frequently commented that the main attention in the debriefing was given to the Victim player, who supposedly had the most painful experience. However, the interviews indicated that the game can be equally rough for the Rapists. The artificially produced experiences of guilt and cognitive dissonance, enhanced by the mechanics of thin alibi, individuation and humanization, primarily targets the perpetrators. On the other hand, the game master role given to the Victim player partially shields her from the self-blame, victimization and the subsequent cognitive dissonance that might otherwise be caused by portraying the relatively passive victim of abuse.[60]

Of course, the Victim has her own trip that is based on external horror, abuse and violation, which are all experienced through the glasses of the first person audience.

Tackling the Paradox of Painful Art

The play experience of *Gang Rape* is disturbing and even painful, but the whole experience is regarded as rewarding. This is the heart of the paradox: how can painful experiences of art be rewarding and even desirable?

Aaron Smuts proposes a *rich experience theory* to answer the paradox. He states that people seek out novel experiences, whether pleasurable or painful, in order to get "relief from boredom." People, at least most of them, have highly developed mental faculties and seeking out novel and challenging stimuli is desirable in itself.[61] Some of the most complex and challenging stimuli arise from threatening, dangerous and painful situations. For example, tragedy is often based on complex crisis structures, such as a loss of a loved one.

What does this mean in the context of *Gang Rape*? According to the theoretical background sketched above and based on the interviews of the participants the actual experience of playing *Gang Rape* was stressful, scary, disgusting, and for most players, very intense: "The entire game was so intense that it is all kind of blurred."[62] The enjoyment, both in retrospect and during play, arising from *Gang Rape* gives support for the rich experience theory.[63] The players wanted to have intense emotions and experiences even though they perfectly well knew that these were not going to be "pleasurable" as such.

> So there's arousal, there's impotence, and there's disgust, at the same time. So you can see why that leaves you feeling rather brainfucked. And that's the [power] of that game, the simple mechanisms are able to create all these three.[64]
>
> I am most certainly happy that I played it. It was a very worthwhile experience and definitely the most intense game I have ever played.[65]

The rich experience theory, however, does not answer the Difference Question, why people do not seek out these experiences in real life but rather in art. Smuts explains this using a variant of *control theory*, which proposes that it is much easier to have these kinds of experiences in response to art than to real life situations. Having similar situations in real life as in much painful art would have disastrous consequences for the involved persons.

The account is still incomplete as it is not entirely clear why persons should have such emotional experiences if they very well know that the situations and events in art are fictional. This paradox of fiction has been puzzling scholars for some decades starting from Colin Radford's[66] initial statement of the paradox. There are many conflicting attempts at solving the paradox.[67] Recent work in cognitive media studies[68] provides one that is close to our approach and consistent with the analysis of *Gang Rape*. According to these theories based on cognitive psychology and neurosciences, our minds do not care if the events are fictional or not to create some kind of emotional experiences, because the cognitive reality status check happens *after* the initial emotional appraisals. Thus, the emotions felt by the players during play were real, which also explains the reported physiological reactions to play. The game mechanics also provided a dampening effect on the reality status check after the initial, subconscious emotional appraisal. Thin alibi, first person audience, and making real decisions during play make the whole experience closer to real life than to pure fiction. In summary: the initial emotional responses are automatic and subconscious and the game mechanics were designed to lessen the effect of the following cognitive monitoring of the reality status.

Some players reported moving their focus between concentrating on the game situation and monitoring their own reactions during the game. Playing *Gang Rape* is similar to taking part in a piece of performance art as a performer. In the case of *Gang Rape* there are no spectators as such, rather, the players themselves are both performers and the audience of the performance. This fact is also highlighted in the structural turn taking employed in the game. While the Victim or a Rapist is performing during his or her turn, the other players take the role of the spectator. At the same time, as in any performance from participating in a ritual to acting on the theater stage, the performer is the first person audience for his or her own performance. Thus switching the focus from the game situation to their own reactions can be understood as switching between being a performer and being a spectator of own performance. Thus, there are three layers of participation in *Gang Rape*: being a performer by taking turns in the game and fleshing out the fictional situation; being the audience for other players taking their turns in the game; and being the first person audience for one's own performance.

After playing the game, and even during the play itself, the players consciously reflected their emotional responses. This reflection, especially during the debriefing, allowed the players to take control and manage their emotional responses. These coping mechanisms[69] allow the players to come to terms with their responses and relieve the cognitive dissonance experienced during play. Such coping may partly explain why the players felt that the overall experience was rewarding in the end. Even though *Gang Rape* tries to make it difficult to detach oneself from the experience, the players do have some room to maneuver, allowing them to push their experience to the very edge of their comfort zone.

Literary Darwinism offers another view on the pleasures of fiction.[70] Even though the focus of this approach is not on explaining the paradox of painful art, it can help in explaining why rich experience theory works from the evolutionary psychology point of view. According to literary Darwinism our capacities for creating and enjoying fiction are evolutionary adaptations, which are part and parcel of how our minds work. Both Joseph Carroll[71] and Steven Pinker[72] agree that there is an adaptive value for fiction and counter-factional thinking in the first place. Our ancestors were living in a world where coordination of group activities and collaborative planning, such as in hunting large mammals, would have been adaptively beneficial. It is difficult to see the adaptive value of enjoying fictional creations, which bear no relevance to the facts at hand, even when most entertainment fiction falls into this category. According to Pinker this is a by-product, a spandrel, of the adaptive value of fictional thought in general.

Pinker claims that the pleasures of listening or reading a good story (or playing a good game) form in a similar way to pleasures gained from eating cheesecake. Our taste for sweet, fatty, and high-caloric foods was an evolutionary advantage when such food items were scarce. Eating strawberry cheesecake hijacks the evolved pleasure circuits. The pleasure caused is considerably more intense as the concentration and combination of preferred food items is high in cheesecake. Pinker argues that the same happens with fiction: stories stimulate the pleasure centers involved in dealing with adaptive challenges, such as group coordination and counter-factual thinking, without needing to actually do the challenging stuff itself. The pleasure can also be more intensive than in the real-life scenario as the content in the stories can be compressed and exaggerated causing more intense excitation of the pleasure centers.

The whole story, however, is more complex. Joseph Carroll and Lisa Zunshine both argue that fiction can help us to organize our socially adaptive mechanisms for understanding and empathizing with other persons' point of view. Fiction allows us to practice, monitor and experience what are other people's cognitive states and motives for behavior without actually being in the factual situation. Through fiction we can understand other people, and ourselves, in a safe, simulated situation. The answer is thus two-fold: at the same time we can gain immediate pleasure from fictional accounts as according to Pinker and also have a more profound effect of understanding what we are as human beings.

The experience of playing *Gang Rape* follows this two-fold path. The immediate experiences arise from the intense fictional situation that titillates the players' cognitive mechanics for coping with a stressful social situation. According to the rich experience theory these experiences, even though they are not pleasurable as such, can be rewarding. The fictional framing, or magic circle, protects the players from real physical harm, making the situation manageable for the players. The overall experience is rewarding as the players gain new insights, both conscious and sub-conscious, into human nature. The player interviews reflect this process. The players state that during the game itself they were having intense experiences, mostly disturbing or even painful, but in the end, and especially after the debriefing, the game was considered rewarding.

Conclusion

It is not rare that players commit brutalities in games; digital games especially have portrayed atrocities from pornographic rape[74] to torture, mutilation and mass murder. Video games generally tend to distance the player from the victim, in order to turn violence into entertainment. David Grossman[75] has argued that video games do this to the extent where they serve as a dehumanizing influence making it easier to pull the trigger in the real life as well. *Gang Rape* does the opposite, it is designed to display abuse up close and personal. In light of the interviews, it does the trick using basic, but powerful psychological mechanisms — mechanisms that do not simulate the psychology of rape, but invert it to drive home an artistic point.

> After playing it I would say that it really hits the nerve it set out to. It really comes down that few mechanics being well placed in that situation that amounts up to be a rape. It really works in these situations.[76]

The play experience of *Gang Rape* is disturbing and even painful, but the whole experience is regarded as rewarding. The analysis of the interviews supports Aaron Smuts' account of the rich experience theory: We can find value in strong emotional responses, whether they are positive or negative. In real life, however, the consequences of the situations eliciting strong negative emotions would be too disastrous for the participants.

According to the theories of emotion used in this essay, the primary appraisals of both real and fictional events cause automatic and subconscious emotional responses. The following cognitive monitoring reappraises the emotional response according to the reality status of the event. While the players' emotional landscapes are not valid psychological simulations of the rape situations, *Gang Rape* nevertheless produces strong and real emotions, which made it a worthwhile experience for the majority of interviewed players.

Notes

1. See Stenros & Montola, *Nordic Larp.*
2. See Hopeametsä, "24 Hours" and Stenros, "Nordic Larp."
3. See Montola, "Positive Negative."
4. *Gang Rape* has been published in Ellemand, et al. *Scenariebogen.* Both games also available for free through http://jeepen.org/games.

5. See Smuts, "Paradox."
6. Hume, *Natural History* and Feagin, *Pleasures.*
7. Carroll, *Philosophy* and Gaut, "Enjoyment Theory."
8. Smuts, "Paradox."
9. The word larp is an acronym for "live action role-playing," now a word of its own.
10. Gräslund, "Europa."
11. Hopeametsä.
12. Gotthard & Zlatohlávek, "Children."
13. Fatland, "1942."
14. Pedersen, "Delirium."
15. Montola, "Positive Negative."
16. Kellerman, *Focus.*
17. See Wrigstad, "Nuts and Bolts."
18. Montola, "Positive Negative."
19. See Apter, *Dangerous Edge* and *Danger.*
20. Montola, "Positive Negative."
21. Translated as "technical difficulties."
22. Montola, "Positive Negative."
23. E.g., Montola, "Social Constructionism" (forthcoming).
24. E.g., Fine, *Shared Fantasy*, Bowman, *Functions*, and Cover, *Creation.*
25. The one male informant who played the Victim of a homosexual rape is referred to with female pronouns, in order to maintain anonymity.
26. Montola, "Positive Negative."
27. Account told by Rapist-6.
28. Account told by Rapist-1.
29. Account told by Rapist-7.
30. Account told by Victim-9.
31. Schechner, *Performance Theory.*
32. E.J. Bond, "Essential Nature."
33. Gaut.
34. Moravcsik, "Why Philosophy."
35. Dutton, "Naturalist Definition" and *Art Instinct.*
36. Dutton, "Naturalist Definition."
37. Tavinor, *Art.*
38. Stenros, "Nordic Larp."
39. For a historically more inclusive treatise see Morton, "Larps."
40. E.g., Montola, "Positive Negative" and Stenros, "Nordic Larp."
41. The players of Brenda Braithwaite's *The Train* (2009) discover that they are running the trains taking prisoners to concentration camps. It has been argued that the ethical response to that determinism is to disobey the rules that make them take fictional people to death camps. In *Gang Rape*, everyone knows the rules in advance, and the Victim is present, expressing her consent to participate.
42. See Montola, "Positive Negative" and Stenros, "Nordic Larp."
43. Robinson, *Deeper.*
44. Hopeametsä.
45. Schechner.
46. E.g., Poremba, "Critical Potential." and McGonigal, *This Might Be a Game.*
47. Salen & Zimmerman, *Rules* and Huizinga, *Homo Ludens.*
48. See Apter *Dangerous Edge, Reversal Theory* and *Danger.*
49. Goffman, *Presentation.*
50. Aronson, et al., *Social Psychology*, cf. Festinger, *Theory.*
51. See e.g., Milgram, "Behavioral Study."
52. Zimbardo, *Lucifer Effect.*
53. Originally Festinger, et al., "Some Consequences."
54. E.g., Bandura, "Disinhibition" and Zimbardo.
55. Account told by Rapist-1.
56. Source: *Gang Rape* booklet. The booklet assumes a female Victim and male Rapists.

According to the author, the game is written in a way that should make the reader feel bad already, and this is one of the many decisions supporting that goal.

57. See Boss, "Collaborative Roleplaying" for discussion on how narrative agency can be distributed between players and game masters.

58. Montola, "Positive Negative."

59. Refer also to Fatland.

60. In *The Journey*, players had to portray passive reactions to abuse. Some players found it highly painful to not be able to confront their abusers or defend their loved ones within the fiction (Montola).

61. See Dutton, *Art Instinct*, Dissanayake, *Homo Aestheticus*, and Ramachandran & Hirstein, "Science of Art."

62. Account told by Victim-9.

63. As our data consists of retrospective narrativizations of play, we cannot comment on how players experienced *Gang Rape* rewarding during play. Hedonic psychology argues that retrospective evaluations of good and bad experiences are subject to significant fallacies (e.g., Kahneman, "Objective Happiness"). However, those our understanding of the past is based on those fallacies.

64. Account told by Rapist-4.

65. Account told by Victim-9.

66. Radford, "Anna Karenina."

67. See e.g., Schneider, "Paradox of Fiction."

68. E.g., Grodal, *Moving Pictures* and *Embodied Visions*; Robinson, *Deeper Than Reason*.

69. Robinson.

70. Carroll, *Literary Darwinism*.

71. Ibid.

72. Pinker, *How the Mind Works*.

73. Zunshine, *Why We Read Fiction*.

74. Martinez & Manolovitz, "Incest, Sexual Violence and Rape."

75. Grossmann, *On Killing*.

76. Account told by Rapist-2.

Jungian Theory and Immersion
in Role-Playing Games
SARAH LYNNE BOWMAN

Theory pertaining to role-playing games remains in its infancy. Pioneered in 1983 by the work of Gary Alan Fine in his seminal sociological study *Shared Fantasy*, this burgeoning field still struggles with establishing common terminology to describe the phenomenon of the role-playing experience. Role-playing shares similarities with many other genres of artistic expression — including film, theater, and literature — and theories pertaining to these genres often prove fruitful to furthering our understanding. At the same time, role-playing is distinct from these other forms in that it emerges as a co-created, improvised, spontaneously shared reality. Role-playing encourages no passive audience, only participants who are all engaged in the evolving creation of the narrative. Therefore, trying to adapt an exact corollary between the theoretical conceptualizations offered by artistic and literary criticism to role-playing often proves problematic.

Difficulties also arise when researchers consider the vast array of different types of role-playing games, from tabletop, to live-action role-playing (larp), to virtual gaming. Other tangentially related activities also exist, such as psychodrama, improvisational theater, Renaissance Faires, reenactment societies,[1] sexual subcultures with role-taking features,[2] etc. Even within the same "style" of game, such as live-action role-playing, staggeringly different types of experiences are classified under the same overall label. By way of only a few examples, the word "larp" is used to refer to each of the following: the sport-like play of fighting with foam weapons, the pretense activity of replicating the imagined political structure of a court of vampires, the recreation of the living conditions in countries occupied during World War II, immersion into projected dystopian futures with deplorable living conditions, etc.[3] Because of the vast array of different themes within these games, the establishment of any sort of general, unifying theories that encompass the experiences of all role-players can be difficult.

31

As a preliminary attempt, I have proposed in previous work that all role-playing games include three of the following basic functions: community building, problem solving, and identity alteration.[4] Three role-playing theories that have proven useful in understanding these functions are social interactionism, liminality, and the "magic circle." Most of these examine either the community building or identity alteration functions of role-playing. However, these theories address role-playing from a social psychological and anthropological standpoint without delving into the deeper psychology involved within enactment. My primary interest lies in the creation of role-playing characters and their emergence as epic, larger-than-life representations of personhood. Role-players often use the term *archetype* to describe the types of characters they play,[5] which leads me in the direction of Jungian theory. If role-playing involves enacting archetypes — a term popularized by C. G. Jung in the early twentieth century — how does the process of immersion into character call upon these age-old symbols, which are consistently represented and replicated in myth and popular culture throughout time and space?

This essay will examine these recent applications of previous theories to the activity of role-playing, while adding a new dimension to understanding the process of immersion from the perspective of Jungian psychoanalysis. I will explain how Jung's concepts of active imagination, the collective unconscious, archetypes, envisioning, dialoguing, individuation, and integration can help role-players conceptualize the process beneath the enactment of their role-playing characters. Then, I will explain Jungian theory's place within the spectrum of the history of ideas in the last century. Lastly, I will offer tracks for further research in the area of applied analytical psychology and role-playing, including: the Campbellian *monomyth*, Erich Neumann's three universal mythic structures, and more detailed analyses of common archetypes. While I do not intend for this contribution to explain all of the psychological factors present while role-playing, I hope to further complexify our understanding of the psychological nature of the fantasy content enacted through characters during immersive play.

Symbolic Interactionism, Liminality and the Magic Circle

Important to the study of role-playing games are the theories of symbolic interactionism, liminality, and the "magic circle" of play. Arising from the work of Erving Goffman, symbolic interactionism explains how each interaction represents a theatrical event in which we portray a particular role in order to fulfill our part of the social contract as established by the norms of the collective consciousness.[6] Largely unaware of this process, we constantly shift between roles depending upon the frame within which we find ourselves; we navigate through the social world by donning what we intuit to be the appropriate "mask" to fit each frame. When social roles and interactions are adequately performed, society is considered stable and dependable, allowing for the group to maintain the inherent structure necessary for dealing with potential uncertainty and crisis.

Community building as a process is further reinforced by group-enacted, ritual activity. According to Arnold van Gennep and Victor Turner, rituals enforce group cohesion and identity, a phenomenon known as *communitas*. In ritual, individuals cast aside their normal social roles in preparation for a performance experienced in a group setting. These performances often include adopting more universal, archetypal social roles — such as "bride," "hero," or "shaman" — in order to experience a shift in individual and communal consciousness. This shift is called liminality and involves entering a "betwixt and between" state of consciousness. The liminal state is one in which normal social conventions do not apply, new rules of reality are established, and temporary alternate social roles are enacted.[7] While those participating in the ritual may not realize the profundity of such an experience, this alteration of social rules during an established space and time creates what Huizinga calls the "magic circle." While within the magic circle, the group accepts this new set of rules and identities for a limited time. Huizinga believes that even the most simple of games take place within this magic circle, an imagined space where liminality can be established and experienced, thereby reinforcing the group itself as a cohesive unit.[8]

Many rituals feature rites of passage, in which one or more participants engage in the activity in order to pass from one socially recognized identity to another. In ritual, the masks normally inhabited by each of us in our daily lives are temporarily cast aside as we make these transitions. Common rites of passage include baptisms, puberty rites, weddings, and funerals; each is an experience that communally marks a shift in social role so that each participant is in acceptance of the change by virtue of their participation. Because of the protective frame of the magic circle, this temporary loss of identity and assumption of a new role is understood and accepted. Therefore, even within liminal experiences, the participants feel a sense of safety when altering their identity and performing unusual acts.

Though less common than standardized social rituals, role-playing games also manifest as a form of ritual behavior where the rules of reality are temporarily altered and new ones are established. While some of these roles can become formalized or standardized — such as the leadership role of the Storyteller/Gamemaster — role-playing differs from other more codified social rituals in that the participants have a remarkable amount of creative control over the experiences enacted within the magic circle. The roles they adopt are often spontaneous and self-generated, even if participants are enacting a particular "type" of character that serves a specific purpose. This co-creative capability provides an almost limitless well of imaginative potential; the only limits are defined by the rules established by the magic circle and the expectations of the player culture within which these performances take place.

Together, these three theories of social interactionism, liminality, and the magic circle explain the process of role-playing on a basic, fundamental level. They provide an overall framework for understanding the often-fuzzy boundaries between "game" and "reality." They contextualize the act of role-playing from the perspective of the fields of social psychology and anthropology; in other words, they describe group behavior and how the individual player relates to the whole. In my estimation, however, a deeper psychological analysis of the practice of role-playing is needed. What "happens" to a person when they remove their previous social identifications and adopt new ones, largely of their own creation? From where do these characters arise? How close do these characters represent the daily social roles of their players? To what degree do the experiences and creations within the magic circle reflect the individual's psyche? To what degree can the events within the game alter the consciousness of participants?

These questions are not merely of interest from the whimsical perspective of the idle philosopher. Because role-playing games represent an emerging art form that is not fully understood by the mainstream or by their participants,[9] the performative activity of co-creating new worlds of reality can raise concerns about the psychological safety of such activities. The concepts of the safety provided by the magic circle, the communal cohesiveness reinforced by liminality, and the normal shifting of roles inherent to social interaction may provide some degree of comfort and comprehension of the social processes at work. However, the psychological effects of such experiences still remain largely unknown.

I believe we need another theory to bridge the gap between the social and the psychological. My previous work has delineated a typology of nine relationships between players' primary sense of identity and that of their enacted characters based on ethnographic research. This preliminary theory is an attempt to make sense of the spectrum upon which characters fall with relation to our "normative" selves — i.e. the selves we perform in everyday life that we have come to identify as "us." Some characters manifest as exceptionally similar to the identities of their performing players, while others are strongly distinct.[10] While I was able to dabble with possible conclusions for why players enact particular types of roles based on their own stated reasoning and my speculations, until further elaboration, the typology itself still represents a rather superficial analysis of the psychology behind character enactment.

I wish to understand the deeper processes behind the act of character creation and the impetus behind performing particular types of roles. Jungian psychoanalysis holds, I believe, some of the explanatory keys to unlock these questions. In the following essay, I will explain how the process of immersion in role-playing games is near-identical to Jung's concept of *active imagination*, only distinct in the fact that role-playing takes place in a group setting rather than an individual one. Active imagination leads to the aforementioned stripping of one's individual Ego identity, allows for the player to tap into their *personal unconscious*, then to further delve down into the *collective unconscious*. According to Jung, within this collective unconscious reside the age-old *archetypes* evolved since the inception of human consciousness, ever-potent and enduring, which emerge during this process of active imagination in a ritual setting. Role-playing a character involves unearthing aspects from within these two deep structures, which manifest as spontaneous creative moments within the safe space of the magic circle. When the player emerges out of the liminal experience and their persona is reactivated, they have the potential to reintegrate the experiences gleaned from the process back into their self-concept and attain a state of higher actualization. Jung refers to this phenomenon as *individuation*. Many role-players report an increase in self-awareness, out-of-the-box thinking, social skill proficiencies, and empathy as a result of their experiences within games.[11] I believe that the individuation process described by Jung is one of the fundamental ways that these benefits are achieved.

Immersion and Active Imagination

This transition from one's previous sense of identity into another is called *immersion* in role-playing theory. Certainly the term can also describe a moviegoer's passive relationship with the images portrayed in film, suspension of disbelief, or identification with the main character. A gallery attendee can find themselves immersed in a particular painting, temporarily experiencing a loss of self while viewing the static images before them. Avid music listeners often become immersed in the "world of the song," allowing the melodies, beats and/or lyrics to take them on a journey away from their immediate lives and into a deeper, more emotive, thoughtful state. Alternately, artists and writers themselves may get "lost" in their work, temporarily shifting out of the mundane reality as they create new works. What makes enacting a character in a role-playing game a unique form of immersion from watching a movie or writing a novel is the combination of the active, performative elements with the creative ones.

Role-playing is a spontaneous, ritualized, co-creation of reality, where each participant draws from his or her own well of imagination and takes part in contributing to the overall experience. A role-playing game is both enacted and experienced at once. Though some elements may be pre-planned — a particularly popular strategy in narrativistic role-playing games — the reactions on the part of the participants are, on the whole, spontaneous and unpredictable. From a creative standpoint, this process may be unique to other forms of art due to its spontaneous nature and the fact that players actively immerse themselves into a new identity for extended periods of time — an identity generally stemming from their own imagination, rather than a pre-scripted role.

From the perspective of Jungian theory, immersion also represents a form of active imagination, a psychological phenomenon that Jung often observed in therapeutic, intellectual, and artistic situations. Active imagination involves the relaxation or temporary suspension of the primary ego in order to delve into deeper levels of consciousness. Jung refers to the first level of the Ego as the *persona*. He adopts the term "persona" to indicate the "mask once worn by actors to indicate the role they played."[12] Like Goffman, Jung defines this surface expression of identity as a "mask," a compromise or unconscious agreement between the individual and the society. When one adopts a persona, according to Jung, they often adopt a name, earn a title, and exercise a certain function as dictated by society.[13] The adoption of a persona — often accompanied by a rite of passage such as a graduation ceremony or a job interview — represents a feigning of individuality in service to the whole, a "semblance" of Selfhood, or a two-dimensional reality.[14] While the Ego consciousness does retain some sense of individuality, society expects the person to filter thoughts and feelings through the persona. These conscious thoughts and feelings arise from the next level, the *personal* or *individual consciousness*.

When a participant engages in active imagination, they take part in fantasy activity that does not overly necessitate the persona or even the Ego identity as a whole. Some common examples of active imagination are drawing, creative writing, and improvisational acting. According to Jung, when the surface persona is relaxed, the mind finds avenues to even deeper layers of consciousness, often unearthing potent symbolic imagery. The first of these deeper levels is the *personal unconscious*, those aspects of the individual's psyche that are repressed in order to maintain the illusion of the stable Ego identity. The personal unconscious is composed, in part, of what Jung calls *complexes*. Deeper still within the layers of the mind dwells the *collective unconscious*, which contains *archetypes*. Jung believed these age-old symbolic images to be inherited from our ancestors, part of the foundational structure of our minds and our use of language. Archetypes resonate with us on a fundamental, primordial level. We do not need training to enact or recognize archetypes, though we may not always share the same interpretation of these universal symbols on a cultural level. Thus, Jung refers to archetypes more as inherited thought-patterns rather than inherited thoughts or ideas.[15]

When enacting role-playing characters, we draw from each of the layers of our consciousness. Some characters manifest as closer to the surface of the normal Ego identity than others; I refer to these character types as Doppleganger Selves, because they only slightly deviate from the player's usual persona.[16] Other characters are enacted to play out particular fantasies or wishes, a *wish fulfillment* in psychoanalytic terms.[17] Some roles are adopted in order to explore darker, repressed avenues of the consciousness, aspects that have been suppressed by the Ego because they threaten to destabilize identity or social cohesion. Jung refers to these aspects as pertaining to our Shadow self, the parts of ourselves that we wish to deny exist at all, so are suppressed in our personal unconscious.[18] Other characters represent idealized or exotic aspects of the Self, archetypal fragments from the collective unconscious that emerge as helpers, mentors, healers, heroes, Tricksters, seductresses, villains, and other universal symbols. When these archetypes manifest through participation in active imagination, they belong not to the Ego or persona, but rather to the realms of the Transpersonal and the universal.

When accessing these Transpersonal elements of the collective unconscious, Jung describes a common reaction amongst participants in active imagination called *inflation*. Inflation is a feeling of "god-likeness," as if the individual is imbued with the power of a divine or eternal entity through interaction with the archetype.[19] When interfacing with or performing an archetype, participants involved in active imagination often attribute qualities of "cosmic proportions" to their state of altered consciousness. Jung lists several unique characteristics reported as a result of inflation: a sense of temporal or spatial infinity; changes in the proportions of the body, such as becoming immensely huge or dwarfishly small; exceptional speed or hyperextension of movement; "astrological" associations, such as relating oneself with telluric, lunar, and solar analogies; the experience of "flying through space like a comet"; mythological or religious motifs; feeling as if one is dead; finding oneself in a strange place; feeling as if one is a stranger to him or herself; the sensation of confusion, madness, disorientation, or dizziness.[20]

Inflation often occurs when in a dream, trance, or hypnotic state, as the person meanders through the personal and collective unconscious in a less fettered manner than when awake. However, many of these qualities can also be attributed to the supernatural characteristics exhibited by certain role-playing characters, particularly within the fantasy, horror, and science fiction genres. The abilities of shape shifting and moving quickly through time and space, for example, are common in superhero characters, as well as attributed to certain werewolves, mages, and vampires in White Wolf's World of Darkness. Shifting planes of reality or traveling to distant planets and stars are possible character abilities in *Dungeons & Dragons* and science fiction games such as *Star Trek* and *Traveller*. While more specific examples are beyond the scope of this introductory study, much of the pleasure involved with role-playing within these genres is tied to the ability to enact superhuman abilities. If we consider the role-playing experience as a form of active imagination that accesses the collective unconscious, inflation offers the "possibility" of imagining these otherwise impossible feats. By accessing archetypes, the characters within our imaginations are lent superhuman attributes, allowing us to perceive ourselves for a short time as something different than what we could normally ever become — perhaps something greater, or more sinister, or more capable.

While the qualities of role-playing characters do not always manifest as positive or god-like attributes, the desire to extend consciousness beyond its normal limits does seem to be a common theme in role-playing games. Even in a small, free-form game devoid of costuming or in an immersive Nordic Larp grounded in high realism, the player expects to be transported to a different place and time. Sometimes, that place is external, such as reenacting a particular moment in history or envisioning a possible dystopian future. Other times, that place is internal, such as experiencing a particularly painful psychological state. While these games may not feature supernatural elements, they still require active imagination to enact the magic circle. The content derived from these characters more than likely arises from a person's individual complexes — their personal unconscious. Alternately, these emotions may be drawn from more universal human experiences, such as love, fear, desire, hatred, suffering, etc. While a participant may not ever have experienced rape or murder, for example, such situations can arise in a role-playing game. The player — as in the Ego identity associated with the persona — still has not undergone rape or murder after the dissolution of the magic circle, as the content arises purely from the imaginative properties of themselves and their fellow participants within the safety of the protective frame. However, players do experience an "as if" state in which these experiences occur, which I believe derives from the depths of the unconscious. Though the individual has no recollection of such an occurrence in their own lifetime, the primordial experience still exists within the archetypal parts of the mind. Also, the residue of the experience remains even after the dissolution of the magic circle, retained in memory as both a role-playing moment and an intensely emotional exchange.

Similarly, that player may never have experienced performing the role of father, mentor, sister, hero, king, or even goddess in their mundane existence, and yet they are often called to somehow emulate these qualities in game scenarios. Certain aspects may have been absorbed into the unconscious by observation of external events or of other people playing such roles in mundane reality. Yet, some characters types remain foreign — even, impossible — to emulate from observation. Elves, vampires, and gods, for example, are usually physically immortal — an experience no player has witnessed first-hand in the "real world." Yet, we find ways to call upon these impossible attributes through the process of active imagination by accessing archetypal information and inflating those Transpersonal qualities through the enactment of the character.

Individuation and Integration into the Self-Concept

Selfhood, in Jungian terminology, does not automatically occur in every person, nor is it equivalent with the Ego identity. Selfhood is not considered a given to psychological development. Selfhood is a result of the Ego becoming aware of the elements of the personal and collective unconscious that are considered alien, frightening, or awe-inspiring. According to Jung, the processes of psychoanalysis and artistic or intellectual pursuits should have the same basic aim. The persona is temporarily disintegrated, which deposes the conscious mind from power. This process produces a state of psychic disequilibrium, which allows for the issues dwelling within the unconscious to become exposed.[21] The individual can then resolve the unconscious difficulty, usually through some combination of *envisioning* and *dialoguing*. According to Jungian theory, envisioning allows the contents of the unconscious to become visible in the imagination and is the genesis for all artistic expressions, role-playing being one of many. Dialoguing allows the individual to discuss a particular conflict with a therapist, a conceptualized projection of someone that they know, or an imagined archetypal figure. Furthermore, role-playing adds the extra benefit of allowing *enactment*. Instead of these processes occurring on an individual or solely one-on-one basis, enactment within the magic circle allows players to envision and dialogue with one other on an archetypal level in a group setting while protected by the frame of the game.

After these processes of envisioning, dialoguing, and enactment occur, the protective frame of the magic circle must eventually end or fade, if only temporarily. The Ego identity and persona must now come to terms with the content unearthed by the liminal moments of the game. The Ego experiences itself as individual in this moment — separate, somehow, from the archetypal entities with whom it has interacted, and yet altered through the experience of interaction itself. Jung dubs this process *individuation*, the sudden awareness of the Ego as distinct from the archetypal, Transpersonal Self and, yet, in contact with the collective unconscious. This awareness of difference and, yet, paradoxical connectedness with the Transpersonal creates a crisis for the Ego that must be resolved.

For Jung, these moments represent great potential for growth. When the individual is knocked off balance and forced to interact with aspects of the Self that are repressed or unknown, the opportunity arises for particular personality conflicts to be resolved and for blocks to be removed, allowing further development. Artists would, therefore, often consult Jung during the time of his practice in order to help them remove blocks from their creativity or emotional barriers to intimacy. Jung believed that if the troubled parts of the personality could understand, digest, and assimilate the automatic, instinctive, and unconscious elements of the Transpersonal consciousness, a new inner balance could be achieved.[22] However, Jung warned against dwelling too long in states of active imagination, for the psychosis of the unconscious could override the Ego and create an even greater imbalance. Thus, a return back to the mundane persona with proper integration of the material experienced in the liminal state must occur for the individuation process to be considered successful.

According to Jung, religious prayer and transcendental meditation also fall into the category of individuation, which is why much of the archetypal imagery we unearth when undergoing the process of active imagination bears a "religious or mythological motif."[23] The extent to which such experiences are *actually* spiritual or religious in nature or merely *imagined* as such is beyond the scope of this discussion. Jung merely observed that such imagery repeatedly surfaces cross-culturally throughout time and space. This concept later developed in the field of comparative religion by such theorists as Erich Neumann and Joseph Campbell. Campbell's delineation of the *monomyth* has proved useful for scholars studying mythology and fairy tales, as well as the popular culture genres of fantasy, science fiction, and even action adventure. The experience of the player-character as star in his or her own *monomyth* has also been explored,[24] as has the idea of the archetypal Fellowship exemplified in *Lord of the Rings* as replicated by the standard adventuring party in *Dungeons & Dragons*.[25]

Erich Neumann further examined not one, but three universal myths: Creation, Hero, and Transformation.[26] In addition to the hero's journey, I believe that the Creation and Transformation narratives also often recur in role-playing content, as I will further explain in later work. In addition, the wealth of different archetypes available for exploration in role-playing games is vast indeed, including, but not limited to the hero, Divine Mother, the femme fatale, the Trickster, the Warrior, and a host of other manifestations. Future work will delineate each of the most commonly occurring archetypes, will include examples from role-playing games that actively encourage players to enact these types of characters, and will present ethnographic data from actual players on their experiences.

Considerations When Applying Jungian Theory

Problems arise when attempting to use Jungian concepts to explain psychological mechanisms in our current academic climate. In the second half of the twentieth century, psychoanalysis in general — and Jung in particular — fell out of favor in the majority of psychology departments. Modern psychology instead tends to prefer behaviorism and cognitivism over theoretical abstractions, methods that insist upon using strict observational practices to procure the bulk of research data. Behaviorism, for example, emphasizes the "Ghost in the Machine" premise; the contents of the psyche are present, but ultimately unknowable outside of the context of the brain, so only the study of human behavior can be considered solid science.[27] Cognitivism has found ways to map where places like creativity, emotion, and imaginative expression exist within the brain, but draws no conclusions about the transcendent aspects of such experiences outside of the cognitive context.

Jung, on the other hand, doggedly explored matters of the nature of the psyche in his work. He considered himself a scientist, extrapolating his interpretations from the empirical evidence of dreams, artwork, cultural artifacts, religion, and mythology. However, his insistence on the existence of a collective unconscious — a vast pool of primordial images and stories that make up the basis of human consciousness — tends to make the more scientifically-minded uncomfortable, if not downright hostile, to his ideas. Jung wanted to understand why certain imagery emerged again and again cross-culturally when civilizations had no knowledge of one another. He also wanted to understand how to unlock the meaning of dreams and other non-rational experiences by establishing a series of archetypal images inherent to our genetic makeup. The existence of inherent archetypes would account for why certain imagery unknown to the dreamer would attempt to "communicate" important concepts also echoed in world religion and art. While Freud emphasized the libidinous bond between child and parents as the universal psychological "story," Jung felt that imagery in dreams and art were far more complex and varied. Because of his attempts to describe and theorize upon the nature of transcendent experiences in a universal context, both Freudian psychoanalysts and the more science-heavy psychologists ultimately rejected his ideas in an official capacity.

In my estimation, just because a theory is no longer popular in scholarly circles does not mean it lacks explanatory power. As Thomas Kuhn famously suggested in his work on scientific revolutions, the adoption of certain new ways of viewing the world often call into question old ones, forcing people to shift their paradigm in order to accept the new information.[28] In the case of Jungian theory, providing universal explanations for subjective experiences such as dreams, art, and even spirituality contradicts the scientific paradigm, which cannot reliably measure these things yet. To say that the source of many of the symbols in culture, for example, lies in the genetic code is a concept that most scientists will reject if they currently know of no evidence of such a phenomenon. In addition, many scientists favor an agnostic, existential, or atheistic paradigm, either shying away from discussion about spiritual matters or reacting with scorn to any serious discussion of a connection between transcendent experience and science. Following Kuhn, the majority of people — even the greatest minds of our time — feel the need to fervently defend their personal truths. Ideas which fall outside of these truths will often be rejected without consideration.

While Jungian theory has failed to establish a foothold in the current permutations of psychological scholarship, Jung's ideas have influenced popular culture on a more massive scale than many might realize. As journalist Mark Vernon recently stated in a BBC News Magazine article, "Alongside Sigmund Freud, [Jung] is arguably one of the two people of the 20th century who most shaped the way we think about who we are."[29] A conversation between Carl Jung and one of his patients emphasizing the necessity for a spiritual belief system helped build the foundation of Alcoholics Anonymous, the 12-Step Program that has hundreds of permutations and has helped millions recover from life-threatening addictions of all sorts.[30] Various New Age movements have been inspired by Jungian concepts. Borrowing from Frazer in *The Golden Bough*,[31] Jung's emphasis on the Great Mother as the most powerful early divine figure influenced neo-pagan groups such as Wicca and ecofeminism, many of whom have recovered ancient female deities from obscurity and developed new religious practices around the worship of femininity. In addition, Jung's theory of Psychological Types has been adopted by the mainstream in the form of the Myers-Briggs Type Indicator personality test, which is often administered by employers as a way to determine compatibility between the subject and the work environment. According to MBTI assessment company CPP, Inc., "As many as 1.5 million assessments are administered annually to individuals, including to employees of most Fortune 500 companies."[32] Thus, while Jungian concepts have failed to establish a strong following in academic institutions, their potency in terms of popular adoption cannot be denied.

Furthermore, Jungian theory, though independently influential in its own right, is best understood within a spectrum of different approaches to understanding human behavior and culture. No theory is developed in a vacuum; a theorist works within the conditions and influences of his or her time. The ideas developed from the theorist are not singular and unrelated to other concepts; in fact, they tend to work best when considered in concert with other related theories, as I have ventured to do by connecting the theories of symbolic interactionism, liminality, and the "magic circle" with individuation. A spectrum approach allows individual ideas to be considered within a larger scope, allowing us to integrate information. I will explain how Jung's ideas relate to other trends present in the twentieth century, including: comparative religion, structural functionalism, narratology, evolutionary psychology, and avant-garde artistic movements.

Jungian Theory Within the Spectrum of the History of Ideas

According to Jung, as previously described, archetypal symbology is present cross-culturally, embedded in our religious mythologies, our fairy tales, our popular culture, and other artistic expressions. Jung believed that while much of culture is specific to its own particular time and place, certain concepts are universal. They emerge cross-culturally regardless of whether or not the societies expressing them had any historical contact. Jung believed these "inherited thought-patterns" to be necessary for survival, evolutionary adaptations built into our genetic code.[33] To Jung, then, archetypes do not represent mere coincidences in imagery; they express aspects of the human experience that would have been important to communicate early in the development of our consciousness. To use the *monomyth* as an example, determining whether or not someone is playing the role of villain, princess-bride, or mentor/donor would have been strategically important to early humans. Interaction with animals and exposure to the elements was more commonplace, so such aspects are emphasized in archetypal symbology. Stories emphasizing the creation of the world, the development of humankind, and the potential destruction by natural or supernatural forces remain of interest in both ancient contexts and in our current mythological narratives. These types of symbols and stories provide both a sense of wonder about the unknown and an explanatory function, lending to their paradoxical nature, which Jung called the *principle of opposites*.

These revelations fell in line with the emerging fields of comparative religion, functionalism, and evolutionary theory, areas which are still studied today to greater or lesser degree. Following Frazer's work in *The Golden Bough,* comparative religion focuses upon charting the major themes in religious narratives world-wide and trying to trace certain central concepts.[34] Though comparative religion has evolved as a discipline since the time of Jung's writing, ideas such as the Great Mother hypothesis, the hero's journey, the concept of the Shadow, and analysis of specific mythological figures as archetypal in nature — such as the Trickster — owe a debt to analytical psychology.[35] Scholars in this field sometimes adopt a Jungian lens for certain narratives that are best illuminated through his theories.

Another popular theory during the first half of the twentieth century was structural functionalism, arising from sociology, linguistics, and anthropology. Functionalism puts forth the notion that scholars can reduce social formations to certain organizing principles that are necessary for the group to function properly. While functionalism does not attempt to explain all aspects of human behavior, proponents of this theory believe that elements of culture such as religion, language, art, ritual, law, economics, etc. are specifically useful in maintaining social cohesion. Turner's work on liminality falls under this general category, as does Durkheim's *totemic principle*, the notion that all social organization originates from early religious categories.[36]

In addition, some scholars during this period sought to unpack narrative structures from a functionalist perspective. Vladimir Propp, Erich Neumann, and Joseph Campbell all attempted to find the "template" for narrative logic, identifying various key roles that characters must take and important dramatic moments that must be enacted in "universal" story cycles. Narratologist Noam Chomsky sought to find the universal grammar behind all language.[37] Lévi-Strauss believed that while surface aspects of myths may change, certain paired oppositions called *mythemes* are present within every myth and exist within all permutations of the story.[38] Similarly, Jacques Lacan believed that opposition was fundamental to the emergence of language in each infant; we learn what things are by understanding first what they are *not*. These conceptual threads also exist within Jungian theory: the idea of certain stories being central to the human experience; the concept of key archetypal roles replicating throughout myth; the notion that these symbols and stories have psychological potency and help hold the fabric of society together; and the *principle of opposites*, where oppositional elements are embedded into archetypes, the paradox of which accords symbols with their psychological power.[39] Structural functionalism has fallen out of favor in many academic circles, replaced by so-called "post-structuralism," where cultural meaning emerges entirely from social construction and is, therefore, malleable. However, I do not believe one can claim to be a post-structuralist without first understanding and respecting the claims of structural functionalism.

Regardless of the trend in the liberal arts toward social constructionism, some fields still seek to identify essential aspects of human behavior. Evolutionary psychology has become increasingly popular in recent years with advances in cognitive and genetic science. Evolutionary psychology seeks to chart how certain human behaviors emerged as the result of environmental pressures and requirements. Theorists such as Steven Pinker hold that complex language became a crucial part of our evolutionary process and that language structures and acquisition are part of our instinctual, genetic make-up. Pascal Boyer claims that religious concepts fall under certain general cognitive categories based on our intuitive comprehension of the world.[40] Originating from the work of Richard Dawkins, memetic theory has emerged as an explanatory model for how ideas replicate through culture from mind to mind. Though memes are gene-like, memetic theory holds that ideas transmit through culture rather than as an essential feature specifically embedded in the code.[41] The instinct to spread information may be inherent, but the information itself is not. While memetic transmission is certainly observable, the question still remains why some symbolic structures more easily replicate than others. From a memetic perspective, archetypes fall within this category. If we accept Pinker's assertion that the faculty for language structures is inherent to our genetic makeup and Boyer's claim that religious concepts fall into certain embedded, intuitive categories regardless of culture, the possibility that certain mythological content is inherent within these structures still exists. As David Lindenfeld suggests, "The notion of archetypes and their structure has undergone a certain rehabilitation in the past several decades thanks to evolutionary psychology, which provides a more sophisticated formulation of instinctual behavior than was available in Freud's or Jung's day."[42] Ultimately, regardless of whether or not archetypes replicate memetically or genetically, we see evidence of them cross-culturally, as evidenced in the work of comparative religion.

Also popular in the early twentieth century was the exploration of unconscious material through art, as evidenced in such experiments as automatic writing and Surrealism.[43] Analytical psychologists such as M.-L. von Franz believed artistic work often expresses archetypal imagery.[44] Jung himself created *The Red Book*, a sixteen year project in which, through active imagination, he delved into what he believed to be the collective unconscious and interacted with archetypal material. The result of these explorations was a massive tome with vivid artistic images and the stories of his imaginings catalogued in medieval-like calligraphy. Emerging from this process, Jung felt himself to be a more individuated person, which compelled him to find analytical language to theorize upon the nature of his own experiences and those of his patients. Jung states:

> The years ... when I pursued the inner images, were the most important time of my life ... my entire life consisted in elaborating what had burst forth from the unconscious and flooded me like an enigmatic stream and threatened to break me. That was the stuff and material for more than only one life. Everything later was merely the outer classification, the scientific elaboration, and the integration into life. But, the numinous beginnings, of which contained everything, was then.[45]

Unlike Freud, who insisted that symbolic content only revealed neurosis, Jung believed that this unconscious imagery may hold the keys for understanding ourselves and the world around us in a more integrated manner.

In summary, Jung's ideas exist within a conceptual spectrum alongside other lines of inquiry already present in various disciplines. Jung was certainly not alone in wishing to understand the evolution of consciousness with regard to language. Though evolutionary psychology and cognition has yet to reliably prove the existence of archetypal content as embedded in the genetic code, the suggestion of language as inherent to human development remains a topic of interest to researchers today. Also, from a more right-brained perspective, the process of active imagination can explain many creative activities and artistic expressions, including immersion into role-playing games.

For example, comparative religion holds that certain imagery repeats cross-culturally; a common symbol is the serpent or dragon, which features heavily in many Creation and Destruction myths around the world.[46] When studying the rich tapestry of mythological symbols, the meaning embedded within a title such as *Dungeons & Dragons*, for instance, ceases to be merely arbitrary. Hook suggests that each player in a role-playing game can be seen as enacting his or her own hero's journey during play.[47] Slaying the dragon becomes a symbol for individuation in the Jungian model, as the individual is able to confront the unconscious — the primordial existence before individuality — and integrate its power into the sense of Self.[48] In addition, descent into the Underworld to reclaim some important part of one's self is another common theme in mythology,[49] a process for which the Dungeon becomes a metaphor. Characters emerge from the Dungeon having gained something; these gains are tangibly articulated as "experience points" that improve their character's abilities and items to help them on future journeys, but psychologically, player-characters also gain the experience of potential individuation.

This short example demonstrates the potency of the Jungian approach when understanding the archetypal content present in many role-playing games. Regardless of a character's archetypal affiliation — rogue, healer, warrior, sage — the metaphoric process of entering the dungeon of the unconscious and conquering enemies that would normally produce terror are central tenants of the individuation process. While not all role-playing experiences feature the explicit symbolic content of *Dungeons & Dragons*, Jungian theory can help to explain the potency of that particular narrative — known in the gaming world as "the dungeon crawl" — and the success of that style of role-playing games. Less fantastical role-playing games still feature challenges that must be overcome, be them physical, social, psychological, or even spiritual. Therefore, the hero's journey need not manifest literally within fictional narratives for individuation to occur.

Role-Playing Theory and Jung

As mentioned before, the most commonly-used concepts in current role-playing theory are the persona, the magic circle, and liminality. Jungian theory provides a psychological explanation for the role-playing experience that complements these more sociological theories. The emphasis on the persona and adoption of different social masks in Goffman's work correlates strongly with Jung's explanation of the pre-individuated Ego, the surface level of which he calls the persona. Unlike Goffman, though, Jung suggests that we can break down this persona and delve into deeper layers of meaning through exploration of our personal and collective unconscious. The two theories can be used in concert with one another to provide a more rewarding explanation of social-psychological experience, one that does not merely emphasize the superficial necessities of social life.

Jungian theory also connects quite strongly with the concept of liminality. Analytical psychologists have correlated active imagination and individuation with liminal experiences. In *Jung in Context*, Peter Homans describes individuation as liminal, stating that it "begins with a withdrawal from the normal modes of social action, epitomized by the breakdown of the persona."[50] In addition, proponents of depth psychology and comparative religion lament the lack of rituals in modern society. In her book on female initiation rituals, Jungian Bani Shorter stresses, "The need to accord space, time, and place for liminal feeling and ritual enactment was largely ignored in Western society for centuries. Now this need once again commands attention."[51] Role-playing games can be viewed, in this sense, as a needed resurgence in ritual behavior, rife with mythological and archetypal content. When role-players enact these rituals and integrate these experiences back into their self-concept through the process of individuation, they participate in an age-old process; however, they also experience a revitalized, imaginative, and new practice of self- and group discovery.

Joseph Campbell, the Jungian comparative religion scholar most commonly associated with the *monomyth*, breaks down the three phases of the hero's journey as such: departure, initiation, and return.[52] These designations directly correlate with van Gennep's phases of the ritual process, later adopted and popularized by Turner, "separation, margin (or *limen*, signifying 'threshold' in Latin), and aggregation."[53] The magic circle can be integrated with these concepts, as it creates a sort of liminal space tied to play behavior. These concepts attempt to put into words the "fuzziness" of these in-between experiences, providing terminology for the social and mental space created when we play. When we add the component of the enactment of a spontaneously-created role, the personal unconscious and mythic/archetypal content can help explain the qualities that characters emerging within that social and mental space possess.

That liminality, a magic circle, or a persona "exists" is just as difficult to prove scientifically as the existence of a collective unconscious or universal archetype. Researchers can only measure these experiences in reports from the player base, just as spiritual experiences cannot be reliably quantified by scientific means. For this reason, much of the academic scholarship on role-playing games emphasizes ethnographic information gleaned from participants. It is impossible to "capture" the experience of enacting an archetype, entering a magic circle, or exploring the liminal game world. These experiences exist in the "betwixt and between" space of reality by their very nature. As Evan Torner explains in his work on role-playing documentaries, attempts to record role-playing experiences often fail to express the entirety of the experience, as much of the "action" takes place within the player's mind.[54] Interviews after the fact are a sort of "secondary revision," in Freudian terms; explaining the experience of role-playing after gameplay can never capture the moment completely, as the subject has experienced the "return" phase, emerging out of the ritual space and integrating back into the daily persona of society. Thus, I would suggest against rejecting Jungian theories as theoretical models due to their "unscientific nature," as the other accepted theoretical concepts regarding role-playing immersion are just as difficult to prove outside of phenomenological ethnographic reports.

Ultimately, I am not advocating a single-minded adoption of Jungian theory as the "answer" to all creativity in role-playing games. Any theory is a lens that we may choose to use or discard when most appropriate. I believe, for example, that the concept of archetypes explains, on some level, the nature of role enactment. It also explains why the vast majority of roles feature epic or mythological content, as fantasy material is rife with archetypes. While many might claim that the reason for the popularity of fantasy role-playing simply stems from the historical condition of *Dungeons & Dragons* being the first and therefore the most influential game, I believe that explanation only accounts for part of the reasoning behind the phenomenon. The enactment of the hero's journey and of age-old archetypes allows for some of the deepest interaction between the individual and the collective. Instead of passively watching a fantasy film or listening to a fairy tale, role-playing allows the participants to act out this archetypal content.

As Jung emphasizes in his discussion of individuation, simply accessing these archetypes is not enough. One must engage in envisioning, dialoguing, and enactment in order to fully establish the relationship between the Ego and the archetype. We can see this process take place in both the role-player's personal relationship with their characters and with their interactions in the game with other enacted characters. Part of the character is most certainly a personal, individual expression on the part of the player, but part of it taps into these deeper archetypes.

When interacting within the game, role-players are engaged in the individuation process on more social scale than Jung originally detailed. His examples of active imagination take place either in solitude — in the cases of personal explorations of art, literature, and dream-work — or in a one-on-one relationship with the analyst and subject. Inherent to this latter relationship is a certain power dynamic established by the social world; even though the therapy session holds similar features to a liminal experience, as "a spatial-temporal frame [marks] off the special kind of reality of a psychoanalytic session,"[55] the subject likely never forgets the fact that the analyst remains in a socially-codified authority position. Role-playing games, however, remove players from the professional world, which makes for a deeper liminal experience. Family members may no longer fully perceive each other as their normative personas when immersed in a role; thus, the power dynamic of a parent/child relationship, for example, might flip if the child in question is the most powerful character in the game or the organizer. Just as in religious rituals, one's social status outside of the game rarely affects the enactments within the game.

Thus, when a player successfully enacts a particularly potent archetype — say, a Villain, Trickster, Sage, Warrior, or Femme Fatale — the group generally responds to the features of that character, not to the social distinction of the player enacting it. An interesting example of this phenomenon occurs when an organizer adopts the role of multiple characters in the game in order to provide a fully imagined world within which the characters can interact. An organizer may play a Sage character, passing on vital information to the group, then switch into the role of the Villain, who the characters must attempt to defeat or evade. The players understand that the organizer is an authority figure within the structure of the game and is portraying these roles in order to advance the story, but the characters respond to these archetypal characters in a manner appropriate to their own psychological orientation. For example, if a player-character is a Trickster archetype — commonly embodied as the

Rogue in *D&D* or the Malkavian in *Vampire: the Masquerade*—they may attempt to foil the Sage or assist the Villain simply to create chaos and force players to adapt.[56] Alternately, a Warrior who wishes to save the people in the hero's role would likely revere the Sage, accept the help offered, and use it to defeat or elude the Villain.[57]

These are merely hypothetical examples; more research is needed into the nature of archetypal enactment in role-playing characters. However, these archetypes are often purposefully embedded in role-playing games. White Wolf directly states Carl Jung as an influence on the immensely popular World of Darkness game *Vampire: The Masquerade* and specifically uses the term archetype in various source books. Tolkien used classic archetypes from mythology in *The Lord of the Rings*, which influenced many of the Races and Classes in *Dungeons & Dragons*.[58] Therefore, I do not believe the question should remain: "Do archetypes exist within role-playing games?" They clearly do. The question becomes: "Why is archetypal enactment important to understand?"

In conclusion, Carl Jung's conceptualizations of active imagination, archetypes, and individuation provide a needed bridge for a psychological understanding of the types of characters enacted within the magic circle. Examining the psychoanalytic potential of these enacted roles can help explain several phenomena. First, role-playing produces a temporary release from anxiety by relaxing the public persona and allowing repressed aspects of the psyche to emerge. Second, the exploration of the content of the personal and collective unconscious may provide assistance in working through psychological and social barriers. Third, the experience of increased self-awareness, empathy, and out-of-the-box thinking that many role-players report as a result of their experiences may arise from the individuation process, creating a healthier balance within the psyche. Finally, the concept of active imagination may prove more useful terminologically for explaining the process of role-playing than the commonly-used word "escapism." Escapism oftentimes denotes a pejorative connotation, as if the individual cannot cope with reality or somehow rejects it. On the contrary, the concepts of active imagination and individuation demonstrate that even if a player is "escaping" the confines of reality to enter the liminal magic circle of play, the work that takes place within that frame can become psychologically powerful, offering the potential for a more balanced and self-actuated psyche.

Notes

1. Bowman, *Functions of Role-Playing Games* 33–46.
2. Harviainen, "Larping That Is Not Larp" 180–181.
3. Stenros and Montola, *Nordic Larp* 25–28.

4. Bowman 7–9.
5. Bowman 143–154.
6. Bowman 47.
7. Bowman 47–51.
8. Montola, *Pervasive,* 10–17.
9. MacKay 157–159.
10. Bowman 155–178.
11. Bowman 1–5.
12. Jung, *Portable,* 105.
13. Jung 106.
14. Ibid.
15. Jung 83.
16. Bowman 164–166.
17. Nephew, "Playing" 122.
18. Jung, *Portable,* 144–148.
19. Jung 88.
20. Jung 108–109.
21. Jung 110.
22. Jung 109–110.
23. Jung 108.
24. Hook, "Larp" 34–40.
25. Tresca, *Evolution* 5.
26. See Neumann 5–220.
27. Ryle, *Concept* 27.
28. Kuhn, *Structure* 111.
29. Vernon, "What Would Carl Jung Make of 2011?"
30. "Bill W — Carl Jung Letters."
31. Frazer, *Golden* 330–362.
32. See "History."
33. Jung, *Portable,* 83.
34. Voth, "Myth and Meaning."
35. Voth, "Continuing."
36. Durkheim, *Elementary Forms* 6.
37. Lindenfeld, "Jungian Archetypes" 223.
38. Gras, "Myth" 477.
39. Lindenfeld 223–224.
40. Boyer, *Religion Explained* 71–91.
41. Dawkins, "Memes" 189–201.
42. Lindenfeld 225.
43. Shamdasani, "*Liber Novus*" 196.
44. von Franz, "Process" 157–254.
45. Jung, *Red Book,* back cover.
46. Voth, "Continuing."
47. Hook 34.
48. Bowman 14.
49. Voth, "Inanna."
50. Homans, *Jung* 207.
51. Shorter, *An Image* 79.
52. Campbell, *Hero* ix.
53. Turner, *The Ritual Process* 94.
54. Torner, "The Theory and Practice" 113.
55. Milner, quoted in Casement, *Learning* 339.
56. Hyde *Trickster* 6.
57. Hook 32.
58. Bowman 143–154.

Circles and Frames: The Games Social Scientists Play

Nathan Hook

This essay explains the two concepts of *protective frame* (from psychology) and the *magic circle* (from the sociology of play), and how their intensity supports and shapes immersive role-playing and *bleed*, an emergent concept in the Scandinavian role-playing tradition. We will begin by defining each of these concepts, and then review some classic psychology experiments that have included some element of role enactment or role-play beyond merely the role of "participants" through the lens of these theoretical metaphors.

Protective Frame and Magic Circle

In his popular psychology book *The Dangerous Edge: The Psychology of Excitement*, Michael J. Apter proposes the notion of a *protective frame* around play that psychologically shields players from the "real world."[1] Though this frame is located in the minds of participants, it sometimes attains physical representation, for example, by the arch of a theater or the boundary line in cricket. It can also be abstractly represented, like with the rules of board game. This frame empowers players of any game by creating a feeling of safety, which allows them to engage in play behavior that might be "silly," shameful or otherwise inappropriate if done outside of play. The protective frame is mostly illusory; a psychological feeling of safety, not actual guarantee from psychological or physical harm.

The presence or non-presence of Apter's frame may determine whether an emotionally potent experience can cause anxiety or arousal. For example, seeing a tiger walking around would be seen as anxiety-inducing, but seeing a tiger inside a cage (a literal protective frame) would be seen as exciting. The frame is not always physically embodied — a rock climber's confidence in his/her own skill and ability might constitute their protective frame. As a hobby, role-playing can also be considered a form of protective frame. According to Apter, assuming a different role such as a shaman in a ritual mask or an actor on stage creates a psychological feeling of safety that empowers the person to engage in unusual play behavior. Under this paradigm, "stage fright" represents a kind of failure to form the protective frame in one's mind.

In his 1939 work *Homo Ludens*, Johan Huizinga describes the social boundary that surrounds play, in the widest possible sense:

> All play moves and has its being within a play-ground marked off beforehand either materially or ideally, deliberately or as a matter of course.... The arena, the card-table, the *magic circle*, the temple, the stage, the screen, the tennis court, the court of justice, etc., are all in forms and function playgrounds, i.e. forbidden spots, isolated, hedged round, hallowed, within which special rules obtain. All are temporary worlds within the ordinary world, dedicated to the performance of the act apart.[2]

While the circle is also physically embodied like the frame, what Huizinga describes is a *social*, rather than psychological, barrier that separates the activity from everyday life. For example, the magic circle stops players from holding a grudge against someone who attacked him/her while playing a competitive sport such as boxing or the board game Risk. The above quote shows how Huizinga extends this concept to play in the widest sense — beyond merely "games" or "sport" to religion, drama, and law. Clearly there is much in common between the frame and the circle, and in some cases they may share the same physical embodiment. They operate on different levels however, with the frame being personal and the circle interpersonal. This essay deals with another modern "hallowed ground" couched within these two principles, and with its own special rules: the laboratory of the social scientist.

Immersion

This essay uses the term "immersion" primarily within the context of individual psychology. In a paper published in 1975, psychologist Mihály Csíkszentmihályi proposed the concept of "flow," meaning a mental state where a person is fully immersed in an activity as active participant. Flow is not a passive state. The term is derived from Csíkszentmihályi interviewees during his experiments, as they used the metaphor of water current. The concept applies to many fields of activity involving intense concentration on a single activity for a long time, including sports, spirituality and games.

Flow is the umbrella concept that relates to many different fields, and "immersion" is a subset of flow that relates to a particular kind of activity. Within the context of this essay "immersion" is used as a concept for a person achieving a state of flow while taking on a particular role. Method acting is one example of this. When reviewing his infamous Stanford Prison Experiment in 1999, Philip Zimbardo applied the term "immersion" to his scenario of ordinary people assuming the roles of guards and prisoners, stating that "immersion in "total situations" can transform human nature." Zimbardo presents immersion as both a possibility and risk in the social scientist's laboratory.

Shortly after Zimbardo's re-evaluation of his experiment, Mike Pohjola published in 2000 the Turku Manifesto in Finland, which highlighted the concept of immersion in a role-playing context: "Role-playing is immersion to an outside consciousness (a "character") and [the interaction] with its surroundings."[3] Pohjola presents immersion as the ultimate goal for a participant in a role-playing game, something that only results from a player's active effort, rather than as something passively achieved. He refers to immersion within a particular character (and his/her own personal diegesis as a facet of that), whereas Zimbardo refers to immersion in the context of a surrounding situation that transforms the participant's "nature." When considered this way, these two immersions stand in stark contrast to one another. In this essay, "character immersion" refers to what Pohjola describes and "situational immerison" refers to what Zimbardo describes. As they can both be classified under the aforementioned concept of "flow," the concepts may not be as opposed as one might think. One term I will avoid using here is "role" as used in that of a job or a character. The term "role" can help define a constructed character, along with a personality, personal history, and so forth. Yet it can also be regarded as a mere facet of the situation, such as being in the role of a "prisoner" in the Zimbardo experiment. "Role" is ambiguous in that it might refer to either a personal or interpersonal level of interaction.

Bleed

The concept of bleed relates to all the previous concepts. Markus Montola describes "bleed play" where the boundary between the real world (player) and play (character) becomes even more porous. While the psychological basis for bleed is unclear, the concept is used as design rhetoric by role-playing gamewrights as such the Nordic *Vi åker jeep*[4] group who describe it thus:

> Bleed is experienced by a player when her thoughts and feelings are influenced by those of her character, or vice versa. With increasing bleed, the border between player and character becomes more and more transparent. It makes sense to think of the degree of bleed as a measure of how separated different levels of play (actual/inner/meta) are.[5]

Annika Waern discusses bleed within computer game context where the player feels the emotions of the character.[6] Both elements of the player him/herself seep into their gameplay (bleed-in), and the effects of play affect the player (bleed-out). These effects weaken the psychological power of the protective frame, while still maintaining the social alibi power of the magic circle.

Montola suggests that direct bleed — when the player experiences the emotions of their character — is quite similar to Pohjola"s character immersion; it might be viewed that direct bleed-out is what happens when immersion does not properly end after play finishes. There is also indirect bleed, where the player experienced diametrically opposite emotions to those of their character. Bleed reminds one that both barriers — circle and frame — are by no means impermeable. The circle is merely a social convention. The frame is merely a sense of safety. Neither of them can prevent real psychological changes from occurring — even if the pretense that they do so is important for the activity itself. The term "bleed" here could inclusively refer to both short term changes, such as an emotional state carrying over beyond the scenario, and a longer term change, such as an experience within play permanently changing a deeply held belief in a person.

Asch's Conformity Experiment

We will proceed by looking at an example of a bleed-in effect, where a cultural trait affected the behavior of participants inside the magic circle. Solomon Asch was an early pioneer of social psychology in the United States, and his Conformity Experiment was carried out at a liberal arts college in Pennsylvania. Asch's work would later inspire the work of Stanley Milgram, whose Ph.D. he supervised. Within the context of this essay, this experiment demonstrates how an example behavioral trait–conformity–bleeds across the magic circle of the laboratory.

In 1951, Asch advertised for participants for a group line judgment experiment — judging relative lengths of drawn lines — but was actually researching the power of conformity to confirm the conclusions found by a experiment carried out by Muzafer Sherif in 1935 that people tend to agree with a group's judgment even when wrong.

In Asch's original run of the test, the participants were individual male students who believed they were seated around a table with seven fellow participants. These "fellow participants" were, in fact, all confederates planted by Asch who were following the researcher's prior instructions. The experimenter showed the group a vertical line drawn on paper and asked them to indicate which of three other lines were most similar to it in length. This was repeated eighteen times. The plants deliberately gave the wrong answer on twelve occasions.

RESULTS — ASCH

- Asch reports a participant faced with a group of others giving a clearly incorrect answer would agree with it 32 percent of the time.
- Sean Perrin and Charles Spencer repeated the experiment and only in 1 out of the 396 trials did the participant conform. They attributed this change to the changing role of students, from conforming in 1950s America to a more questioning role in the 1980s.
- Marie-France Lalancette and Lionel Standing also found no conformity when they repeated the experiment.
- Nigel Nicholson, Steven Cole and Thomas Rocklin found 12 of 38 UK and 8 out of 21 U.S. students conformed at least once.
- Felix Neto repeated the experiment with female participants at a Portuguese university and found 59 percent participants conformed at least once, with 28 percent conforming three to twelve times. Participants also reported considerable distress under peer pressure.

ANALYSIS — ASCH

The results above seem mixed: while conformity does occur, it is in fact an unreliable outcome. Even in Asch's original experiment, some participants did not conform at all. It may very well be an expression of a particular social class/subculture than a universal psychological principle. The ecological validity, or how well the experiment approximates a real world situation, is somewhat low given the artificial nature of the task. But one would find it ecologically valid within the sphere of experimental design: pressure to conform can be identified as a possible confounding variable in any group experiment. From a role-playing game perspective, the issue is less of a concern, since role-played situations are themselves often removed from everyday experience. This removal is usually the basis of the circle. The game-like task of the experiment may have reinforced a circle within the experiment.

What this experiment shows us is an example of a bleed-in effect. Despite being within the physically defined magic circle of the laboratory and carrying out a game-like activity, the participants nevertheless felt a need to conform. In some of the later runs, their socially based reluctance to conform is also evident. In Asch's experiment, the rituals of being recruited as a participant, entering the laboratory, having the rules explained and doing an abstract task do not form a strong enough circle to prevent bleed-in. In summary: the weaker the circle, the higher the level of bleed-in.

A ROLE-PLAYING CONTEXT — ASCH

Let us consider a fictional variant on this previous experiment, or what might have happened had Asch and his successors included a protective frame mechanic in the situation. Would the conformity as shown by Asch arise if one requested the participants to role-play a *character*, rather than themselves? If participants with full knowledge of Asch's experiment were asked to then assume the roles of 1950s American college students in a fictional experiment, what would they do? At first glance one might expect the participants to display conformist behavior due to their faithfulness to the historical scenario.

People conform out of fear of a negative social reaction. Within the role-playing context, a strong protective frame should protect the player from those negative reactions, much as a stage actor should not have to fear the long-term consequences of his/her villainous character's actions. The participant might be sufficiently empowered by the protection the frame provides to the extent that they fail to immerse in their character or the situation. To reiterate: a participant's awareness of Huizinga's circle provides a social alibi for character action, and Apter's frame provides psychological protection which can actually prevent "realistic" immersion in the situation. The issue of ecological validity arises again: a person asked a question in everyday life may respond differently than they would under experimental conditions.

A real example of this mechanism being deliberately used is the work of Augusto Boal in *Games for Actors and Non-Actors*. Boal uses the protective frame of role-playing in theater activity to empower people to overcome their conformity and challenge the social status quo. For example when he organized "forum theater" in rural village of Godrano, Sicily, he empowered the residents to publicly argue with their mayor in the village square by giving them characters to play, even when the mayor entered the fiction and played himself. Boal achieved his results via the protective frame, and not the magic circle; an actor is not separated via the fiction, but by the psychological sense of invincibility conveyed by the role. Asch's participants let their conformity bleed-in through the circle because they have no character; Boal uses the frame of the participants wearing the metaphorical "mask" of a character to overcome their conformity, with the aim their experience will then bleed-out into their real lives.

An added wrinkle is that players with a strong protective frame may feel more inclined to create drama for the sake of doing so; seeking dramatic scenes rather than character immersion. Related to this would be the taking advantage of a strong protective frame to explore repressed facets of their personality or engage in taboo play. Sarah Lynne Bowman describes role-players displaying this type of play and terms it "Repressed Self" and "The Taboo Self."[7] The participant engages in childish or mischievousness behavior that would not be acceptable in everyday life, or breaks social taboos by discussing topics such as murder, incest and sexual abuse.

If the protective frame is weak, this sense of empowerment may not apply and conformity displayed may be an expression of the player's own conformity. Any distress felt *bleeds-out* to the participant. This would not represent immersion in the character or the character's culture, but may represent "situational immersion" in the experience of the situation present — the sense of fear or shame they feel disagreeing with the group becomes real for them. This appears to be what happened in 1995 when Felix Neto repeated Asch's experiment with female Portuguese participants.

In summary:

- A weak frame results in situational immersion.
- A strong frame results in character immersion.
- A very strong frame can result in game play, dramatic play, or repressed / taboo play.

Milgram's Obedience Experiment

In 1961, Stanley Milgram performed his classic obedience experiment at Yale University where participants were instructed to torture another person. We will look at this experiment and interpret the results under this model to show the distinction between the Circle and Frame and to demonstrate long term bleed-out.

Milgram recruited men aged 20–50 under the pretext of taking part in a memory experiment. He later carried out another run with women participants which found broadly similar results but they reported higher levels of stress. The experiment started with the participant drawing lots with a "plant" pretending to be a second participant. This was a rigged draw such that the actual participant was assigned the "teacher" role and the plant the "learner" role.

As the situation appeared to the participant, they were taking on the role of teacher by giving the learner a small sample electric shock and then teaching word-pairs to the learner. The teacher then asked the learner a multiple-choice question about the word-pairs, which the learner would answer by pressing a button. Each time a question was incorrect, the teacher would pull a lever giving a gradually increasing electric shock.

The real learner was, in fact, an actor. He would merely listen to a pre-recorded sound to indicating the shock level, and would role-play receiving an appropriate kind of shock. At high "voltages," the learner would bang on the wall and complain about his heart condition. After that, he would go silent. If the real participant (the teacher) expressed doubts, the experimenter dressed in a lab-coat sitting behind them would verbally encourage them to continue by speaking from a list of scripted statements and assuring them they would not be held responsible.

RESULTS — MILGRAM

In the first run of the experiment, twenty-six out of forty participants (65 percent) administered the maximum electric shock of 450 volts. Every participant had questioned the situation in some way to the experimenter at some point. Only a single participant actually stopped before getting to 300 volts. Various attempts to repeat the experiment produced different results. Milgram repeated it in an office location in a nearby town rather than Yale University and found the results dropped to 48 percent, but this difference was not statistically significant and thus dismissed by Milgram. Proximity between the teacher and learner made more of a difference with people more reluctant to torture someone in the same room as them — which one could say would be a more ecologically valid situation. None of the twenty-six participants who went to the maximum charge left the room to check on the learner without asking permission to do so first.

Charles Sheridan and Richard King challenged the validity by suggesting the participants already suspected the electric shocks were faked. They repeated the experiment with a puppy receiving real electric shocks and also looked for a gender difference. Out of twenty-six participants, all thirteen women went to the maximum charge (100 percent obedient), but many were disturbed and some cried. Six male participants refused to do this (54 percent obedient).

ANALYSIS — MILGRAM

92 percent of participants responded to a follow-up survey. Of those, 84 percent said they were "glad" or "very glad" to have participated, and 15 percent gave a neutral reply. Many offered to join Milgram's staff for future experiments. This compares well with Markus Montola's recent research into extreme role-playing in scenarios designed to elicit negative emotion. Participants expressed afterwards they were glad of the experience, despite stressful reactions at the time.

It seems likely that the special location (the laboratory), props (the machine with a long bank of levers), special costume (the authoritative white coat of the researcher) combined with the entry ritual of drawing lots produced a magic circle effect in the minds of participants. It generated a feeling of social safety that protected them from the moral and legal consequences of torture. These results affirm the power of a strong magic circle to override "common sense." Under this model, the reason for the difference in behavior in different locations was that the resultant magic circle was somewhat weaker in the office location than in an impressive university; I suggest the building itself may have contributed to forming the magic circle since for participants from the surrounding community the university building is a space apart from their everyday life.

In his 1974 book *Obedience to Authority: An Experimental View* Milgram describes how six years after the experiment one of the participants wrote to him explaining that due to his experience in the experiment he was refusing the Vietnam War draft. Assuming we accept this statement at face value, it means that an experience within the magic circle of the experiment room had permanently altered their world-view and life course. This is in stark contrast to the usual limited nature of the aforementioned bleed effects. While some might regard this as a positive change or personal growth, it also shows the weakness of the protective frame to protect from psychological changes — the participant was permanently altered by the experience.

Despite being within a very strong circle, the participants in the experiment were still themselves without a frame. They conform to the new social rules but they lack a sense of psychological safety from the consequences. This is most clearly shown in the case of the women crying (a sign of psychological state) while still torturing a puppy (because of social rules).

In summary, this example shows:

- It is possible to have a strong circle and a weak frame — the two do not have to go together. This also reaffirms they are not the same thing.
- Most people are glad to have had "negative experiences" within a circle, even if not expecting it. At the risk of over-generalization, Milgram's findings appear to suggest this is "normal."
- Long term, significant bleed-out is possible
- The weaker the frame, the higher level of bleed-out.

Slater's Reprise of Milgram

Slater, et al. repeated Milgram's obedience experiment in 2006 using a virtual reality "learner" to make it clear to participants the situation wasn't real.[8] The purpose was to see if this altered their responses. We will look at this briefly to establish the power of situational immersion even in situations in which the participants are aware the events aren't "real."

As in the original experiment, the participants carried out a memory association recall test on a stranger; teaching word-pairs, except the role of learner was played by a graphically crude female virtual reality human. 23 participants saw the "learner" and 11 had only a text interface. In the visible condition, the learner shows signs of distress, claimed she "never agreed to this" and wanted to stop. In the text interface condition, there were no protests.

RESULTS — SLATER

In the hidden / text-based condition, all participants administered all twenty levels of shock. In the visible condition, 16 of 23 gave all levels of shock, 3 gave at least sixteen shocks, and 3 stopped after nine shocks. The participants were asked afterward if it had occurred to them to stop (those who had stopped were counted as "yes"). 12 of 23 visible participants and only 1 of 11 text participants answered yes, citing their negative feelings. Of those 12 participants who wanted to stop 5 claimed knowledge of Milgram's experiment, but this was not found to be statistically significant.

Questionnaires showed increased anxiety after the experiment. Heart rate increased at the start for all but was higher at the end only for visual participants. I suggest that the participants in the text condition without the interruptions of protests may have slipped into a state of task-based flow or immersion as described earlier.

ANALYSIS — SLATER

From their perspective, the researchers point out these responses could also be obtained by watching a violent film, but also cite that the participants made unscripted comments back to the virtual person. Two participants appeared to and later admitted to trying to emphasize the correct answer from the multiple choice list to the virtual character. In the visual condition, the participants were also recorded as giving the learner much longer to answer since they had been briefed that failing to answer should be treated as incorrect. The researchers claim this shows the participants were experiencing the situation not in the same manner as watching a non-interactive, movie but in a situation where their behavior could alter the outcome.

The researchers own conclusion is that "humans tend to respond realistically at subjective, physiological and behavioral levels in interaction with virtual characters notwithstanding their cognitive certainty that they are not real."[9] As noted earlier, Annika Waern describes emotional bleed in a computer game context, another example of realistic response to virtual characters. In some respects this is a remarkable finding — players of computer games do not generally report these feelings when inflicting pain on virtual characters, so one might question how these results withstand the reality test.

This experiment shows that at least in some cases that even in a clearly unreal situation participants display a similar response as if the situation was real. Slater et al. point out that if we accept this finding then it would overcome some of the ethical issues that have prevented research of this kind in recent years such as experiments into the psychological effects of committing torture. This is particularly interesting from a role-playing game perspective and could be considered strong evidence of the validity and potency of actions within a fictional context. The participants know that what they are doing isn't "real," yet their feelings and behavior is real. Physiological reactions might be seen as very strong evidence for immersion in the situation. In summary, immersion can happen even in clearly unreal situations. The "unreality" of the situation is a form of strong magic circle, in the same way as players carry out unreal military aggression playing the board game *Risk*. However, this research suggests that even in such an unreal situation participants physiological and behavioral responses are the same as if the situation is real.

Zimbardo's Stanford Prison Experiment (SPE)

Philip Zimbardo conducted his famous prison experiment in 1971. I will include only a brief summary of the experiment in the context of this essay. This experiment is used here as a defining example of *situational immersion*.

18 male college students took part, and were assessed as "normal" and assigned roles of prisoner or guard. The informed consent forms warned their "basic civil rights" would be violated if they choose the prisoner role rather than the guard role. "Virtually all" of these indicated a preference for being a prisoner. Zimbardo says this was because they could imagine being imprisoned and felt they might learn from the experience. This shows remarkable uniformity in choice of preferred role and keenness for a disempowered role. Regardless of preferences, roles were assigned randomly by coin toss.

The motive for their preference may relate to the wider social frame. The participants had volunteered to take part in a psychology experiment — something "serious" and "formal." Since deriving pleasure from this is therefore inappropriate they focused on treating it as a learning experience. Being paid $15 per day to participate may have compounded this by encouraging a professional attitude towards participation. This is a form of bleed-in effect as the nature of the social circle shapes their agenda. The prison guards underwent a battery of psychological tests which concluded there were within the normal range. Sam McFarland and Thomas Carnahan noted that none of the eight personality scales they were rated on equate to or predict abusiveness or aggression. Stephanie Cox argues the personality tests would fail to detect sadism or other traits rooted in the subconscious mind. Assuming this criticism is valid — that hidden subconscious traits could surface within a magic circle — this would also apply as a possible danger to a great many other social circles. This might be an example of the "taboo play" that Sarah Bowman describes.

Zimbardo made himself part of the experiment by casting himself as the prison superintendent. He later recognized the error of this, with his own judgment being affected by his role. The nine guard participants were brought in a day early for group orientation and to select their uniform. The guards were given minimal directions beyond maintaining order and not to use their billy clubs as actual weapons — a rule which was not always maintained.

The nine prisoners were arrested by real police officers at their homes, read their rights, spread-eagled, searched and booked in at a real police station. This could be considered an early example of "pervasive gaming" as described by Markus Montola, Jaakko Stenros and Annika Waern in their 2009 book *Pervasive Games*.

The prisoners were then taken into the venue — a "prison" of three cells and a closet, a corridor and some adjoining rooms in the basement of Stanford University Psychology department. They then underwent a "degradation ceremony" of being stripped and sprayed; a ritual to firmly establish the act of crossing over into the magic circle, but not a protective frame, since being degraded broke all feelings of psychological safety.

The prisoners were dressed in smocks with prisoner numbers sewn in, and ankle chains, and wore nylon stocking caps to simulate having their hair shaven. The prisoners were not permitted underwear. Zimbardo recognizes in the article this is not how real prisoners are treated, but the treatment was to create a specific psychological effect:

> It should be clear that we were trying to create a functional simulation of a prison — not a literal prison. Real male prisoners don't wear dresses, but real male prisoners do feel humiliated and do feel emasculated. Our goal was to produce similar effects quickly by putting men in a dress without any underclothes. Indeed, as soon as some of our prisoners were put in these uniforms they began to walk and to sit differently, and to hold themselves differently — more like a woman than like a man.[10]

Under rules made up by the guards the prisoners could only refer to themselves and each other by their numbers and to the guards as "Mr. Correctional Officer." This constantly reaffirms the power relations and the immersive game aspects with the dehumanizing effect of numbers and the empowering effect of titles.

Zimbardo notes that it took a full day for the guards to get fully into their role. While the prisoners went through an elaborate ritual to enter the magic circle of the experiment the guards did not. They each worked an eight-hour shift, then went home which made them only "part-time participants." They never turned up late or called in sick.

Results — Zimbardo

By the second day, the prisoners rebelled against their treatment by barricading themselves in their cells, ripping off their numbers and shouting abuse at the guards. It should be noted how prisoner-participants had proactively devised a diegetic "solution" to their situation rather than the non-diegetic solution of asking to leave the experiment. Both groups seemed to be immersed in their roles. All nine guards came in together and crushed the rebellion using a fire extinguisher as a weapon. The guards then had the prisoners stripped naked, deprived of meals and blankets and broke prisoner unity by creating a privilege cell and rotating prisoners in and out of it. The guards' abuses grew more extreme, including solitary confinement in a small closet for hours, excessive physical exercise of the prisoners and what Zimbardo calls "simulated sodomy." Worse abuses were recorded on the late-night shift when the guards wrongly believed that the experiment staff were asleep.

A visitor day included the participant's friends and relatives. They too complied with arbitrary prison rules and the concerns of the participant's parents for their son's welfare was easily brushed aside by Zimbardo himself staying immersed as prison superintendent.

A real Catholic priest who had been a prison chaplain visited the prison. Zimbardo describes how he played his role more like a "movie version of a priest than a real priest" and speaks of this "adding to the uncertainty we were all feeling about where our roles ended and our personal identities began." Note the bleed effects to which these statements refer. The prisoners went through a parole board hearing headed by the experiment's prison consultant, who had been a prisoner for seventeen years himself; thus he had experience of sixteen years of parole requests being rejected. Zimbardo describes how this consultant "became the most hated authoritarian official imaginable" and felt sick afterwards at whom he had become. This is an example of *indirect bleed* as described by Markus Montola — strong feelings felt by the player that do not correspond to those of the character.[11]

Thirty-six hours in, prisoner 8612 was released after displaying extreme stress reactions and appeared pathological. Other prisoners copied this strategy, resulting in three other prisoners being released over a short period of time. It's unclear to what extent these were real or faked. Assuming at least some of them were genuine, this would show the lack of psychological safety. Participants were responding in a powerful fashion to the situation, yet didn't simply ask to leave the experiment. This is another example of reacting authentically to an unreal situation

A rumor went round that prisoner 8612 planned to break back into the jail and rescue the other prisoners. The prison authorities planted an informant prisoner in his old cell, relocated the whole prison to a different location nearby and even plans laid to lure 8612 back in order to capture and imprison him again. The break-in never happened but this showed how immersed in the roles everyone had become.

Prisoner 819 had developed a full body rash and asked for a doctor. He was taken to a side room with the superintendent and priest. The other prisoners chanted that he was bad prisoner and he broke down in tears. Zimbardo suggested they leave — ambiguously unclear whether this is within the diegetic fiction or not. 819 replied diegeticly that he could not leave and said he wanted to go back to prove he was not a bad prisoner. At that point Zimbardo broke the diegetic fiction by telling 819 who both of them were, stating it was an experiment not a prison. He describes the reaction of 819 as "looked up at me like a child awakened from a nightmare." 819 had been deeply immersed in their role and perhaps also displaying the signs of Stockholm syndrome, where a prisoner identifies with the captor.

The experiment was ended after six days, despite having been intended to run for two weeks. The parents of the prisoners had called the superintendent — having themselves been contacted by the priest — to arrange for legal aid, showing how pervasive the experiment had become. A visitor to the prison — who Zimbardo was dating at the time and would later marry — remarked on how terrible the situation was. She was the first person to raise a moral objection to the experiment — the parents, lawyer, priest and others had failed to do so.

A Role-Playing Analysis — Zimbardo

Two months later, prisoner 416 described the experience in a follow-up interview: "I began to feel that that identity, the person that I was that had decided to go to prison was distant from me — was remote until finally I was not that, I was 416. I was really my number."

This appears to be an account of achieving deep immersion. Their own identity has been suppressed by their new role. There is a question or whether to take the participant's later account at face value — how self-aware are they of their own mental state and how able are they to recollect it afterwards and to express it in words?

We might question to what extent this total immersion has really happened. Playing a character is normally more than merely assuming a social role and a new name or number. In that sense the very term "role-play" is misleading. Immersion in a social role has been achieved, but immersion into a character has not been achieved or even attempted. I consider this a form of situational immersion — the people are caught up in the circumstances fully but are still themselves. They were not seeking to portray a different character in the way an actor would.

Note also the prisoners and guards reacted in different ways to each other. Some prisoners led the rebellion while others tried to be "good prisoners" and a few broke down completely and had to be removed. Some guards were particularly sadistic, others merely passive of the abuses committed by others. While Zimbardo claims that individuality has been suppressed, their different reactions and choices show it manifesting. As Martyn Shuttleworth points out Zimbardo plays down the fact that not all the guards took part in the abuses in the prison.

Martyn Shuttleworth also notes that in a real prison guards receive extensive training and are given orders from higher authorities. Had Zimbardo given the guard stricter guidelines their behavior might have been very different. This doesn't invalidate the results but it does suggest the results may not generalize as Zimbardo has assumed.

In 1999, Zimbardo wrote a list of ten lessons learned from the experiment. One of them is:

> Role-playing — even when acknowledged to be artificial, temporary, and situationally bound — can still come to exert a profoundly realistic impact on the actors. Private attitudes, values, and beliefs are likely to be modified to bring them in line with the role enactment.[12]

What the SPE clearly shows is the power of the magic circle and its ability to distort the behavior of those within it. Its entry point was clearly marked but the limits were not causing it to expand and draw in others. He waxes philosophically in a way that appears relevant:

> Good people can be induced, seduced, initiated into behaving in evil (irrational, stupid, self destructive, antisocial) ways by immersion in "total situations" that can transform human nature in ways that challenge our sense of the stability and consistency of individual personality, character, and morality.[13]

It is this usage from which I derive the concept situational immersion defined above.

In summary:

- Many normal people seem glad to seek out negative (unpleasant) experiences for personal growth in the right context.

- The magic circle can override our moral sense in a profound way
- Ritual and ceremony can be used to create a magic circle without a protective frame.
- A circle without the protection of a strong frame results is powerful situational immersion, but without necessarily character immersion.

BBC Prison Study

In 2001 the BBC carried out a variation of the SPE, shown as a four part TV series "The Experiment" in 2002. In stark contrast to the SPE, this example demonstrates what happens with a strong protective frame in place. The outcome was very different to the original SPE. The guards did not naturally slip into their role, and attempts to manipulate the prisoners against each other strengthened their prisoner group unity. On the sixth day they staged a breakout and turned the prison into a commune. This itself collapsed and a group including both former prisoners and guards set up a new regime along much harsher lines — much closer to the SPE results. The external ethics committee terminated the experiment as this happened, two days early.

The general findings show that the results of the SPE may not generalize and are limited within the culture that created them. Middle-class male American white college students in the seventies behaved in one way, the ethnically varied British adults a generation later behaved in a very different way. Some of the participants in this prison study (PS) even had knowledge of the SPE and the prisoners actively used psychological techniques to divide the guards. This represents a bleed-in effect that transformed the whole situational dynamic much as later repeats of Asch's conformity experiment produced different results to the original.

My interpretation of these results is that while a magic circle was established by being in the prison the protective frame was much stronger than in the SPE. The prisoners were overly confident they were safe which meant they took risks without being afraid of real consequences — essentially acting like a game player, rather than someone immersing in a role. This might also be related to the participants knowing it was a TV program — that may have framed it in their minds as a "game show" rather than an "experiment."

Analysis — Circles and Frames

Circle and Frame shapes Immersion
Both the circle and frame exist on a scale from "strong" to "weak." For ease

of presentation, I'll refer to these scales as if they were binary pairs. Taken together this gives us a range of four possible combinations:

- A **weak circle** and **weak frame** is the status quo in everyday life. We might go into a place where particular social rules apply such as the social frame/script of behavior in a supermarket or restaurant but the experience is still regarded as a direct part of everyday life.
- A **weak circle** and **strong frame**; this is a very hard situation of which to find an example. Possibly private immersion such as prayer would fulfill this but I would argue that privacy is a form of circle. This combination is mostly non-viable — that is, that the circle is necessary prerequisite of the frame. To put another way, to feel psychologically safe, a person must first feel socially safe.
- A **strong circle** and **weak frame** produces situational immersion, where the person becomes immersed in the situation they find themselves in. The Stanford Prison Experiment is a good example of this happening. Another example would be a tightly scripted work place.
- A **strong circle** and **strong frame** produces character immersion where person becomes immersed in their character or character's culture. The Prison Study is a good example of this. Other examples would include stage drama and some forms of live role-play.

An additional level is that if the frame is "too strong" repressed or taboo play results instead. Unrealistic game-type play or deliberately playing to create drama may also result from this, such as acting in an aggressive fashion and feeling safe from the consequences of doing so. An example of this would be a typical person displaying highly aggressive behavior in a board game.

In summary:

- A circle is a necessary prerequisite for a frame.
- A weak frame results in situational immersion.
- A strong frame results in character immersion.
- A very strong frame results in game play, dramatic play, or repressed / taboo play.

Returning to the quote from Huizinga, one might find the magic circle applied to a great many things. Clearly the feeling of being on a tennis court is not the same as being in a court of justice. I suggest that the concept of frame offers us a way to better break down those different concepts. For example, a conventional routine workplace might be said to have a strong magic circle with a weak protective frame — encouraging people to immerse in the situation and fulfill their job role, rather than display more personalized behavior.

Analysis — Bleed

Based on considering these experiments under this model, I believe that bleed-in and bleed-out actually function in entirely different fashions. In light of my review of these experiments, it is misleading to consider the two concepts as the same.

- **Bleed-in** is based on the strength of the circle. The weaker the circle, the stronger the bleed-in effect. Asch's experiment demonstrates how personality traits such as conformity can bleed-in. To put it another way: we are ourselves unless we have a social alibi to not be so.
- **Bleed-out** is based on the strength of the frame. The weaker the frame, the stronger the bleed-out effect. Milgram's experiment demonstrates how changes to personality traits can bleed-out. To put it another way: the less protected we feel, the easier it is to be psychologically altered by our experiences. As an example of this, consider that physical torture causes much stronger psychological changes than suffering consensual pain from a dentist.
- The weaker the circle, the higher the level of bleed-in.
- The weaker the frame, the higher the level of bleed-out.

Conclusion

We have looked at bringing together these different concepts from different fields and combining them into a new model that allows into reinterpret classic experiments in a new light. We have seen that there are distinct kinds of immersion and that the kind of immersion that takes place is shaped by the strength of the psychological sense of safety the participant experiences. We have seen how porous the barriers around such experiences can be and that people have experienced permanent change within the innermost cave of the laboratory.

In summary, my findings are:

- A frame (psychological) requires the presence of the circle (social).
- A weak frame produces immersion in the situation, a strong frame produces immersion in character, very strong a frame leads to repressed, taboo or game-like play.
- Bleed-in depends on the strength of the circle. The stronger the circle, the weaker the bleed-in.
- Bleed-out depends on the strength of the frame. The stronger the frame, the weaker the bleed-out.

Notes

1. See Apter, *The Dangerous Edge* (1992), *Reversal Theory* (2006), and *Danger* (2007).
2. Huizinga, *Homo Ludens* 10.
3. See Pohjola, *Manifesto*.
4. Found on http://jeepen.org/dict/
5. See Waern, "I'm in Love."
6. See Bowman, *Functions of Role-Playing Games*
7. Cf Slater, et al., "A Virtual Reprise"
8. Ibid.
9. See http://www.prisonexp.org/psychology/10
10. See Montola, "Positive Negative."
11. Zimbardo. "A Simulation Study."
12. Zimbardo. "Reflections on the Stanford Prison Experiment."
13. Ibid.

Part 2. Role-Playing Breaches Reality

Role-Playing Communities, Cultures of Play and the Discourse of Immersion

WILLIAM J. WHITE, J. TUOMAS HARVIAINEN
and EMILY CARE BOSS

"Immersion" is the fundamental ideal of a variety of emerging ludic or quasi-ludic forms (i.e., games and game-like activities), particularly those characterized by the spatial, temporal, or social extension of the Huizingan "magic circle." Because immersion is central to many participants' understanding of their own experience in these activities, it can serve as a foundational problematic for the study of that experience as a cultural form and enable connections to be made across fields of study and types of play. However, its very centrality also makes immersion problematical in a larger sense. Specifically, as it is used to mean different things by different people, difficulties in productive conversation often arise. This essay addresses the issue by examining the discourse of immersion in two different communities of play: (1) the U.S.-based "indie [tabletop] RPG design community" centered on an online discussion forum called "the Forge," on the one hand, and (2) the Scandinavian larp/tabletop hybrid movement known as "jeepform," on the other. In both cases, the ambiguity of immersion as a concept can be shown to have been recognized by members of those communities, and alternative conceptual schemes that nonetheless valorize some form of immersive experience (while at the same time eliding the language of immersion) to have been adopted. For example, the "Big Model" of Forge theory identifies three different types of "Creative Agenda" that shape the aesthetic experience of play. Since identifying a group-level Creative Agenda is a matter of seeing what play-behaviors are socially reinforced, Forge theory implies an immersive ideal that is related to a mutuality of experience — a game that "clicks" for all participants. In contrast, the jeepform notion of "bleed" centers on an individual experience

71

of play where engaging as a character in a game feeds back (or "bleeds out") into the player's psychological reality. This suggests an immersive ideal where the point of play is to create psychologically or emotionally resonant individual experience. The paper concludes that understanding the specific kind, quality, or type of immersion that is valued within a particular community of play is an important analytic precursor in discussing the varieties of ludic experience.

Immersion and the Ludic Turn

The emergence of new digital media enables myriad forms of playful expressiveness[1] ranging from hypertextual fictions to multimedia and multi-voiced alternate-reality games.[2] Efforts to make sense of these new media have spurred intense arguments about their nature — e.g., can videogames be productively understood as narrative form, or are they rather *sui generis?*[3] — as well as widening recognition of the social and cultural importance of games, an importance that Joost Raessens calls the "ludification of culture,"[4] wherein (computer) games take their place alongside film, radio, and television in their impact on the production and reproduction of identity and culture.

But Kendall Walton's argument that aesthetic expression has *always* been fundamentally about imaginative play rather than about representation *per se* pre-figures a broader ludic turn in our understanding of the operation of mediated fiction. In other words, in contradistinction to Greg Costikyan's famous complaint (within game design circles at least) that games are not stories, it is possible to point to an emerging understanding of fictional forms that proceeds from the perspective that *stories* are indeed *games*. In addition to Janet Murray's treatment of hypertext and digital media, Henry Jenkins's explorations of fandom and participatory culture (e.g., *Convergence Culture; Textual Poachers*) show how individuals' creative engagement with a fictional medium functions as a kind of play — how "textual poaching," that is to say, is in and of itself a game of make-believe. The key to understanding fiction as play — the hinge of the ludic turn, that is — rests in the concept of immersion, central as it is to ideas about the operation of both fiction and play. Murray says that "a stirring narrative in any medium can be experienced as a virtual reality because our brains are programmed to tune into stories with an intensity that can obliterate the world around us."[5] This understanding of immersion as a separation from the everyday world restates Johan Huizinga's notion of the "magic circle," in which those at play are separated for a time from the usual social and moral orderings of their world. Huizinga defines play as "a free activity standing quite consciously outside 'ordinary' life as being 'not serious' but at the same time *absorbing the player intensely and utterly.*[6] Bernard Suits' conception of a "lusory attitude," which is needed to render a player willing to strive toward the game's goal using only the methods prescribed by its rules, implies a similar kind of bounding off play from other activities — even those that may superficially appear similar. Many games researchers orient their investigations toward experiential concepts redolent of immersion, such as "presence" (Tamborini and Skalski), "flow" (Wan and Chiou), and "passion" (Wang et al.), and game designers concern themselves with how to entice players to cross the threshold of the magic circle and remain within "until the goals of the game have been met."[7]

"Immersion" is thus valuable in considering the varieties of ludic experience, as the idea points to that which seems to be for many people the point of playing games in the first place. Mark Barrowcliffe, for example, in his memoir of playing *Dungeons & Dragons* as a boy, writes:

> One of the misconceptions held about D&D is that it involves casting spells or summoning devils. This is akin to looking at Ralph Fiennes playing a concentration camp commander and demanding that he be tried for war crimes.... However, when the game is working properly, it certainly feels like you're casting spells or fighting people for real, and the emotions conjured up can seem deep ones. Very rarely, in my experience, do people refer to each other by their character's names.... People are identified very strongly with their characters, and they identify very strongly with them.... Losing a character, that you've had for some time, maybe years, can be a major emotional experience. At fourteen years old it can be the first real grief you've known in your life.[8]

Jennifer Cover suggests that a tabletop RPG is "valuable to players because of the way it immerses them in a narrative experience."[9] She reports on her own participation in a D&D game. During one break in play for her, while her character was resting in a cottage in-game as other player-characters hunted for her, she wrote in her blog: "For those that don't play, I can't really explain it to you. But I've had a total adrenaline rush going on since about 4:00. The tension, the excitement ... all maxed out. It's amazing. And the story. Oh, my god ... the story is *so good*."[10]

Compare those accounts to this one by a fan of *Star Trek* when it originally aired during the 1960s:

> My friend and I met some other girls a grade ahead of us but ga-ga over [*Star Trek*]. From the beginning, we met each Friday night ... to watch *Star Trek* together.... We re-wrote each story and corrected the wrongs done to "Our Guys" by the writers. We memorized bits of dialog. We even started to write our own adventures. One of us liked Spock, one liked Kirk, one liked Scotty, and two of us were enamored of McCoy (Yes, I was a McCoy fan). To this day, I can identify each episode by name within the first few seconds of the teaser. I amaze my husband by reciting lines along with the characters. (I had listened to [audio recordings of the shows] again and again, visualizing the episodes.)[11]

Arguably, the role-player's engagement with his or her embodied-narrative-as-game is of the same general type as the media fan's engagement with a favorite show. In both instances, the experience is *immersive,* involving the active co-production of character and narrative on the part of participants. It is this kind of engagement with the "text" that seems central to participatory culture of all kinds, including on-line and digital gaming. Therefore, a key task in making sense of the "ludic turn" is understanding what immersion is and how it works.

The rest of this chapter contributes to an understanding of immersion by comparing how it is used in the discourse of two different communities of role-playing gamers. The first is the "indie [tabletop RPG] design community" that emerged from the on-line discussion site called the Forge, and which is interested in enabling game designers to craft rules that evoke a particular kind of shared experience that may be unique to a given game, as indicated by this description of an "actual play" session of a game designed to emulate movies like *Fargo* and *A Simple Plan* and the novels of Elmore Leonard:

> My group tried *Fiasco* for the first time this weekend and had a blast. There were four of us, 3 lifelong roleplayers and 1 a more recent convert. We used the "In a Nice Southern Town" playset. I played Butch, a middle-aged former high school football star with bad knees and a good heart. Butch ran a landscaping business where he occasionally employed day laborers and members of the high school football team looking to make an extra buck. Butch was married to Tina who worked over at the New Outlook Tanning Salon & Weightloss Center on Commerce Street. Unbeknownst to Butch their marriage was in rough shape.... We had a fiasco in the making.... All in all it was a real hoot. We had a great time coming up with the setup and playing out the scenes. There were a couple "laugh until you cry" moments involving Tina who ended up being the star of the show despite hardly ever leaving the weightloss center. And everyone really enjoyed playing their characters and fell right into picking up background characters as needed in other scenes.[12]

In contrast, the practitioners of the larp/tabletop RPG hybrid known as "jeepform" are more interested in facilitating an intensity of psychological experience in their game-play, the production of strong emotions on an individual basis rather than a collectively satisfying experience, as this excerpt from an interview with the player of one jeepform game indicates:

> Not only was I disgusted with what I did come up with, I also felt a very strong sense of inadequacy and impotence on not being able to come up with more shit, and not being able to perform better and without repeating myself. Since [the game] is about intercourse, and across of me is a rather beautiful girl ... of course [I have] a sense of arousal. So there's arousal, there's impotence, and there's disgust, at the same time.... And that's the power of that game, the simple mechanisms are able to create all these three.[13]

In what follows, the difficulties, contentions, and confusions that accompany the term "immersion" within each community are discussed, and the devices employed to work around those difficulties are described in order to argue that, ultimately, ideal-types of immersion are used in discourse to orient members of a specific gaming (or, more broadly, fan) community to issues of design and play.

WHOSE IMMERSION?

Before turning to specific cases, however, some discussion of the idea of immersion is needed, as it is sufficiently elusive a concept as to defy easy definition. Matthijs Holter lists the variety of ways in which it has been understood by larpers and role-players, including (1) as a player's complete and total psychological identification with a character, (2) as the players' locus of engagement with the game, (3) as "flow" *à la* Mihaly Csikszentmihalyi (4) as "channeling" a character, (5) as immersion in the situation or story, (6) as a kind of trance state, (7) as having an emotional bond with a character, and (8) as a cathartic or similar reaction to the events of play. These disagreements about the proper or true meaning of "immersion" have generated enough conceptual confusion that a number of observers advocate simply abandoning it as a covering term, since it obscures more than it reveals. Additionally, the adoption of unexamined commonplaces about the relationship between reality and the game experience has been called the "immersive fallacy."[14] This is a way of reading the history of technologies of communications that sees it as inexorably and ideally leading toward "more and more powerful systems of simulation."[15] However, in the context of the history of art, it is not the case that purely mimetic representation is the end-all and be-all of expression; *trompe-l'oeil* is after all a curiosity rather than a culmination.

This means that pursuing "realism" as a tool for facilitating immersion is rather a will-o'-the-wisp, regardless of medium. Something more complex is going on. As Alexander Galloway notes in the context of video games,

> Representation refers to the creation of meaning about the world through images. So far, debates about representation have focused on whether images (or language, or what have you) are a faithful, mimetic mirror of reality ... or conversely whether images are a separate, constructed medium.... Games inherit this same debate. But because games are not merely watched but played, they supplement this debate with the phenomenon of action. It is no longer sufficient to talk about the visual or textual representation of meaning. Instead the game theorist must talk about actions, and the physical or game world in which they transpire.... One is prompted to return to Aristotle's notion of mimesis in the *Poetics*. And indeed this is crucial. But as Johan Huizinga reminded us many years ago in his writings on play, "It is *methectic* rather than *mimetic*."[16]

"Oh man," Matthijs Holter concludes. "We have to stop saying 'immersion.'"[17] Instead, as Ron Edwards says, "we're better off deconstructing the issue [of immersion] into independent parts that address anything substantive and leaving the term to evaporate slowly, if possible."[18] Moyra Turkington (in her "Abandoning Immersion" blog post) comes to a similar conclusion:

> When I could find some precious time to look around, I found that with distance, my brain was becoming more and more frustrated with the discourse of gaming in general, and in particular, with immersion. It's a word I've been using for a long time now, and a word I really was rather fond of once, but I think it's long lost any semblance of meaning.... So from here on in ... I will be using words like goal and socket and payoff as a kind of matrix to point to specific things rather than try and situate things that are clearly different in a catch all word like immersion. Rather than saying You are immersive or I am not immersive, which really tells you nothing, because too many people assert too many conflicting qualities to immersion, I will talk about the means of play, the motivations of play, and the path of play....[19]

Immersion's conceptual elusiveness may be attributed to the diverse range of immersive experience noted by role-playing theorists and game studies scholars. Douglas and Hargadon differentiate between *immersion* and *engagement*, a distinction that is not always carefully made in discussions of the experience of play. Cover identifies four types of immersion in tabletop play, three oriented toward one's engagement with the diegetic "storyworld" (spatial, temporal, and emotional immersion) and one directed at the others with whom one is playing (social immersion). Similarly, J. Tuomas Harviainen suggests in the essay "Multi-Tier Game Immersion" that there are three types of immersion — in the *character* one plays, in the *narrative* one experiences, and in the *reality* one perceives — with which participants engage differently, depending on their play preferences.[20] Laura Ermi and Frans Mäyrä, in turn, split the experience into sensory, challenge-based and imaginative immersion, the last of which can be considered to contain all three of Harviainen's immersion categories.[21] In coming to grips with the variety of immersive experience, some theorists attempt to identify its essential quality or character. For example, Lauri Lukka claims that immersion involves "attempts to grasp the whole personality (creative role) rather than [adopting] one specific (everyday) role of a different person,"[22] a definition that focuses on character immersion. In other cases, the essentialist move amounts to a recapitulation in other terms of the notion of a magic circle of play, in which the make-believe game-world is taken seriously (even if not "for real") for the duration of the play experience. Thus Tobias Harding considers the essence of immersion to be a change of perspective regarding the world, rather than adopting an alternate personality (pace Lukka). Similarly, to Ari-Pekka Lappi, immersion means that "a player takes temporarily things included in (her) imagined space for a part of everydayness."[23] And for Myriel Balzer, immersion involves the player using the game-world instead of his or her own life-world as a primary referent.[24] Elsewhere, Balzer says:

> *Immersion* thus means that the players plunge into the alternative world of live role-playing and experience a decrease of self-awareness because the game-world functions as an isomorphous model of reality for the duration of the event. During this experience, they interact with the game-world in their role, in the same way they interact with their environment outside of the game.[25]

However, the proposition that immersion is somehow the essence of role-playing has at times generated vehement objections. For example, Mike Pohjola's intentionally provocative "Turku Manifesto" positioned itself as a radically immersionist approach ("Role-playing," it begins, "is immersion"), in contrast with what it called fundamentally mistaken "gamist" and "dramatist" approaches. The (possibly ironic) certitude with which Pohjola advanced this notion at times drew heated responses, particularly within the Nordic larp (live action role-playing) community to which it was primarily directed; In his essay "Turku Manifesto Turns Ten," Pohjola later recounts a particularly severe critic gleefully burning his copy upon receipt.

Beyond outright dismissal, the theoretical contestation of Pohjola's immersionist essentialism took place on at least two levels. One response was to identify an alternate element as the in-fact essential component of role-playing. For example, both Satu Heliö and Aksel Westlund developed views of role-playing that centered on its narrative dimension as a key element. On another level, the existence of character immersion was itself problematized, in a manner similar to an atheist critique of religious experience. For example, Henri Hakkarainen and Jaakko Stenros offered a definition of role-playing as interaction within a diegetic (i.e., make-believe) frame. "There is no need to differentiate," they told their readers, "between the roles the player assumes within the diegetic frame and the roles assumed outside of it."[26] Other conceptions of role-playing similarly seek to do away with the language of immersion. Turkington advances the metaphor of the *socket* as "the place in the RPG which serves as the participant's locus of enjoyment. It's the place where people plug themselves into the game and give and take their focus and energy to and from."[27] She identifies the character, the setting, the story, and the social dimension as examples of places where players plug into the game, and notes that different players will experience difference payoffs for a given socket. "For some, the payoff is simply 'completely forgetting I am me for a couple of hours,' for others 'engaging in an actively creative co-operative endeavor with people I like' might be the payoff."[28] This disparity in understanding operates at the level of play as well as within theoretical disputes and formulations.

Harviainen used survey and interview data from larp participants to construct a typology that differentiates playing styles on the basis of how they deal with different types of in-play information — seeking out some kinds, rationalizing some others, and rejecting still others, for example.[29] He notes that beliefs exist about the appropriate use of out-of-character and meta-game knowledge; these allow players to make judgments about how well or how correctly others are playing. Nonetheless, Harviainen suggests, players of disparate styles do in fact manage to play together with some success, and to some extent that success may be a product of the complementarity of different styles. In other words, despite differences in philosophies of role-playing that often center on immersion, individual players within a given game or "campaign" are often able to accommodate those differences in order to play together successfully, especially since they cannot assess during play how immersed or story-driven anyone else is, and because their interpretations of the game need not be identical. In this essay, we suggest that something similar occurs at the level of discourse on role-playing games — that relatively broad or diverse communities of play (i.e., beyond the immediate play-group), which since develop alternative conceptions of immersion that enable them to table questions of what immersion "really is" while at the same time enabling the development of a shared immersive ideal. The following sections examine two such instances. The first case is the notion of "Creative Agenda" that lies at the heart of the "Big Model" of role-playing created on the on-line discussion site for the U.S.–based "indie" table-top RPG design called the Forge.[30] The second is the concept of "bleed" as it has come to be used by the Scandinavian live-action/table-top hybrid game community known as "jeepform."[31] In both instances, the language of immersion was regarded as unhelpful or divisive while at the same time participants in game-related discourse were oriented toward a shared project that required some degree of mutual understanding of "what gaming is about." The discursive solution in both cases appears to have been the development of an alternative conceptual framework that set up an implicit "quasi-immersive ideal" around which that project could continue. As Hjørland and Albrechtsen have shown, discourse communities function as the vital context for determining the meanings of concepts. This is true of both professional knowledge domains as well as hobbyist communities of practice. Therefore understanding the nuances of a concept as central as immersion and its variables is essential to comprehending the aims and means of each player and game designer community, as well as to integrating information from one such group to another (per Søren Brier). As semiotician Kristian Bankov notes,

> Cultural entities exercise *a relative resistance* (which is the same as saying that these phenomena, society, culture, impose some criterion of truthfulness), which is the resistance of habit, of convention, of common sense, of common usage, of ideology,

of power relations, of logic, of rhetoric, of legislation, and so on. All these entities, at the same time (in principle), are also discursively constructed, and subject to transformation, due to discursive (including social interaction) activity of the interested community.[32]

Our two examples, while in some sense marginal, illustrate this point. They have been chosen because they both represent formalized yet loose groups that have crystallized around central theses of what is important to play, yet undergo constant debate on the fine points of those theses, the significance of immersion very much included. Thus we do not wish to suggest that the matter of immersion is "settled" within these communities; rather, we assert that they represent contexts of discourse — positions, participants, and histories — that illustrate the fundamental and ongoing "constructedness" of immersion as a concept.

"Creative Agenda" as Communal Immersion

The concept of "Creative Agenda" — orientations that shape players' experience of the role-playing game — comes out of electronic conversations conducted at the Forge, an on-line community devoted to discussing the design, publication, and play of "indie games" (i.e., small-press, creator-owned tabletop RPGs).[33] The Forge was founded in the late 1990s with the intent of directing the attention of gamers to the raft of small-press games that had by then been published in some form but not become widely known or disseminated. It was then revamped at the turn of the century in order to serve as a "design resource" for independent games.[34] Central to the project of the Forge was the development of a vocabulary for discussing the impact of a game's design on the experience of play. The essential dictum of the Forge is encapsulated in the title of an article written by Edwards early in its history: "System Does Matter" — where "system" refers to the mechanisms used to establish and modify the fictional situation of the game.

System matters, according to Edwards, because the character of the procedures used to create the fiction of the game directly affect the different paths through which players enjoy the game, the different "aims or outlooks" with which players approached their play. These paths — not yet called "Creative Agenda" in 1999 — grew out of earlier Internet discussions about role-playing, and were explicitly assigned to players as individuals. According to Edwards, the *gamist* wanted "a contest in which he or she has a chance to win," the *narrativist* hoped for "a role-playing session [that] results in a good story," and the *simulationist* sought a game system that created "a little pocket universe without fudging."[35]

As the on-line conversations at the Forge went on, producing a "Big Model" of precisely how system matters in RPGs,[36] these orientations became recognized as "Creative Agenda"; that is, as "aesthetic priorities and other matters of imaginative interest regarding role-playing."[37] The possibility that other Creative Agendas might exist, albeit not as yet seen to be such, was implicit in Edwards' formulation, which stated that three Creative Agenda were "currently recognized." That tacit admission might be seen as a tactful sop to advocates of an immersionist orientation to play, e.g. John H. Kim,[38] although as we have seen Edwards himself along with other participants at the Forge found the term "immersion" inherently problematic — and numerous Forge conversations attest to that problematic character.[39] Additionally, Forge conversations bruiting the possibility of additional agenda[40] or of the derivative or subordinate character of recognized agenda[41] underscored the centrality of Creative Agenda to the Big Model.

However, the "official" Forge position came to be that, rather than being a distinct Creative Agenda, immersion was instead a response to the enactment of play, and could conceivably emerge in response to any Creative Agenda. "It's what role-playing ... *feels like* when a particular set of techniques ... is put into action and works in that particular group/activity context."[42] Immersion is experienced "in the moment" of play as an output of the creative and communicative effort that goes into forging a coherent game, as a "reverberation" feeding back from the specific techniques of play being employed through the semiotic and diegetic levels that shaped the use of those techniques all the way to the social situation in which that use takes place. "This reverberation," says Edwards, "is the ultimate expression of the arrow" of Creative Agenda, which proceeds from top-level *Social Contract* (i.e., the social situation in which play is embedded) through diegetic and game-systemic *Exploration* to specific game-mechanical *Techniques*.[43] The specific Creative Agenda in operation at the table, Edwards goes on, "becomes the backbone of play, without any need to reflect upon it, remind people of it, remember it and try to accord with it, or anything else that is outside of the moments of play themselves."

This explanation exemplifies a shift in how Creative Agenda was understood to operate by the participants in Forge discussions. Edwards originally conceived of it as a relatively stable attribute of individual players. Over time, Creative Agenda began to be seen as an emergent property of play itself. In other words, while its earliest formulations regarded Creative Agenda as something that players brought to the table and which made it more or less possible for them to play together based on their degree of compatibility, the development of the idea and particularly its *applications* to talk about "actual play" saw players' aesthetic preferences as at least potentially fluid, so that they were able to enjoy a variety of play styles. In other words, it was increasingly recognized that a given player might at different times enjoy (1) the agonistic competition of Gamist play, "stepping on up" to show his or her tactical chops in a tabletop melee, (2) the mimetic diegesis of a Simulationist "sandbox" or open-ended game-world, and (3) the dramaturgical integrity of a character making thematically meaningful choices in Narrativist play.

Creative Agendas thus inhered not in the player (since players' preferences were not absolutely fixed) nor in the design of the game (since the same game text could conceivably support a variety of Creative Agendas)[44] but rather in the group dynamic created during play. The critical desideratum for play in the Big Model's terms is thus *coherence*; that is, "the degree to which one or a combination of Creative Agendas are accepted and reinforced among members of a role-playing group."[45] This is important because it makes Creative Agenda only accessible or measurable in the observation of actual play as a group activity. As one participant in an on-line discussion about how to see Creative Agendas in play explained to his less well-informed fellow participants:

> First of all, talking about Creative Agenda outside a group context is pretty much useless. By definition, individuals don't "play Sim" or "play Gamist," just like there's no actual such thing as a "Narrativist game design." The shorthand exists because it gets tiresome to write "plays in a way that might be highly endorsed in a Gamist environment" or "is ideal for supporting a Narrativist agenda at the table" over and over again. Historically, taking that shorthand literally has muddied up the discussion a lot more than I'd like. So, if you pull off the awezume combo of phat moves and wipe out the big orc leader, and no one else cares, and no one else ever cares, Gamism is simply not happening at that table. The social emphasis and support has to be there as a trend, a pattern of behavior in the group. That's what CA clash is — other people failing to support and engage the stuff that turns you on, and you failing to support and engage the stuff that turns other people on.[46]

In "The Whole Model," Edwards says the same thing with admirable concision: "The only variables that really make sense, in discussing GNS [i.e., Creative Agenda], are the social interactions and communications that go on among the real people at the table, during play." He goes on:

> What is reinforced among them? Who praises whom, for doing what, and how often? When is a staged or proposed action disallowed, often in very subtle form? What gets everyone listening with undivided attention to a single person's announcements? When do people laugh? When do they not laugh, or socially squelch someone else's amusement?

Thus, coherence around a particular Creative Agenda emerges as an ideal for "functional" play in Forge terms — indeed, much Forge model-building and discussion was motivated by the desire to diagnose and allow the correction of dysfunctional play. What makes this goal at least quasi-immersive is the way that the Big Model ties Creative Agenda to "Exploration" (i.e., the diegetic elaboration of some element of play, such as character, situation, setting, and so forth). Creative Agenda, in other words, is the specific orientation to play that unites a group of players in the act of playing. It can be seen as a kind of communal immersion that is enabled by the players' mutual engagement with a specific chord of the magic circle, or as a form of shared imaginative immersion whose presence is signaled by the emotional engagement[47] experienced by the members of a gaming group in response to their recognition of the coherence of their play around a specific Creative Agenda at a given moment.

"Bleed" as Immersion via Identification

"Bleed" is another example of a community-specific quasi-immersive ideal that has the advantage of highlighting what that community values while avoiding the language of immersion. In this case, the term has been adopted by members of a subset of the Nordic larp community who have devised a freeform approach to role-playing characterized by an emphasis on developing and disseminating techniques that highlight the psychological experience of play. This "jeepform" style[48] has been described as a hybrid of tabletop and larp, and has had some influence on the North American indie game design community.[49]

Montola describes bleed as a "design rhetoric" that orients jeepform gamewrights toward "brink play" in which "the magic circle of play serves as an alibi for non-ordinary things." He identifies "bleed-in" as leakage from player to character, and "bleed-out" the reverse, from character to player — where playing the character, in other words, has an impact on the cognitive, emotional, or psychological state of the player. Some games produce a kind of bleed-out called "direct bleed," in which a player's psychological response to the events of the game closely resemble those that could be attributed to the character. "Direct bleed," says Montola, "is similar to character immersion." Not all bleed, however, is welcome.[50]

The concept of bleed refers to "leakage" (both informational and emotional) between character and player. According to the on-line jeepform dictionary:

> Bleed is experienced by a player when her thoughts and feelings are influenced by those of her character, or vice versa. With increasing bleed, the border between player and character becomes more and more transparent. It makes sense to think of the degree of bleed as a measure of how separated different levels of play (actual/inner/meta) are.[51]

As we have seen, essentialist approaches to immersion such as that of the "Turku Manifesto" claim that in order to be truly immersed, players have to be so thoroughly in character that they lose their sense of mundane identity. The concept of bleed, on the other hand, resembles the narrative-identity view promoted by role-playing researchers such as Hakkarainen and Stenros (i.e., the Meilahti school)—who saw themselves as writing in response to Pohjola—and Dennis Waskul and Matt Lust; specifically, that role-playing characters are effectively just more drastic versions of the social identities people switch between when they move from one context to another.[52]

Tobias Wrigstad's discussion of jeepform makes clear that, as a general principle, "immersion" is supposed to emerge from avoiding obtrusive out-of-character distractions by means of subtle coordinating moves. These techniques of coordination include "telegraphing"—sharing in-game information via inobtrusive gestures, vocal cues, and generic props. However, the purpose of those techniques is not to facilitate the "obliteration" of the world outside the magic circle; rather, it is to allow players to participate in the unfolding of a jointly constructed narrative through the enactment of an in-game identity. Thus, jeepform designers are supposed to consider how to make use of— in addition to the "actual game level" of the interaction of characters—the meta-level of the social relations among *players* and the inner level of a *character's* psychological state. At the level of meta play: "If there is an important hockey game that same evening [as the game], can the players' desire to learn its outcome be exploited in any way? If two players are an item, can that be used to achieve an effect? If most of your players have played your previous games, can this be used?"[53] Similarly, at the inner level of play: "If Tom [the character], secretly, flirts with a barmaid while Julia [another character], his girlfriend, is there, Julia's monologue [where she gets to say what's on her mind while the other players pause] can make the scene much more interesting."[54] Another technique for exposing the inner level of play is *insides/outsides*, in which "the player gives running comments discussing what goes on inside the *mind* of the character (insides) regarding what happens in the actual play (outsides)."[55]

This non-essentialist, narrative-identity approach to immersion has been explored by the Nordic role-playing community at some length. J. Tuomas Harviainen advances the notion of *perichoresis*, in which player and character are complete, individual selves that exist in a state of reciprocal interpenetration.[56] The perichoretic character is supposedly "complete" enough so that it in theory could exist as an individual, yet information flows between the two personas, so that what affects one affects the other, though not in an identical manner. Lauri Lukka takes this further, claiming that the character and player actually exist in constant overlap, excluding short moments of flow experiences.[57]

Jeepform-inspired designers may manipulate bleed experiences by intent, increasing their likelihood.[58] Games focused on bleed-out play capitalize on the emotional resonance held by the fictional events or aspects of character to create and heighten internal experiences in the player. Markus Montola describes the jeepform game *GR*, "an intentionally repulsive short scenario that examines ... a particularly ugly form of violence."[59] The techniques employed in the game are intended to create "an intense emotional experience," and include the requirement that an attacker maintain continuous eye contact with the victim while describing actions during the assault. Additionally, Montola points out, "characters are paper-thin so as to discourage players from 'hiding' behind them"— in other words, there is little established in the way of alternate persona to enable players to distance themselves from the acts "committed by" their characters, thus forcing them to seek alternative defense mechanisms. The notion that bleed is a design rhetoric that focuses attention on creating an immersive "brink play" experience by employing techniques that heighten a player's identification with his or her character is important to our argument here. Equally important is the notion that this design rhetoric emerged in a discursive environment — the Nordic larp community — in which the concept of immersion was highly charged. Just as in the conversations at the Forge, immersion was a concept that incited strong passions and allegiances, as can be seen in the contention between the Turku doctrine and the Meilahti School (i.e., Hakkarainen & Stenros).

Conclusion

The point of this argument is to suggest that "immersion" is a fundamentally contested concept; perhaps because there are many different paths into the magic circle of play. Rather than attempting to resolve the contest by offering a top-down definitive description of what immersion "truly is," it seems that a more fruitful approach would be to see how different communities of play (in the broadest sense) employ ideals of immersion to orient themselves toward shared aesthetic goals. In the case of the Forge, the concept of coherence around a Creative Agenda leads to an ideal of communal engagement with the play experience. In the case of jeepform, the concept of bleed leads to an ideal of psychological resonance across the player/character boundary. Understanding the sometimes subtle differences in the immersion terminology of such communities of play is essential to understanding the communities themselves, as the central part of role-playing deals precisely with the issue of temporarily pretending to be, possibly even becoming, someone else.

Beyond the particular and peculiar concerns of role-playing, understanding the ways in which the idea of immersion ramifies throughout the far-flung precincts of participatory culture can highlight the nature and extent of the "ludic turn," as well as providing a tool for examining how members of audiences and fan communities engage with the fictive objects they favor as well as with each other. Arguably, larp and tabletop role-playing are manifestations of the same impulse that drives the creation of fan fiction, the production of *machinima*, and even the identification of MMORPG players with their avatars: the desire to engage with a fictional world through the lens of character.

Notes

1. See Murray; Harrigan and Wardrip-Fruin. *First Person.*
2. E.g., McGonigal, *Reality Is Broken*
3. See Frasca, "Ludologists Love Stories."
4. Raessens, "Playful Identities" 52.
5. Murray, *Hamlet* 98.
6. Huizinga, *Homo Ludens* 13, our emphasis added.
7. Salen and Zimmerman, *Rules of Play* 333.
8. Barrowcliffe, *The Elfish Gene* 34–35.
9. Cover, *The Creation of Narrative* 107.
10. Cover 106, emphasis and ellipsis in original.
11. Jenkins, *Textual Poachers* 52.
12. See drhoover.
13. Montola, "Positive Negative"
14. Salen and Zimmerman 450–55.
15. Salen and Zimmerman 451.
16. Galloway, *Gaming* 71–72, emphasis in original.
17. Holter, "Stop Staying Immersion" 19.
18. Edwards, "Feeble Attempt."
19. Turkington, "Abandoning Immersion."
20. See also Harviainen's "Information, Immersion, Identity" for an account of how these differences interact.
21. See Hopeametsä, "24 Hours."
22. Lukka, "The Dual-Faceted Role" 164.
23. Lappi, "Playing Beyond Facts" 77.
24. See Balzer, "Das Erzeugen von Immersion im Live-Rollenspiel."
25. Balzer, "Immersion as a Prerequisite."
26. Hakkarainen and Stenros, "The Meilahti School" 56–57.
27. Turkington, "Covering the Bases."
28. Ibid.
29. Harviainen, "Information, Immersion, Identity."
30. http://www.indie-rpgs.com
31. http://jeepen.org.
32. See Bankov, "A Sociosemiotic Model."
33. More at http://www.indie-rpgs.com
34. Edwards, "Understanding the Pool."
35. Edwards, "System Does Matter."
36. See Boss, "Key Concepts in Forge Theory" for a summary of the Big Model.
37. Edwards, "Provisional Glossary."
38. See Kim, "Immersive Story;" "Simulationism Revisited."

39. E.g., Boss, "Thoughts on Why Immersion"; see also Ravenscrye Grey Daegmorgan, "Immersion, Childishness, and Understanding."

40. E.g., Charvill, "Invention."

41. E.g., Edwards, "All-out Dissection."

42. See Edwards, "Beating a Dead Horse," emphasis added.

43. Ibid.

44. See Lehman, "CA Classification."

45. Edwards, "Provisional Glossary."

46. See Balsera, "Do We Really Know."

47. See Wang, et al., "Passion."

48. http://jeepen.org.

49. See White, "Blurring the Boundaries."

50. See Schick, "Breaking Frame" for an example.

51. http://jeepen.org/dict/

52. As per Hall, "Minimal Selves;" Holstein and Gubrium, *The Self We Live By*.

53. Wrigstad, "The Nuts and Bolts" 135.

54. Ibid.

55. Wrigstad 136.

56. Harviainen, "Corresponding Expectations."

57. See also Tea and Lee, "Reference and Blending" as well as Hendricks, "Incorporative Discourse Strategies" on character-player blending.

58. Harviainen, "Corresponding Expectations;" see also Montola, "Positive Negative."

59. Montola, "Positive Negative."

Note: The order of names of this essay's authors has been corrected from the original printing of this book.

Gary Alan Fine Revisited: RPG Research in the 21st Century

KATHERINE CASTIELLO JONES

Gary Alan Fine's 1983 book, *Shared Fantasy*, has been called a seminal work on role-playing games (RPG),[1] defined as "any game which allows a number of players to assume the roles of imaginary characters and operate with some degree of freedom in an imaginary environment."[2] Fine identifies three goals of his research, based on participant observation and interviews with RPG players in a Midwestern city: (1) RPG as an urban leisure subculture, (2) the cultural systems created by RPG players and (3) how RPG induces engrossment and identification.[3] Fine argues that RPGs "engross" their players within multiple systems of meaning. In addition to the game rules and the fantasy content, RPG players are also immersed in the cultural and material systems of "commonsense reality." Players shift between these multiple systems of meaning and the different systems interact with each other in interesting ways, such as a player using their personal knowledge to help their character successfully navigate a challenge in game.[4]

By taking RPGs seriously and arguing that they had implications beyond the confines of their subculture, Fine's ethnography helped legitimate the academic study of role-playing.[5] It is widely cited by much of the contemporary scholarship on RPGs, and on game culture in general. Since the study was conducted, however, role-playing gaming as a subculture has expanded and changed in many critical ways. Not only has the subculture itself grown in numbers, but it has also expanded in terms of variety of games, players, and spaces available for interaction among participants. RPG players can now draw on the Internet, conventions and other spaces to have discussions about their experiences in RPGs and theorize about writing, running and creating them. Science fiction and fantasy, often an integral part of RPGs, has also become much more prevalent in everyday discourse through popular media such as movies, television shows and video games.[6] This trend has the potential to shift the demographics of the subculture as well as its relations with the mainstream culture.

Drawing on Fine's study, as well as more contemporary studies of RPG, this essay examines how these changes have affected the RPG subculture in ways that deserve scholarly attention. Rather than making a definitive statement about the current state of the RPG–something far outside the scope of a single article–this document instead highlights potential areas for further academic exploration. I argue that drawing on perspectives from cultural sociology can aid the study of RPGs: players, games and subculture. Cultural sociology provides tools to expand RPG research in several promising directions: (1) locating the hobby in the context of other leisure subcultures, (2) interrogating the interplay between RPG structures and interpersonal interactions during actual play, (3) more systematically exploring the variations among RPGs and among RPG players, and (4) examining how material and cultural production shape the fantasies available to RPG players. First, however, it recapitulates the major observations of Fine's study of the role-playing subculture and points to subsequent changes within the hobby.

Role-Playing: Then and Now

Gary Alan Fine states in the Preface to *Shared Fantasy,* "The observations and interviews described in this book reflect the state of the hobby in 1977–79; I have made no attempt to revise the manuscript in light of the changes in the games or players since that time."[7] In addition to being one of the first serious studies of RPG, Fine's book also provides a snapshot of the early days of RPG as a hobby and subculture. The first commercial RPG, *Dungeons & Dragons* (D&D), had gone on the market in 1974. Fine documents the burgeoning market of new RPGs, born out of dissatisfaction with D&D, or from hopes of reproducing its financial success.[8]

Since the time of Fine's study, RPG consumption has increased and RPG players have grown in number. 7,000 copies of D&D were sold in March of 1979 and market researchers estimated about 300,000 individuals played D&D at that time.[9] Fine's own estimate was that there were about 500,000 RPG players in 1979.[10] But according to marketing research done in 1998, 2.5 million people between the ages of 12 and 35 played a tabletop RPG monthly in the U.S. Of that 2.5 million, 1.5 million played D&D monthly.[11] At the time of his writing Fine estimates there are "dozens" of role-playing games being sold.[12] Currently about twice that many new games are published each year. In addition to a growth in sheer numbers, the hobby has become much more complex and varied. Not only are there more RPGs on the market, they have expanded in terms of their genre, setting and mechanics.

During the era of Fine's fieldwork stores specializing in RPGs were just beginning to appear, whereas today RPG players can often visit stores in their area that sell RPGs exclusively or as part of a broader specialization in a more general "geek culture," that includes some combination of comic books, anime and manga,[13] video games, collectible card games, miniature figurines, and specialty board games in addition to table-top RPGs. Large conventions devoted to RPGs were beginning to be held in the 1970s, but the numbers of attendees have grown. For example, 3000 attended Origins, a convention devoted to hobby gaming, in '77, growing to 4200 in '78.[14] But by June 2011, Origins recorded 11,502 people in attendance.[15] A similar convention, Gen-Con, had 5,000 attendees in 1981 and had 36,733 in 2011.[16] Many additional regional and local conventions have also formed in the intervening decades. This growth could be expected to strengthen, but also change, the budding RPG subculture documented by Fine in 1979.

Fine argues that RPG has a distinct subculture, though it overlaps with those of war gamers, science-fiction enthusiasts and medieval history buffs.[17] Fine partly defines this subculture through its use of in-jokes, cant and common expressions. Fine even includes a chart of selected terms used by fantasy gamers. The use of technical talk, e.g., regarding how best to roll dice or the weight of medieval armor, is also given as evidence of a distinct RPG subculture.[18]

But the RPG players Fine observed were also connected by their subcultural networks. In 1979, he identifies several ways that communication structures sustain and build the RPG subculture: (1) multiple group membership, and (2) weak ties maintained through amateur press association magazines, conventions, and play-by-mail campaigns. Fine also identifies structural roles as a key for disseminating subcultural information, especially the roles of game creator or publisher. Finally, mass media helps create a subculture of shared information. These include science fiction and fantasy novels, books about medieval weaponry or armor, and professional gaming magazines.[19]

It is important to note that Fine's discussion of the gaming subculture's social and communication network structure predated the emergence of the Internet. While "some have even discussed computerizing these games," according to Fine, the growth of computer games and computer-mediated communication systems was still on the horizon. The rise of computers and the Internet has clearly changed the hobby, and its subcultural networks, in important ways. The Internet especially has been an important, yet understudied, aspect of subcultural within the gaming subculture. It has opened spaces for community, scholarship and niche marketing within the RPG subculture. The 1990s saw the growth of Usenet list serves like RGFA.[20] A site called "the Forge" was founded in 2001 as a location for discussions on RPG theory and independently published RPGs, helping to foster an online community, an independent publishing movement, and a body of analytical RPG theory.[21] RPG players today communicate with each other using a proliferation of listservs, blogs, podcasts, social networking sites and websites devoted to RPGs. These online forums not only help build subcultural community ties and help disseminate subcultural information, they have also helped advance theorizing about RPGs by players themselves and fostered niche communities devoted to particular systems (like *Amber* or *Dungeons & Dragons*) or particular types of games (for example "story games"). These developments have clearly changed the subculture that Fine examined in the 70s. Yet while RPG scholars recognize that Fine's conclusions may be outdated, there has been little systematic attention paid to how these changes should shape the directions of future RPG scholarship.

I find that cultural sociology has much to add to the study of RPGs, in terms of players, games and subculture. Fine himself is a cultural sociologist and his interest in meaning and subculture clearly influenced the direction his study took. However, much like RPG, cultural sociology has developed and changed a great deal since the late 1970s. Several perspectives that have expanded or developed since then can point us in useful directions for future RPG research. These perspectives can provide future researchers with tools to expand our knowledge about RPGs and can also give researchers a framework for contributing to existing bodies of scholarship beyond game studies. It is my contention that the study of RPG can produce rich data useful to many different fields of study, especially in the realm of meaning and culture, but this means that researchers must be ready to engage with scholarship outside the topic of RPG itself. I believe this project will prove fruitful not only for deepening RPG scholarship, but also for making RPG scholarship relevant to an audience who may have no prior interest in, or knowledge of, RPGs.

Studying a Leisure Subculture

A growing body of literature has focused on exploring the importance of leisure activities as sites for the creation of individual and collective identities. Exploring the findings from this literature provide fruitful directions for the study of RPG as a leisure subculture. These leisure-based "social worlds" actually have much in common with RPG even though they encompass hobbies as broad as folk dancing, long distance running and quilting.[22] In each of these subcultures, members build skills and create interpersonal relationships, experience autonomy, and forge individual and collective identities.[23] Past studies of RPG have tended to emphasize the uniqueness of the hobby, and while it is certainly the case that there are aspects of the RPG subculture that make it distinct from hobbies like running or quilting, similar processes are at work in every case.

For instance, past studies have examined leisure subcultures as sources of both skills and relationships, as well as sources of conflict as practitioners attempt to balance their leisure activity with other aspects of their lives. Research has examined negotiations over resources such as time, money, and space within families.[24] RPGs certainly function in a similar way as gamers negotiate with family and friends about how to divide these resources between gaming and other hobbies or activities.

Other research has focused on how leisure activities are often gendered. Much of this research has focused on the realm of sports and masculinity,[25] but research on quilting has also shown how negotiations with family members have a gendered aspect to them.[26] Other studies examine how participation in leisure subcultures is used to construct masculinity or masculine spaces, as well as the experiences of women in these spaces.[27] Some researchers have argued that these masculine leisure subcultures function as an "escape hatch" for changing cultural understandings of masculinity, providing a space removed from the "real world" where men can enact more traditional forms of masculinity.[28] But the view of any leisure subculture as an "escape hatch" has been challenged by leisure subculture researchers who argue that the interplay between these social worlds and the "real world" is more complex.[29] RPG seems like a hobby that is well-suited for making contributions to this literature. While RPG players are predominantly male, some authors further argue that RPG is a "masculine" space.[30] While individual players might discuss their experiences as male or female RPG players,[31] or experiences of playing characters with a different gender than their own.[32] RPG scholarship lacks a systematic exploration of the construction of masculinity and femininity within RPGs, including the experiences of both male and female players. Such a study could help explore the interactions between the social world of the leisure subculture and the construction of masculinity and femininity in the wider culture.

In *Shared Fantasy*, Fine discusses the reasons for a lack of women gamers in the hobby, giving a quite detailed analysis of the social factors discouraging women from becoming involved. While RPG remains a majority male hobby, the presence of female gamers (both in terms of sheer numbers and in terms of recognition) has changed since Fine's research was conducted. Small-press fan publications like *RPGirl* have worked to give female gamers a voice and call attention to their presence in the subculture. An exploration of this change could be useful both for understanding contemporary RPG subculture and for understanding leisure subcultures more generally. Other authors have examined how women players may still feel marginalized, both by the source material used in RPG creation, and in their interactions with male gamers.[33] Drawing on existing literature from other leisure subcultures may help researchers to explore these gendered experiences among RPG players.

Finally, researchers of leisure subcultures, often also called "serious leisure communities," have highlighted a common concern about how subcultural activities are viewed by the wider culture. The marginalization of RPG players, and RPG culture, tends to be a common theme in existing RPG research, often argued to stem from the "uniqueness" of RPG itself.[34] But studies of other leisure subcultures, such as gun show participants or sky-divers, demonstrate similar experiences. Members of these subcultures often tell "identity stories" that position them outside the mainstream culture.[35] They take pride in their subcultural membership, while simultaneously working to mediate the negative stereotypes about their activities by the broader public.[36] Anderson and Taylor argue that members often use "aligning actions" to challenge these negative perceptions.[37] Individuals may use "disclaimers" in conversations to verbally challenge their association with negative stereotypes.[38] On a community level, subcultural organizations often affiliate with popular social causes to give themselves positive press or engage in "dramaturgical stereotype busting" by staging events that counter negative stereotypes about their activities or members.[39] Many of these same techniques can be found among RPG players and organizations. By viewing RPG as a leisure subculture, this common process can be explored with more detail and could give us information not only about RPG experiences, but how these experiences fit into a larger framework of leisure subcultural processes.

In the following sections, I turn to cultural sociology to examine potential tools to expand RPG scholarship. First, I examine the formal and cultural structures provided by official RPG rulebooks and texts and use Ann Swidler's "culture as tool kit" theory to explore the interplay between structure and agency in RPG interactions. Next I examine the heterogeneity of RPGs, both games and players, examining how Michele Lamont's theory of "boundary work" is useful in studying how these variations play out in terms of interactions between RPG players. Scholarship on the "production of culture" also points to interesting directions for the study of RPGs, particularly how the material and cultural production of RPGs shapes the experiences of players and their construction of identities. I also examine how network analysis can be combined with the study of culture to provide a more nuanced understanding of how and why certain cultural "tools" are used by some RPG players and not others. Finally, I end with a plea for scholarly reflexivity in the study of RPGs.

The Culture of Role-Playing — Formal and Cultural Structures

It may seem odd for a sociologist to point to the importance of RPG texts, meaning the given rules and books supporting play, rather than social interactions, when it comes to studying RPG culture. However, official RPG texts, open as they are to change and manipulation by players and Game Masters (GMs),[40] do provide an important *structure* to play that should not be overlooked. Daniel MacKay identifies both cultural and formal structures as shaping RPG play. Thus, official texts are important because they provide a cultural structure, the setting, references to other cultural phenomenon (books, movies, TV shows) as well as more ideological elements: what types of characters are encouraged, what types of stories are promoted. Connected to this are the formal structures enforced by the game rules: how outcome is determined, how power is divided among players and GM (if there is one), how do the rules structure the types of narratives that are created? I am not arguing that official texts should be prioritized over the real world interactions, which are so central to RPG. Rather, scholars need to take seriously the interaction between the structures of the text and the actual play done by individuals. Much like social structures, the structures (both formal and cultural) of game texts constrain the actions of player and Game Master. Individuals can exercise agency and may throw out whole chunks of text or rules to better suit their individual preferences, but they are also still working within the structure of the game.

Cultural sociologist Ann Swidler's conceptualization of culture as a "tool kit" provides a useful lens for studying these types of interactions within RPG subculture.[41] Swidler is primarily interested in how culture shapes capacities for action. She focuses on how culture is used by actors, asking how cultural elements can constrain or facilitate patterns of action.[42] For Swidler culture is more than just cultural products, culture provides moods and motivations, ways of organizing experience and evaluating reality, and rules for conduct and the creation of social bonds. Culture can sustain some strategies of action while constraining others; alternative forms of action or interaction come to seem unimaginable or implausible.[43]

As Fine points out, RPG is an excellent site for the study of culture because RPG players engage in meaning-making at multiple levels, both "in-game" in the creation of a shared fantasy, and in the "real world" of small group interactions.[44] Swidler's theory could be used to explain the capacities for actions at both these levels. What patterns of action are constrained or facilitated by the rules in a rulebook? Similarly, what patterns of action are constrained or facilitated by the shared culture of a particular gaming group? How does this culture shape the interactions among players, or players and GM, in the "real world?" And how does this culture equally, but perhaps in different ways, shape the shared fantasy that is created? Research drawing on this theory would be poised to offer some interesting contributions to the sociological study of culture, showing how culture operates in shaping different types of actions at different levels of meaning.

Swidler's theory was also created to better account for cultural variety. She argues that cultures are not unified systems but rather contain diverse symbols, stories and guides to action.[45] The theory can be used to explore how these diverse modes intersect, interact and compete. Culture can be viewed as an oddly assorted tool kit containing implements of varying shapes and sizes, which challenges the portrayal of individuals as cultural "dopes."[46] She instead argues that individuals use a variety of cultural tools depending on the situation or problem at hand.[47] Swidler seeks to examine the variable ways individuals hold and use culture, viewing them as skilled and active users of their cultural "tool kits."[48]

This aspect of Swidler's theory also has much to offer the study of RPGs and their players. Cultural variety exists among different game systems, different gaming groups and different players. How do individuals navigate these differences? How do actions shift depending on the context? For instance, how do players choose between the motivations for competition versus cooperation, or between the values of pacifism and violence? Based on Swidler's argument, we would expect these choices to vary by the situation or the problem experienced, in some cases competition may be a more useful "tool" than cooperation. In this way RPG research can recognize both the particular modes that are enabled or constrained by rules, small group culture, or other factors, while still recognizing the agency and interaction that is so key to the experience of role-playing. Similarly, there may be competition between the cultures of the "real world" and the game world. Strategies, such as violence, that may reward players within a game world may not be valued by those same individuals within the "real world." Drawing on Swidler's concept of cultural variety, and the variable ways culture can be *used*, allows for an exploration of culture at multiple levels, accounting for interactions between different cultural modes and for the agency of players in deciding how and when to use particular cultural modes. Exploring how players and GMs choose between these competing modes offers a more nuanced understanding of how RPG players cross between the different "frames" and adds to a broader understanding of how individuals actively use culture. Swidler's concept of culture as a "tool kit" can be used to help researchers bring in role-playing texts in a way that recognizes both their power and their limits in shaping actual play. As writers for the *Forge* have pointed out, rulebooks are not RPGs, RPGs only happen when players sit down, interact and play a game.[49] This is certainly true, and yet to overlook the ways that rulebooks, systems, etc hold a culture that enables and constrains certain actions, whether it be playing without a GM or dice, or creating a female character in a "historically accurate" medieval campaign, is to miss an important aspect of these interactions. Swidler's theory of culture not only accounts for the variety in cultural modes, it also calls for researchers to pay special attention to the way individuals actively use culture.

In this way, research on RPGs can more thoroughly explore the complex cultural world navigated by RPG players.

Variations Among RPGs and Players — Distinction and Boundaries

Demographic profiles of RPG players often highlight the homogeneous nature of the subculture: mostly white, male, middle-class, and higher than average levels of education.[50] Studies of RPGs have also tended to focus on the sense of community among members of the subculture, portraying them as a community of outsiders or at least a group of individuals united by their common hobby that can overlook other, unimportant, differences.[51] Studies may also focus on a single role-playing group, treating conflict as the result of personality clashes or friendly disagreements.[52] Yet these aspects of the subculture also mask important variations: among RPG players, among RPG games and among the contexts available for interaction. A recognition of these variations within the RPG subculture will help paint a more complete picture of the subculture and may help future research to explore what these variations mean for players' experiences.

Fine himself was cognizant of the differences among gamers that sometimes led to conflict or tension. While Fine discusses the lack of women in his study–drawing on many structural explanations such as the recruitment of players to do so–he also highlights the conflicts between players of different ages.[53] Fine found that RPGs function as social worlds with existing status systems.[54] But RPG has the potential to have multiple levels of status systems in operation: those that operate in the "real world" those that operate in the "game world" and the way status in the "real world" impacts status in the "game world." Some identity categories or attributes can be transcended by players and their characters, but others such as intelligence or maturity cannot be transcended under any circumstances.[55] It would be interesting to explore how different status categories are challenged or reinforced within different play experiences. Standard categories such as race, gender, religion or sexuality may be viewed as open to transcendence in different contexts.[56] Other status systems may also prove to be more important, for instance age may come to matter less than years of experience with a particular game system, or members may accrue status as writers or creators of RPGs. Paying attention to status differentials among RPG players, as well as how and when they are transcended, provides a more realistic portrait of the subculture and may provide information about how these "real world" status systems are challenged or maintained.

As mentioned earlier, status systems may operate in RPG subculture that mean little in the outside world. These differences represent ways for RPG players to distinguish themselves from others, often in ways that create moral or status boundaries. This quote by Ron Edwards, the author of the independently published RPG *Sorcerer* and one of the founders of the Forge, in his essay "A Hard Look at Dungeons and Dragons" is an excellent example:

> I did find a lot of people to role-play with, including women my own age, but always on the basis that we 'weren't like those gamers.' Conversations about role-playing ceased instantly if anyone nearby evinced interest in D&D. We played *Champions* and *Stormbringer*, and looked forward to the buzz of *GURPS*.[57]

Michele Lamont, another cultural sociologist, uses the term "boundary work" to define how individuals construct similarities and differences between themselves and other groups. Through boundary work, individuals use certain standards to define both who they are, and who they are not. This "boundary work" delimits an imagined community of "people like me" who share the same values and may also share resources. Boundary work is often used to establish moral worth, many times challenging other forms of status such as socioeconomic or appearance, and involves a claim that "people like me" are better than other groups. Edwards' quote demonstrates a common form of "boundary work" within the RPG community. He draws a boundary between himself and his friends in relation to "those gamers" who play a system (D&D) viewed as inferior to the systems preferred by Edwards and his friends. He and his friends identify as role-players but they are different from, and better than, "those gamers." MacKay argues that there has been a growth in smaller "sects" within the RPG community.[58] These players limit themselves to particular literary or cinema settings or to particular game systems. He argues that these sects often form part of a hierarchy of gaming where players of "high concept" systems distance themselves from players of "less advanced" systems.[59] Yet which systems are "high concept" or "less advanced" is not purely an objective categorization. For instance, MacKay identifies *Everway*, a system that relies on a deck of cards rather than dice to drive the narrative, as better for "inexperienced" players while D&D allows for "less formulaic" stories.[60]

This boundary work may help function as an "aligning action" mentioned earlier, allowing RPG players to claim the identity while distancing themselves from negative perceptions of the subculture.[61] Boundary work may also be a way for individuals to accrue subcultural status if other routes are not available to them. More exploration of this type of boundary work would help to recognize the variations among RPG games, players and networks, but would go further than simply recognizing variation by examining how these variations function to draw boundaries within the RPG culture and may be related to larger issues of status, power, or stigma management.

Boundary work may also be the result of real differences in preference that exist among RPG players. *Forge* theory of "creative agenda"[62] argues that players have different reasons for playing RPGs and often want different things from the experience.[63] Some players privilege the story above all else, seeking to be co-authors of a fully developed narrative containing literary themes and coherent plots (Narrativism), some players enjoy the challenges and puzzles presented by the game, seeking to successfully master them and "win" (Gamism), some players are most interested in creating or exploring the world of the game, immersing themselves in the time period and setting, or character they are playing in the game (Simulationism).[64] Recognizing that these different preferences exist, and that they shape the way players experience RPGs, challenges a monolithic explanation of "why" people play RPGs. But this view also opens up potential areas for exploration including how these preferences are shaped by networks, past experiences or other factors, how these preferences remain static or change over time and how these preferences lead players to use different "tools" from their RPG tool kit when playing an RPG.

In response to *Forge* theory, many game designers began to more consciously structure their games to fit a specific play agenda. Designers also began to experiment with mechanics, often dropping taken-for-granted aspects of RPG such as the use of dice or having the game be led by a Game Master. Independent games, those that were self-published or published by small presses, were more able to tweak some of these conventions and have led to a proliferation of different mechanics, genres and styles of play available. RPG research must attempt to make some sense of how this diversity impacts RPG subculture. Though marketing research has shown that most RPG players most often play "mainstream" games like *Dungeons and Dragons* or *Vampire: The Masquerade*, a more systematic examination of how other types of games influence players, distributors or game stores is still necessary.[65] It is quite possible that some games are played by only a limited network of friends and acquaintances, but how these games travel through different networks or are introduced to new players is interesting research in itself. And while play might not be widespread it is also possible that designers draw on each others' ideas so that a mechanic or theme from a relatively unknown game comes to influence a later game that becomes quite popular. Taking the way that games are designed, produced, marketed and sold can tell us a lot about RPG subculture.

Material and Cultural Production

Drawing on a similar view of culture as situational and variable are theorists working in the production of culture perspective. These scholars examine how the symbolic elements of culture are shaped by the situations in which they are created, distributed, sold, and so forth.[66] They argue there are six facets that impact this production: technology, law and regulation, industry structure, organizational structure, careers, markets.[67]

Expanding from this perspective some scholars have looked at the production of culture in terms of individual identities.[68] Similar to Swidler's view, this perspective argues that people use elements from traditional and mass-mediated symbols to produce their identities. Individuals take products and recombine them, often in quite creative ways, to give expression to their identities. This may take the form of resistance, challenging the original meaning or purpose of a product, or appropriation, changing the meaning or purpose of a product to communicate something new.[69] Often these individuals use resistance or appropriation to fabricate "authenticity," to create an identity that is position as more "real" or authentic because it challenges mainstream culture or uses it in ways contrary to the original intent.[70] In the following section, I examine each facet and theorize how it affects the symbolic content of RPG subculture. I also highlight where these facets may also play a role in the production of RPG player identities.

TECHNOLOGY

Changes in technology, such as the rise of the Internet, have clearly had an impact on RPGs. Ron Edwards argues in his piece "The Nuked Apple Cart" that the Internet acts as important resource for independent RPGs. He suggests independent author/publishers run their own ordering services, "and make sure you can meet any demand with quick, efficient service. The Internet would seem the way to go, insofar as no one has to man any phones or leave insincere messages on the machine about 'being away from our desks.'" Similarly, to cut costs he advocates that independent RPGs minimize print advertising and convention appearances, instead relying on the Internet to market a small-press game. "Advertise like a hurricane on the Net, from trading links to amateur sites to hitting chat rooms and usenets with a team of partners." he says, "Get a good web page made and keep it updated." While Edwards' piece recognizes the new marketing possibilities made available by the Net, he is also arguing that this new technology will allow for a more interesting cultural product.

> As customers, too, each of us faces a personal decision: are you a practitioner of an artistic activity or a consumer of a advertising-driven product? I urge you to consider your role in role-playing economics, and to consider whether a shelf of supplements and so-called source material really suits your needs, as opposed to a few slim role-playing books with high-octane premises and system ideas.[71]

By foregoing "glitzy design" for interesting system ideas and cutting distribution and advertising costs, independent RPG designers, according to Edwards, are able to create a product that better suites the needs of RPG consumers.

Whether or not one agrees with Edwards' main premise, his argument fits into the production of culture perspective on multiple levels. First, he argues that since how an RPG is produced will impact its symbolic content, independent RPGs are able to be more creative. Specifically, because they aren't focused on profit they can break new ground in terms of new systems, design, subject matter, and so forth. Next, he calls on consumers to reconstruct a more authentic identity as role-players: as "practitioners of an artistic activity" rather than simply "consumers of an advertising-driven product." Thus technology is used to produce not only a symbolic product, an independent RPG, but also an identity, an "authentic" role-player rather than a dupe of the advertisers.

Theorists working in the production of culture perspective also call for scholars to take into account the meaning of the cultural products being produced. Edwards is calling for a certain kind of RPG subculture, one that rejects advertising and profit. He quotes Paul Mason of Imazine: "RPGs are undergoing a punk rock-and-roll Renaissance, impudently ignoring the approval of the money-men, their agents, and their pinkie rings." How are the meanings produced using older forms of technology different from games that have made use of new technological advances?

LAW AND REGULATION

Copyright law, regulation and censorship have all been identified as shaping the production of symbolic culture. RPG production must also navigate these issues. MacKay theorizes that overlap between different media: movies, novels, television and RPGs, have created what he terms "imaginary-entertainment environments."[72] These media are in communication with each other, contributing to the growth, history and status of a particular intellectual property. This communication may be enabled or constrained by laws and regulations. While unofficial games using particular movies or TV shows may exist, there are also "official" licensed RPGs that have obtained the rights to use the characters and settings from other media products. Drawing on the production of culture perspective would lead us to examine how these laws and regulations impact the RPGs produced and their symbolic content. We might also ask how these regulations contribute to players identities, giving them access to or preventing them from accessing, stories that resonated with them and their personal identities.

INDUSTRY STRUCTURE

Winkler's piece "The Business and the Culture of Gaming" examines the industry structure of RPG. He argues that while the industry can be divided into four categories: manufacturing, distributing, retailing and consuming but that focusing on these categories overlook the unique industry that is RPG.[73] This is in part because RPGs are part of a larger sci-fi and fantasy industry and serve as a niche market in the U.S.[74] The industry structure is also complicated by the fact that many individuals involved in manufacturing, distribution or retail are also consumers of RPG and view themselves as part of the RPG subculture. Winkler argues that this leads to a loyal consumer base and to "friendly rivalry" as opposed to "cut-throat maneuvering" among competitors.[75] Expanding on Winkler's argument using the production of culture perspective means examining how this industry structure impacts the symbolic content of RPGs. How does the loyal consumer base or "friendly rivalry" shape the types of RPGs that are produced? How does this niche market lead to the production of certain types of fantasies or ideas?

ORGANIZATIONAL STRUCTURE

The RPG industry is comprised of large manufacturing firms, small publishing operations of one or two people, distributing firms and specialty retail shops that may also sell other types of products. Winkler argues that the RPG industry is primarily selling ideas rather than items and "ideas require a different business environment than mass-produced commodities."[76] Peterson and Anand, in their review of production of culture literature, argue that bureaucratic, entrepreneurial or variegated organizational forms are characteristic of the cultural industry.[77] It would be interesting to explore how the unique business environment (or environments) of the RPG industry compare to those of other cultural industries.

Winkler highlights the need for a different business environment, one that allows for creativity and experimentation.[78] Yet it is unclear what the organizational structure of different aspects of the industry actually is, or how this structure impacts the kind of products that are created. The Forge helped spur a self-publishing movement in the industry and the organizational structures of these small publishers may be different than the structures of the larger RPG publishers. There are also industry organizations like the Game Manufacturers Association (GAMA) that have their own distinct organizational structure. Outside of personal narratives, no existing scholarship has examined these organizational structures in terms of their effect on the production of RPGs. Future research could examine the organizational structures of different aspects of the gaming industry, or compare different organizations within the same level (different retail stores for example) to explore how organizational structure impacts the production of RPGs and related products. This research would be of potential interest to scholars working on the production of culture and those who study organizations or organizational structure.

CAREERS

The working relationships and networks of creative workers are often part of a larger "career" system that distributes creative, craft, entrepreneurial occupations. Sometimes careers follow a predictable path, while other times they are chaotic and lead to cultural innovation. Careers may be hindered by gatekeepers who judge work by particular standards, and some industries may have differentiated career paths, such as writers who produce "literary" versus "light" works, that lead to status differences and influence the type of products created.[79] Winkler's work highlights the overlap between different aspects of the RPG industry but raises questions about how individuals progress through the structure. Do most industry producers start as consumers, do designers become retailers — do there seem to be set career paths that people follow or is RPG an industry with more chaotic and variable paths? Studying the career paths of some different individuals, those who have been both consumers and manufacturers, designers, or retailers, would help expand our understanding of this aspect of the RPG subculture and could then be expanded to examine how this career structure impacts the symbolic content of RPGs.

MARKETS

In order to be successful an industry must cater to the tastes of its consumers. The production of culture perspective, however, is concerned with examining how consumer tastes become reified markets and how the creation of markets both enables and constrains the products available to consumers.[80] Past research has demonstrated how different products like movies or television shows gain legitimacy or credibility based on their stars, director or writer.[81] Products that are able to demonstrate their legitimacy are more likely to be produced shaping the types of movies and television shows that are available. In a similar fashion, designers or manufacturers may seek to gain legitimacy for their RPG concept. Understanding how these claims to legitimacy are constructed would help us to understand how markets influence the creation of RPGs. While RPG is already a niche market, we have already discussed the differential preferences that exist among RPG players. How do RPG creators and retailers attempt to understand the tastes of their consumers? What ideas are seen as legitimate and which are seen as too risky? And further, how have changes in the industry, such as the rise of independent RPGs or the growth of online retail, changed the way that markets are viewed within the RPG industry. By exploring these different aspects of RPG production scholars would have a more complete understanding of how the "ideas" sold by the industry are tied to larger structures. As the scholars of the production of culture argue, the factors of production will shape the symbolic content produced, this is undoubtedly true for RPGs as well, yet we have little information about this aspect of the RPG subculture.

Exploring Subcultural Networks

Expanding on Swidler's theory of culture Lamont argues that structural conditions shape which culture resources are used by different groups.[82] Structural conditions, such as market position, networks and community characteristics, push individuals to draw on particular "tools" from their cultural tool kit. Especially in the realm of RPG subculture networks may be key in understanding how culture is utilized in different interactions.

RPG players are often part of several different types of networks. Most players have a *local network* made up of friends they game with or acquaintances who they play with at gaming stores or local conventions. They may also be part of *regional networks* fostered by larger regional conventions, colleges in the same area, or friends who live outside their local area. The presence of national associations, and national conventions like Origins or GenCon Indy may also help some RPG players to become part of *national networks*. Though perhaps more important at this point are *virtual networks* composed of websites, blogs, podcasts, message boards, etc. Some RPG players may be members of multiple listserves, message boards or blogs while others may limit their involvement to one or two sites. Finally there may be other types of networks: *system-specific networks* (like AmberCon) which are devoted to specific game systems or those devoted to specific types of games (story games, horror games, etc). Some players may act as links between different local or regional networks, while others may not have many connections outside their local area. Some players, who may also be creators, dealers or association leaders, may gain status because they relay information to and from multiple networks.

Fine argues that gaming groups create their own idioculture, a system of knowledge, beliefs, behaviors and customs peculiar to an interacting group.[83] The local, small group culture produced by these groups is key to understanding how meanings are created during games and how culture is employed in interactions. But while local idiocultures maintain their importance, the Internet has expanded the culture that impacts gaming. RPG players are now able to move beyond their physical location and connect with gamers across the U.S. and the world. Furthermore, the growth of websites like *the Forge* or *story games* create a more unified RPG culture at the national and international level.

Future research should be cognizant of how different players are positioned within multiple networks and how this impacts interactions and play. Researchers might also wish to explore the existing networks of RPG players at these multiple levels and trace how information, game systems or other cultural material, is passed among different groups through these networks. Like the other topics I've explored in this essay the study of RPG networks could make valuable contributions to network analysis more generally and draw a potentially wider audience for RPG research.

Speaking to a Wider Audience — Reflexivity

Many contemporary studies of RPGs and their players are conducted by individuals who are also part of the subculture. This clearly has both benefits and drawbacks. Many studies are drawn from "convenience" samples: gaming groups the researcher is already part of, friends who are also gamers, conventions attended by the participant. While I personally would love to see more studies that interrogate and explore the variance of role-playing experiences across ages, regions and locales, convenience samples do provided a much easier and more feasible way of conducting research (especially in the face of limited funding for this type of research). However, future studies *should* be more reflexive about not only their sampling but also their own biases as RPG players and members of the subculture. All researchers have biases that they bring to their research. Being an "outsider" does not guarantee objectivity. However, being an "insider" does give researchers particular experiences that they draw from when making claims or demonstrating their findings. "Insider" researchers may be less aware of how these experiences shape their research or they may be unaware of the particularities of their local gaming culture. Self-reflexivity has been used by anthropologists and feminist researchers to deal with the problem of bias in research. Since true objectivity cannot be obtained, researchers rather focus on describing their own positionality and how it may impact their findings and experiences.[84]

Researchers explain their relationship to their topic, but also reflect on how this relationship shaped their research, their relation to their research subjects, their analysis of their findings. For instance, I might explain that my early experiences with D&D have led me to look less favorably on that particular system. I might also talk about being the member of a gaming community with a large number of game creators who are proponents of independent and "story" games. Thus my experience of what an RPG is might differ from someone whose gaming experience is more centered around "mainstream" or traditional RPGs. It would probably also be useful for me to explain my own personal preference for "story games" so that readers don't mistake my personal preferences for objective statements of fact.

As Fine points out, RPGs take place in group cultures, the location of the game (a private residence vs a gaming store) and the individuals who make up the gaming group create their own idioculture.[85] Rather than generalizing from the experiences of one group of players researchers should attempt to think about how their unique group culture shapes the role-playing experience. While Fine's fieldwork took place in several different settings, he was still operating largely within one group culture. Most contemporary studies also draw from a group culture for their sample. Future research that attempts to explore multiple cultures: a gaming group at a private residence and one at a more public location, a group of college friends who game together vs. a group assembled over the Internet, could provide some interesting information not only about RPGs but about group cultures more generally. A more systematic examination of convention play would also be fascinating.

Conclusion

RPGs as a subculture have grown and changed in the decades since Gary Alan Fine conducted his research. Not only have the numbers of RPGs, players and conventions grown, the subculture has also increased its diversity in terms of the types of games, players, and contexts for play that are available. The subculture has broadened and expanded its connections to other "geek" subcultures focused on movies, comic books, video games and other pop cultural phenomena. The Internet has played an important role in shaping the RPG community, offering new arenas for networking, discussion and role-playing. Sites like the Forge have provided spaces for RPG players to theorize about RPG play, creation and GMing as well as encouraging more grass roots game creation and production.

All of these changes mean that the RPG landscape today is quite different from that documented by Fine in the 70s. Documenting how these changes have affected the RPG subculture is of interest for those of us who view ourselves as members of it. At the same time, research exploring these historical changes and their effects on the RPG subculture may also be of interest to scholars outside the subculture.

Scholars since Gary Alan Fine have added to the body of RPG scholarship. These authors have made important contributions to our understandings of RPGs. However, much of RPG scholarship is still marketed to the RPG subculture. While this has created a strong scholarly community, it has limited the knowledge and interest in RPGs in other scholarly fields.

Focusing particularly on cultural sociology, I have demonstrated that concepts from this tradition have much to offer to RPG scholarship. My aim was not to stop there, however, I also hoped to demonstrate the contributions that could be made to these different literatures from RPG research. RPG research has much it can offer the study of leisure subcultures, material and cultural production, identity and networks. Research focusing on RPGs could also contribute to wider understandings of how texts structure interactions, how culture is created through interaction, how distinctions and boundaries are created and maintained, and how status systems are challenged or bolstered through interaction.

RPG scholars limit the impact of their work when they target their research to the narrow realm of RPG scholarship. By engaging with other scholars, concepts and questions outside the field of RPGs, researchers have the opportunity to demonstrate the relevance of RPG scholarship to wider fields of study. While I have focused on sociology, I am confident that RPG research could engage with a myriad of fields including (but certainly not limited to) theater, literature, media studies, psychology and communication studies. This wider dialogue would help enrich fields like sociology by bringing them new insights gained in the field of RPGs. It will also help enrich the field of RPG research with new data, concepts and literature.

In order to make our research interesting and applicable to a wider audience, RPG scholars must engage with work outside the narrow body of RPG literature. Concepts created and honed by past scholars can help us better understand our own experiences and data. By holding our research to a more rigorous standard, being reflexive about our own biases, data limitations and group cultures, we make our research conversant with others who may have little interest in RPG per se, but who may be extremely interested in and excited by the findings of our research. RPG scholarship has much to offer the wider intellectual community, as Fine argued when he first published *Shared Fantasy*, and it is still true today.[86]

Notes

1. Fine, *Shared Fantasy* (1983) uses the term Fantasy Role-Playing (FRP) which he identifies as the term most common among his research subjects. However, for the purposes of this paper, I substitute this term with Role-playing Game (RPG), which is the more common term among contemporary gamers.

2. Lortz "Role-Playing" 36, cited both in Fine 6 and Mello, "Invoking the Avatar" 175.
3. Fine 1.
4. Fine 3–4.
5. See Williams, Hendricks and Winkler, *Gaming as Culture* (2006).
6. Williams, Hendricks and Winkler 2 (2006). See also MacKay, *The Fantasy Role-Playing Game* (2001).
7. Fine xiv.
8. Fine 15.
9. Ibid.
10. Fine 27.
11. See Kim, "Who Are Role-Players?"
12. Fine 15.
13. Japanese animation and comic books.
14. Fine 33.
15. http://www.originsgames.com/
16. Compare Fine 33 and Kirby, "Gen Con Indy 2011."
17. Fine 25–27.
18. Fine 28–30.
19. Fine 35–36.
20. Especially rec.games.frp.advocacy.
21. Boss, "Key Concepts" (2008) 232.
22. Anderson and Taylor, "Standing Out While Fitting In" (2010) 36.
23. Anderson and Taylor 35.
24. Gillespie, Leffler, and Lerner, "If It Weren't for My Hobby" (2002) 290. See also Hodman and Jacquard, "Leisure Activity Patterns" (1988) and Orthner and Mancini, "Leisure Impacts" (1990).
25. See Kimmel, "Consuming Manhood" (1994), *Manhood in America* (1996).
26. Stalp, "Negotiating Time and Space" (2006) 128.
27. Pelak, "Women's Collective Identity" (2002), Laurendeau and Sharara, "Women Could Be" (2008)
28. Hunt, "But We're Men" (2008).
29. Anderson and Taylor 37–38.
30. See Nephew, "Playing" (2006), and Schut "Desktop Conquistadors" in that same volume.
31. See, for example, the *RPGirl* zine.
32. Bowman (2010).
33. Cf Nephew.
34. Williams, Hendriks, and Winkler 8–9.
35. Anderson and Taylor 41.
36. Ibid.
37. Anderson and Taylor 47.
38. Anderson and Taylor 48.
39. Anderson and Taylor 51–52.
40. The Game Master, also sometimes known as a Dungeon Master or Storyteller, is the referee of a game. She is often in charge of generating monsters, plot and setting for the game.
41. Swidler, "Culture in Action" (1986), Swidler (2001) 24.
42. Swidler (1986) 277, Swidler (2001) 25.
43. Swidler (1986).
44. Fine 196–200.
45. Swidler (1986) 277, Swidler (2001) 22.
46. Swidler (1986) 277.
47. Swidler (2001) 25.
48. Swidler (1986) 284, Swidler (2001) 25.
49. See Boss, "Key Concepts" (2008). See also Edwards, "GNS" (2001).
50. Fine 39–47, Kim, "Who Are Role-Players?" (2008).
51. Waskul, "Role-Playing" (2006), Winkler, "Social Movements and Culture" (2006) 145.

52. See MacKay.
53. Fine 62–71.
54. Fine 153.
55. Fine 153, 162, 177–180.
56. See Bowman.
57. Edwards, "A Hard Look."
58. MacKay 23.
59. MacKay 48.
60. MacKay 48.
61. Anderson and Taylor.
62. As also mentioned in White, Harviainen and Boss in this volume.
63. Boss, "Key Concepts" 236.
64. Boss 236–238.
65. See Kim, "Who Are Role-Players?" (2008).
66. Peterson and Anand, "The Production of Culture Perspective." (2004) 311.
67. Peterson and Anand 313.
68. Peterson and Anand 324.
69. Peterson and Anand 325.
70. Peterson and Anand 326.
71. Edwards, "Nuked Apple Cart."
72. MacKay 29.
73. Winkler, "The Business and Culture of Gaming" 142.
74. Winkler 143, 150.
75. Winkler 146–147, 150.
76. Winkler 151.
77. Peterson and Anand 316.
78. Winkler 151.
79. Peterson and Anand 317.
80. Peterson and Anand 317–318.
81. Peterson and Anand 318.
82. Lamont, "The Dignity of Working Men" 7.
83. Fine 136–145.
84. For example, see St. Pierre and Pillow, *Working the Ruins* (2000), or Naples, *Feminism and Method* (2003) 37–66.
85. Fine 136.
86. Fine 252.

The Agentic Imagination:
Tabletop Role-Playing Games
as a Cultural Tool

TODD NICHOLAS FUIST

Early in the history of American sociology, George Herbert Mead suggested that children are socialized through play by trying on the roles they observe in adult society, ultimately developing an awareness of the multiplicity of social roles and a sense of self.[1] Despite this early theoretical innovation, it is only recently that play has been treated as a serious sociological topic.[2] With some notable exceptions, however, much of this research examines the rise in popularity of video games,[3] ignoring the form of play referred to as tabletop role-playing games.[4] This is curious as TRPGs represent a particularly fruitful field to explore some of the most central areas of concern to sociologists, including, but not limited to, social interaction, identity, community, role-taking, and textual representations. This essay has two interconnected goals:

1. To develop the concept of "agentic imagination" which can be used to analyze participation in TRPGs by examining how role-players "imagine-in" to the shared fiction they create and "imagine out" to the social world.

2. To analyze how role-players use TRPGs as a cultural tool to shape their identities through *self-exploration*, *world exploration*, and *connectivity*.

These theoretical concepts are supported with evidence emerging from semi-structured interviews with 20 role-players. To situate the analysis, I will first briefly discuss the history of TRPGs and situate this essay within current literature on gaming.

Roll a Knowledge Check: Current Academic Work on TRPGs

With the release of *Dungeons & Dragons* in 1974, TRPGs entered the public consciousness.[5] Since then, there have been numerous role-playing worlds, systems, and styles, representing a number of different approaches to role-playing. This has spawned a large and very loose gaming community that includes people playing games in highly divergent ways.[6] The kind of gamers specifically discussed in this essay play games in which:

1. Players play at least one character (or similar facet of the game world) over which they have a very large (but not necessarily exclusive) degree of narrative control, including history, appearance, interactions, abilities, etc.

2. There is a shared, narrative game world over which players, taken collectively, have almost total control.

This narrows the focus of the essay to any game in which participants create characters, or other actors within the game world, and "play" them in the shared imagined space, predominantly through face-to-face interaction — as in the seminal games *Dungeons & Dragons* and *Traveller*, or in more recent small-press games such as *Fiasco, Apocalypse World*, and *Sorcerer*.[7]

There are several reasons for the focus on TRPGs in this essay that relate to what we can sociologically learn by studying role-players. First, as Jennifer Cover[8] and Thomas Malaby[9] point out, these games provide a significant amount of agency to the players, which is useful for the concept developed below that relies on social imagination. Second, these games allow participants to project cultural representations into the shared imagined space of the game, what Gary Alan Fine[10] calls the "fantasy world" frame (see below), as well as gives players the ability to pull understanding out of the "fantasy world" frame, potentially shaping their behavior and social identities in the "real world."[11]

There are multiple layers of interaction in TRPGs: the layer of social actors actually communicating with each other in the real world; the level of players playing a game with rules and internal logic; and the level of the fiction, or the diegetic level.[12] Johan Huizinga called this level of play within games the "magic circle,"[13] designated as a space set apart, with permeable boundaries, where special rules apply." This level has more recently come to be called the *shared imagined space* in many discussions of role-playing and the term will also be employed here as it stresses both social interaction and imagination, which are central to the analysis in this essay. The shared imagined space is the fictional game world collaboratively created by participation in a TRPG.[14] The creation of the shared imagined space in gaming drives role-playing because it provides a shared framework in which participants can explore other worlds or enter the "headspace" of people other than themselves.[15] Along these lines, Thomas and Brown suggest that that the imaginations facilitated by gameplay are more "learning to be" than "learning about."[16]

Also important is recent work that has treated role-playing as the creation of texts and art.[17] Groups and individuals are increasingly taking part in the production of their own entertainment in a variety of ways, blurring the line between creator and consumer.[18] As MacKay notes, role-playing in particular creates "a cathartic structure that encourages identification with [a game's] content and that persists after the performance has disappeared."[19] My interviewees confirmed this assertion about role-playing, with every single participant claiming that narrative creation as the primary reason they play, regardless of the genres or styles of TRPGs played. When asked what TRPGs are "most like," *none* of my participants have responded that they are most like board games, sports, strategy games, etc. Instead, fiction, usually novels or plays, are suggested as the most appropriate comparison. A typical response came from Ned, a role-player in his late 20s, who said "[gaming is] like going to a party with your friends, and watching and acting in, at the same time, the greatest improv show you've ever seen."

The important elements to consider in the current literature on role-playing then would be the multiple layers of interaction, the agency of the players, and the understanding of gaming as the creation of narratives and texts. With this as the orientation towards the topic material, we turn now to various bodies of academic literature to develop a theoretical perspective to analyze sociological data collected from gamers.

Towards a Theoretical Concept: The Agentic Imagination

What fields of sociological knowledge assist in the studying of role-players, and what can be learned about the social world from an analysis of participation in TRPGs? There are various existing models for describing the interconnected layers of interaction within role-playing united by an understanding that role-playing is a social activity in which some kind of rules system (defined broadly), along with a social contract between players, structures the creation of a shared imagined space in which the interactions of participants in the "real world" create the "game world," including imaginary characters, environments, and situations.[20] Implicit in these models is an understanding of the greater TRPG community and the norms, values, and culture it promotes. Understanding this, the theoretical concept outlined below draws on current literature on identity, social practice within communities, and the use of culture. These literatures situate the practice of role-playing within our current sociological knowledge and help develop a theoretical concept I call the "agentic imagination" that can shed light on analyses of participation in TRPGs.

Identity has enjoyed a complicated history in the social sciences, often meaning different things to different disciplines.[21] Conceptualized by Erik Erikson[22] as the constant reproduction of a self-recognition over the lifecourse, the concept later became associated within sociology and social-psychology as the idea that one "derives [one's identity] from his [or her] knowledge of his [or her] membership of a social group (or groups)" leading to emotion and value based "social categorization" which can be "considered as a system of orientation which helps to create and define the individuals place in society."[23] In this conception, identities are fluid, hierarchical and changing; the result of various social networks that dictate how important our various identities are in a given situation.[24] For example, one's identity as a role-player may be highly salient in the context of gaming, but play into one's work life only minimally.

Following this, sociologists understand identity not as an essential self-concept that is individualistic and unchanging, but rather as a dynamic social process that requires constant work and maintenance through imagination and social interaction.[25] In fact, Anthony Giddens suggests that the "reflexive project of the self" has become the key project for social actors in late modernity.[26] One's identity is predominantly performed in the context of one's various social groups, but this performance also inculcates a parallel social imagination. As Wenger states,

> Through imagination, we can locate ourselves in the world and in history, and include in our identities other meanings, other possibilities, other perspectives... it is through imagination that we conceive of new developments, explore alternatives, and envision possible futures.[27]

It is "imagination" as constitutive of identity that Mead had in mind when he suggested that games assist in the identity formation of children. A concept of identity is useful for analyzing TRPGs because it provides a handle helping us to understand the kind imaginations Wenger suggests we use to "explore alternatives" and "envision possible futures." By situating ourselves in social groups and within time and space, we actively construct our identities. By imagining ways that these situations could be *different*, however, we actively imagine alternative constructions of how we could fit into our social worlds.

I have so far discussed identities at the individual level. What about identity with regard to collectives or communities? While not all role-players seek connection with a larger "role-playing community," almost all of my interviewees suggested that a positive aspect of playing was social both in terms of local interaction with one's gaming group as well as a sense of belonging to a greater role-playing community through attending conventions, consuming gaming products, and community online with other gamers. We may turn to literature on collective identity and community to understand how these elements come together in the world of role-playing.

Within sociology, collective identity has most consistently been discussed with regard to social movements. Sociologists often see collective identity as a "we-feeling" among a group of people and, for an individual, the sense that one is connected to a broader "community, category, practice, or institution."[28] A collective identity may be generated through a combination of factors including shared narratives, texts, rituals, and identification of boundaries between groups.[29] To provide examples relevant to TRPGs, participants in TRPGs often circulate "gaming stories" through interaction networks which may include stories about particularly good play sessions, examples of poor behavior by participants, or other narratives about participation in the TRPG community. Texts include the books and other objects used to run games themselves, but also include various forms of gaming media including magazines, podcasts, blogs, novels, and write-ups of actual play that are posted on the internet for others to read. The practice of getting together with one's gaming group may constitute a ritual, but so would smaller actions such as dice superstitions[30] and larger events such as attending gaming conventions or participating in other forms of sanctioned plays such as the RPGA community.

All of these elements serve to delineate boundaries between participants in TRPGs and other people, allowing for the formation of the imagined community of role-players and the associated collective identity. Someone who knows the jargon from books ("...did you bring your d20?"), understands the references in gaming narratives ("...of course the munchkin at that table is playing a barbarian!"), and participates in the rituals ("...the con was great this year, you should go next year!") is able to understand and communicate effectively via the collective identity of role-playing. These elements interact with each other. Participating in a gaming ritual generates narratives that may be circulated, reading a text teaches one concepts which may be used to better understand narratives, and so forth. As such, participation in gaming involves a social and ongoing process of learning in which the "identity work" of aligning one's individual identity with the collective identity of the greater community both through interaction with other role-players and appropriation of cultural objects produced by the role-playing community.[31] While one may only interact directly with a small number of people in the "gaming community," one's engagement with this small number and the cultural objects of gaming allows one to imagine a greater community of role-players and, through participating in the practices of the community, align one's identity with the collective identity of the community. None of this differs from what happens in most communities, but it is important for the present analysis because the ability to imagine oneself as part of a gaming community is what justifies and normalizes the types of imagination which gaming entails, which are central to our understanding of how gaming may be used as a cultural tool.

Finally, we turn to the use of culture to explain what gamers "do" with the narratives they create in the shared imagined spaced. Rhys Williams defines culture as "the symbolic and expressive dimensions of social life."[32] As a concept, it is often connected with how people and groups create meaning via symbols and interactions.[33] Particularly important for the purposes of the present analysis are the notions that culture is shared and social, and groups and individuals may appropriate elements of culture for the construction of actions and identities. To examine this appropriation, I turn to work on the use of culture, what Henry Jenkins, following Michel de Certeau, calls "textual poaching,"[34] as well as work on cultural tools.

Contemporary sociologists of media and culture, notably Henry Jenkins, Paul Willis, and Ien Ang, have examined the ways in which audiences "construct their cultural and social identities through borrowing and inflecting mass culture images."[35] These authors suggest that popular culture can become a part of our identity work through "textual poaching," in which we use extant cultural objects, often in creative ways, to give meaning to our lives. Willis, for example, examines the creative re-purposing of articles of clothing by punks while Jenkins explores fan-fiction that actively repurposes the characters in ways unintended by producers to explore areas of interest to fan communities. Especially given Celia Pearce's insight that gamers "produce their own entertainment media"[36] while simultaneously borrowing from existing cultural archetypes,[37] the above media studies perspectives provide a useful component of a framework to examine TRPGs.

Likewise, in this volume, Katherine Castiello Jones suggests that TRPGs may serve as "cultural tools" in the sense suggested by Ann Swidler.[38] I agree, and wish to explore this notion further. Swidler provides one of the most thorough understandings of how culture may be used in social life by suggesting that culture can be understood as a "tool kit" that can "constrain and facilitate patterns of action" by providing the materials with which individuals can navigate the social world.[39] Swidler suggests that extant repertoires of action and the context in which a social actor is embedded shape the ability of social actors to construct pathways of action. Cultural elements may, as Swidler suggests, be used as tools in dynamic and creative ways, but not in an unlimited way. The shared nature of culture means that existing systems of meaning loom behind our use of any element of culture.

To summarize: there is widespread agreement that culture may be used as a "tool" in creating pathways of action and/or constructing identities. Contemporary work in cultural sociology and media/cultural studies suggests that culture is both external to the social actor, representing shared repertoires of meaning not reducible to any one individual. Yet they are also available for use by actors for interpretation and appropriation in the creative and dynamic creation of patterns of action or the construction of identity. Connecting this to the above work on identity and community, we can understand how shared cultural elements as well as cultural texts, including the fictional worlds created by participants in TRPGs and the cultural objects generated by the wider role-playing community, may be used as material in the imaginations necessary for identity work.

To tie elements from the above work on identity, community, and culture together, I propose the theoretical concept of the "agentic imagination," by which I mean the active ability of social actors to shape their identities through immersive imagination. As established, to be a role-player is to participate in several levels of social practice and interaction. I will draw attention to three as important for this concept: (1) one's immediate gaming group, usually in the form of face-to-face interaction in the practice of gaming; (2) the shared imagined spaces of the game world and; (3) the level of the greater collective identity of the imagined role-playing community, which individual role-players engage with through interaction with other role-players as well as engaging the cultural objects of gaming such as narratives, texts, and rituals. What connects these levels is an active, social imagination that has the agency to shape the individual: an agentic imagination.

All three of these levels occur simultaneously, interacting with and shaping each other. They are connected through the two parts of the multi-directional agentic imagination as I conceptualize it here, which I am calling "imagining out" and "imagining in." The ability to imagine oneself as connected to a role-playing community mediated and engaged by the cultural objects detailed above, as well as to imagine oneself entering the larger social world as a gamer, is "imagining out." By aligning one's identity with the collective identity of the imagined role-playing community, taking on the norms, values, and assumptions it implies, the practice of role-playing is normalized and given meaning and importance. In other words, the existence of an imagined gaming community and the ability of a gamer to align their identity with it separates role-playing from less structured or more individualistic forms of imagining such as daydreaming or playing make-believe by the social meaning the practice of role-playing is imbued with by the community.

The raw materials of role-playing, the texts, styles, assumptions, behaviors, etc., can then be used to "imagine in," or to project representations into the shared imagined space created through collaborative storytelling during game sessions. Out of this "imagining in," which occurs through the practice of role-playing with a gaming group, role-players are able to extract meaning which can be used to reify their interactions, both in the shared imagined space and in the real world, into cultural objects. These reifications include but are not limited to narratives which are told about particularly memorable games; gaming rituals which shape the way groups interact; write-ups of play sessions which turn the interactions into texts; blog or message board posts which analyze events in the interactions; podcasts which discuss experiences as a role-player; "in-joke" objects such as funny t-shirts or comic strips; and gaming resources which role-players use to play games such as rulebooks and strategy guides.

Finally, because these practices shape the identities of participants in TRPGs, role-players may use imagining in and imagining out in an agentic way, as cultural tools. While the ability to use TRPGs as a cultural tool is not limitless and is constrained by the norms of the gaming community and other social fields, role-players are ultimately able to use their agentic imaginations to construct identities and engage with the "real world" in meaningful ways through their use of TRPGs. In the remainder of the essay, the concept of the agentic imagination will be applied to data collected on role-players to create a typology of ways in which gaming is used as a cultural tool towards the ends of self-exploration, world exploration, and connectivity. To begin, I briefly explain my methods before moving on to an analysis of the data.

Methods

Twenty qualitative, semi-structured interviews were conducted with members of role-players in Chicago, Illinois and Seattle, Washington.* The interviews were recorded and transcribed, then coded to find emerging themes. To find interviewees, I used personal connections and posted a notice at a local gaming store in Chicago to build an initial set of respondents. I asked these individuals to pass my information along to other role-players they knew, widening the sample beyond the initial participants. These network or "snowball sampling" selection methods guaranteed a more diverse group including people who play different games, play in different styles, do and do not participate in the community at the game store, and do and do not know one another, which minimizes the possibility that my sample is representative only of a particular gaming group, rather than the wider community of TRPG players. It is difficult to say with certainty how representative my interviewees

---

All interview subjects in this essay are referred to by pseudonyms to retain anonymity.

are of role-players more broadly, but the process-oriented questions I am asking rely little on generalizability. The participants in this study are predominantly straight, predominantly white, and mostly men.[40] Among the interviewees, however, were two individuals who identified as gay, five women, and two individuals who are racial minorities. All names and several pieces of identifying information have been masked for all participants to ensure confidentiality.

Three Ways Role-Playing is Used as Cultural Tool

There are three primary ways that gaming has emerged as a cultural tool in my analysis: role-playing as self-exploration, role-playing as world exploration, and role-playing as connectivity. In this section I will use my framework to discuss this typology. There are several important things to note at the outset about this typology.

1. These are not "types of role-players," nor "play-styles." They are ways that TRPG participation is used as a cultural tool by gamers.
2. These are not exclusive categories. They are pathways to identity construction, problem solving, and community life by TRPG players via play. As such, one can be using two or three of these tools simultaneously, or, conversely, none at all.
3. This typology is not rigid. The boundaries between these tools are porous. They, in many ways, are connected and even embedded within each other. The appropriate spatial metaphor would not be boxes, nor a continuum, but instead a Venn diagram with a fair amount of overlap.
4. This typology is not exhaustive with regard to the possible ways gamers could use TRPGs as cultural tools. This typology, however, represents, the three most common pathways emerging from my data.

ROLE-PLAYING AS SELF-EXPLORATION

"I think, gaming is a kind of therapy for me," Ben, a 36-year-old role-player, told me over coffee. "It shows me the things that I repress by showing it to me in others." As an example, he said that said that he dealt with his divorce by creating a world-weary character in a fantasy setting who was powerless to stop the dissolution of his adventuring party around him. When he began talking about playing other characters in an effort to understand people in his life who were very different than him, we had the following exchange:

TODD: It sounds like what you're saying is you want to understand how someone can do something that you wouldn't do or that doesn't make sense to you.

BEN: Yeah. How to get out of my own mindset and somehow imagine someone doing something, one of my characters doing something that I wouldn't do.... How I, nevertheless, can feel that. Feel what that character is intending, feel what that character's motivation is, where that character is coming from, and that's what's most appealing to me, in some ways, about gaming. It's not escapism, it's a kind of finding myself, in some weird way, in Otherness.

Finding oneself in Otherness, as Ben puts it, forms the core of role-playing as self-exploration. Role-playing as self-exploration deals with learning about oneself through the game. This works simultaneously through the fiction of the shared imagined space as well as through the interactions at the table. It could be described as a sort of self-performed therapy and, in fact, one gamer jokingly referred to gaming as "poor man's therapy" during an interview. In the above exchanges, Ben discusses the way he uses the "imagining in" inherent in role-playing both to work through personal issues (divorce) as well as to understand other people in his life, all towards the end of greater self-knowledge and the reconfiguration of his identity.

Additionally, multiple players suggested that gaming makes them better personally or professionally. Hal, a 24-year-old role-player who worked as a teacher, related a story of feeling particularly good at being able to help young people write stories because he had been an avid player of *Dungeons & Dragons* for so long. Mary and Tom, a married couple in their 40s, agreed that gaming involved problem-solving scenarios as well as a focus on collaborative work which carried over into their work lives. Mike, a parent of two young girls, said that gaming has made him a better parent by equipping him with the tools to play make-believe with his daughters in a way which takes their imagination seriously. More than one role-player suggested that role-playing helped them in their creative career, including Dirk who said that the constant immersion in collaborative storytelling helped him as a writer, and Patrick who found a great affinity between the world of theater, particularly improv, and role-playing.

Most frequently, role-players expressed an interest in donning the metaphorical skins of others in an effort to get a better perspective on their own self. For example, Darla, a 35-year-old role-player, said "Sometimes I use characters to sort of work out and play out things that happen to me in my own life.... It's a way, for me, as an individual, to explore ideas, a way for me to explore parts of myself, a way for me to see what it's like to try and do something different." When I asked her to elaborate, she said, referring to one of her characters, "there's sort of a crazy aspect to her. Which is something that I, actually, as an individual, have issues with because of an illness I've got."

Trying on "the skins of others" to find oneself can have significant real world effects. An interesting story came from Joel, a 26-year-old Latino gamer who talked about gaming as part of his coming out process. When I asked him how gaming has shaped his interaction with other people, he said:

> Like, you figure out that you can summon up all these sorts of personas and personalities that you never knew you had, and maybe, just maybe, one of them sticks, or you adopt certain traits, and that kinda helped me, even (with) coming out.... That's you practicing who you're going to be.

When I asked him to elaborate on this, he talked about playing one of his favorite characters, "an inner-city Latina named Maria," which he described as "me throwing out some girliness."

Looking at these vignettes with the concept of agentic imagination, we can understand self-exploration through TRPGs as using both the "imagining in" of the projections into the fiction as well as the "imagining out" of figuring out how one's experiences as a gamer relate to other fields of social life as the kinds of imagination necessary to conceptualize alternative trajectories that one's identity may take. One respondent, Ed, put it this way: "I want to play someone interesting, someone effective ... I'm projecting myself. I want it to be me, but me who succeeds. I don't want to be, like, some random stranger who succeeds. Why do I care about that? I want to get that feeling." Through participating in the practice of gaming, role-players are provided with, as my respondent Mary suggested, a "safe place" to try on alternative ways of interacting or being which have real fictional consequences in the shared imagined space, but minimal consequences in the real world. This concurs with the insights of Sarah Lynne Bowman[41] and Myriel Balzer,[42] suggesting that this may be a common way of understanding participation in TRPGs.

Role-players I interviewed used cultural material available to them such as various social and literary archetypes, projected them into the shared imagined space, used them to inhabit an imagined world, and then pulled out lessons about what kind of person they could be for use in their everyday, non-gaming lives, demonstrating the dual process of imagining in and imagining out which is central to the active conception of identity formation I am positing with the agentic imagination. The narratives that emerged from the collaborative storytelling in the shared imagined spaces, in fact, were appropriated by the role-players as tools in the creation of efficacious identities and self-understanding. Role-players also related narratives about exploring issues larger than their own personal identity, however. Many suggested that gaming was a way to explore social issues, as well as other issues embedded in communities and societies. In the next section, I will explore role-playing as world exploration.

GAMING AS WORLD EXPLORATION

While many of the role-players I interviewed suggested that self-exploration was a positive result of participation in TRPGs, this was often understood in connection to larger social issues which role-players explored to better understand their feelings towards. Like self-exploration, this occurred at both the level of the shared imagined space and the level of the real world and, like self-exploration, relied on the connection between these two levels in many ways. In this section, I will examine the ways in which TRPGs were used as a tool in exploring various real world social issues by role-players.

Connecting her own experiences to the exploration of a wider social issue, Francine, a role-player in her 30s, told me:

> I've been [tall] since I was 12 years old and well over 200 lbs.... So exploring that as a teenager, getting to try on the pretty, pretty princess, you know, the Mary Sue with the shining black hair and the brilliant green eyes and all the guys want to do her [we laugh]. It's an exploration of what femininity means when you're not sure of it yourself.... And it's fun to play with the characters.

In this exchange, Francine explains how her own insecurities with regard to her looks and "femininity" led her to try on different characters in different game settings to play with different social conceptions of femininity. After this exchange, we discussed memorable characters she had played and I found that when Francine was in high school she tended to play characters that were beautiful and talented in what she deemed stereotypical ways, whereas now she is more interested in playing characters that "just kick ass" and have a "fearlessness" about them. When I asked her what has resulted in this progression she said:

> I think as a teenager you start with what you think society expects out of you, because, especially as a teenage girl, there's this whole lack of identity, because what you are and what you feel is so at odds with what the media is jamming down your throat.... But after growing up a little bit [you get] away from that, and getting away from that kind of one-note attention to "here's how real people, here's how real relationships function and they're complex..." There are all sorts of different levels to that that actually drive the role-playing and make it interesting.

In these statements, Francine expresses the way she increasingly used characters in TRPGs to pose a critique of cultural conceptions of gender and femininity. We can also see in these passages the way in which self-exploration and world exploration blend into one another. Francine is simultaneously struggling, through her characters, with her own place in the gender system of our society, at the same time that she uses her characters to explore the symbolic boundaries of it and critique it.

A similar narrative was related to me by Hal, who said that the character he's learned the most from playing is a Drow, or "dark elf," (i.e., a member of a "bad guy race" — evil elves from the underworld) in *Dungeons & Dragons*. When I asked him what he liked about the character, he said:

> When we play, it's a very story heavy game. We try and take it pretty seriously and, you know, act in character, and stuff like that. I thought it was an interesting storytelling challenge. How does this character who, in the game world, is out of type and an immigrant and doesn't necessarily belong in the culture we're playing in, how do you play that character? How does he respond to these situations?

I asked him to describe a situation in which he was able to immerse himself in the head of this character and see things from the character's point of view and he replied:

> There was one scene where ... we're at a posh dinner sort of thing ... and he was all decked out in his fancy clothes that he didn't want to wear to begin with, and he kind of just tore off this fancy shirt and just stormed out.... And so, to me, it is sort of like that character who is struggling to help out with this group he's a part of, but in situations which are just so unfamiliar to him and kind of intolerable to him.

Later in the interview, I asked Hal to explain the connection between player and character and what it means for learning about the social world and he referred back to the Drow character, saying:

> If you're a Drow from this brutal, jungle territory where people are murdered everyday for stupid reasons, that might make sense in the [game] world ... but it's something you might be uncomfortable with [in real life], so you have to come to terms with all of that, and ask yourself those kinds of questions.

This led to a discussion about how he has used his character to explore political philosophies he's uncomfortable with, especially more libertarian philosophies, joking that he would draw the line at "playing Glenn Beck the Drow," but that he learned to glean appreciable things from philosophies he was previously unable to see any good in.

Several other interviewees related similar stories to me during conversations. One male participant described a scene in which his character, who was normally mild mannered, became so incensed at his character's sister that he slapped her. The interviewee described being so immersed in the game world that he actually leapt up from his chair, swung his arms, and shouted as he described his character's actions. After the game was over, he said he felt so sick about his character's behavior, as well as his own imagined identification with it, that he was able to say with certainty that he was against violence in the real world. Another player explained that she is an atheist who has difficulty understanding the religious viewpoints of others and, as such, likes to play characters who are religious in different ways in an effort to better understand how religion motivates social behavior in society. When I asked Patrick, a 19-year-old role-player what participating in TRPGs has taught him about the world, he immediately replied:

> Racism. It's so easy for people to slip into this mode.... It's so easy for people to jump to hating. Even people who I know are nowhere near that in real life in gaming are like "oh, let's kill him because he's an orc!" Or the same thing with humans and elves. Like, it's a fantasy setting, but it's still interesting that people go there.

Bowman's essay "Jungian Theory and Immersion in Role-Playing Games" in this volume discusses the Jungian concept of the Shadow self,[43] or the parts of ourselves we wish to deny exist. There is a similar process at work, here, but rather than the bubbling up of suppressed, unconscious fragments, I suggest that these stories demonstrate the ways in which gamers often *actively* explore social pathologies for the purpose of world exploration. This exploration often has real world consequences for interaction at the table. Ned, a role-player in his late–30s, said he is increasingly tired of men playing "stereotypical, oversexed women" as characters and is trying to negatively sanction gamers who do that as much as possible. Darla related a story about confronting a sexist man during a game of *Dungeons & Dragons*:

> I feel like I'm in a minority in the gaming world. There just aren't as many women.... I feel like if things change a little bit at the table there could be more women involved.... Like, [one time I was] sitting at the table of a *D&D* game and this guy made a really sexist comment. We were trying to negotiate with this goblin chieftain, trying to set up a trade thing, and he was like "we can give you gold, or we could give you food, or we could have our human women come and redecorate your place." And I turn to him and say, "as the human woman at the table, fuck you!"

Ed shared a different kind of story, one in which he realized, through interacting with his gaming group that *he* was the problem.

> [I like games] with somewhat of a feminist bend to them, games that kind of force you to examine your assumptions about women's roles. And that's partly because so many of the people I've met through gaming happen to be super intelligent and articulate people into other issues. I've encountered a lot of feminists ... like, through nerdery in general, things like gay rights that I never really would have come into contact with. The first gay people I met were gamers. Prior to that, I was sort of a homophobe.

In all of these instances, we see engagement with the practice of role-playing in one's gaming community as providing the space to manipulate cultural archetypes ("woman," "immigrant," "racial minority," etc.) as one *imagines into* the shared imagined space, allowing the participants to gain understanding about social issues from their ongoing immersion in and identification with the fiction.[44] This allowed players to *imagine out* into the real world, sometimes having immediate social consequences that included negatively sanctioning other players, as well as more diffuse consequences such as developing a greater understanding of social issues. In the final section, I attend to how role-playing serves as a cultural tool to achieve connectivity.

ROLE-PLAYING AS CONNECTIVITY

Steve, discussing gaming with me in his Spartan apartment on a warm day, summarized the way many gain connectivity out of participating in TRPGs, saying:

> The escape from reality, the fiction element, has a lot to do with it.... I'd much rather be a fighter that's big and brawny and can kill things than a short, fat white kid that gets beat up on.... In terms of gamers themselves, my impression of gamers has always been that gamers are, I think in part because of the oppression they feel as a nerdier group of people, nicer to each other than most people are to each other.

In this statement, we see several things going on simultaneously. Steve is suggesting that there is such a thing as a wider gaming community whose members share certain qualities that emerge from a shared "nerdy" identity. It is worth pointing out that Steve is neither "short" nor "fat"; he is in fact tall and slender. This suggests that he identifies with the cultural conceptions of "nerdiness" even when those conceptions don't describe him. Also notable is the language of group oppression. Taken together, these statements suggest that participating in the practice of gaming does, in fact, both create a collective identity we can call the role-playing community as well as suggest that one may imagine out into it to align one's identity with the community. Likewise, Steve's statement indicates a degree of imagining in through which one can make connections with the narrative that provide emotional solace.

The ability to align oneself with the collective identity of a gaming community or the fictional world of a shared imagined space role-playing is *connectivity*. By this I mean role-playing as a cultural tool to make connections both with other people as well as with ideas greater than oneself. This is, to a degree, similar to what some see as "escapism." Many of my participants were aware of pejorative stereotypes of gamers as people who wish to "escape" into fantasy worlds, and some suggested that these stereotypes may be true, but I posit that a more fruitful way to approach this idea is to suggest that rather than "escaping," role-players were seeking to establish social, emotional, and intellectual connections with ideas and people.

Francine echoed Steve's sentiments. When I asked her to talk about what people in the TRPG community share, she replied:

We're not the well-adjusted football jocks, you know? [We're] the escapists, like myself who would be off reading Tolkien ... and all that stuff. Just the geek universe. And getting that level of comfort with each other, like, when you click together and find your people that you can be yourself with, we all have these kind of dark sides because of what you could call the abuse or the scorn of our peers and the internalization of having to deal with, again, "I'm not what the media says is a perfect person." You internalize that.

Here, the "geek universe," of which Francine conceptualizes role-playing as an element of, is conceptualized as a haven from a world in which one doesn't fit. The reified objects of the geek universe are imbued with meaning by their appropriation by this "nerdier group of people," and then used as both the tools of collective and individual identity for people looking to make connections.

This often related directly to the sorts of self-exploration and world exploration I have already discussed. One female participant, for example, said:

My mother ... has borderline personality disorder. And so part of growing up was escaping from her. Things like role-playing, or fantasy, where I could go be somebody that was more heroic, that could have dealt with her, I mean, she was very much the monster of my childhood, and I really wanted that +3 sword to slay her! Knowing that there were these ideas out there, where you could be heroic, where you could fight the monster, was comforting.... It gives you hope that there's something better. That there's a better thing that you can be a part of, you know?

Here, the interviewee uses the connectivity she found from gaming, as well as the other cultural objects of the geek universe, as a part of the self-exploration discussed earlier. By connecting with ideas greater than herself through appropriating cultural objects she was able to imagine herself as someone who could have "dealt with" her mother.

Almost all my interviewees repeated these kinds of narratives to me. Gaming was both a way for them to connect directly with others as well as a way for them to find an outlet in the collaborative narratives developed at the gaming table. Much recent sociological literature has suggested that our society has become increasingly fragmented, leaving many feeling isolated and longing for social connections.[45] Yet, as Dmitri Williams suggests, gamers pose a useful counterpoint to these findings because they aren't "bowling alone," so to speak.[46] Many participants, such as Mary and Ned, discussed being shy and said they were unsure if they would be able to make friends if it wasn't for their participation in TRPGs. Others, such as Patrick, Tom, and Dirk, said that they received a great deal of validation from being able to immerse themselves in fictional worlds and live out the dramatic lives of complicated characters. The use of TRPGs as a cultural tool in the creation of connectivity relies on the ongoing and continued practice of gaming with other individuals connected to the community through a combination of social networks and the texts produced for and by the gaming community. This allows for individuals to engage with gamers in ritualized social interactions as well as engage with the shared imagined spaces created through role-playing, and imagine themselves as part of a coherent whole, and ultimately align their identities with the collective identity of the larger gaming community.

Discussion and Implications

In this essay, I have used existing sociological literature as well as my own investigation of the role-playing community to argue that the practice of playing TRPGs creates the space for agentic imaginations which allow role-players to use TRPGs as a cultural tool to perform self-exploration, world-exploration, and connection with other people and with ideas. While many things in a society may be used as cultural tools, TRPGs make for a particularly rich analysis because they represent one of the few ways in which social groups come together to weave meaningful narratives through unfolding social interaction, allowing for the multi-directional processes of imagining into the shared imagined spaces and then imagining out into the larger gaming community or other fields within the real world.

The analysis here has several implications for the social sciences. First, it contributes to work in cultural and media studies which analyzes the ways in which the content of narratives and texts, even those we create ourselves, may be instrumental in our identity work at the level of both individual and collective identity. The analysis also contributes to our understanding of how participation in communities and social groups can shape our identities. Finally, the present analysis represents an example of the use of cultural tools in action, demonstrating the ways in which a single, albeit broad, cultural tool may be used in a variety of ways, often simultaneously, suggesting a multiplicity of meaning in practice.

For role-players, the analysis may help them reflect with greater self-awareness upon the processes through which they glean meaning and enjoyment from gaming. Similar to how Ron Edwards suggests that players with complementary creative agendas may often find more enjoyment in role-playing together than players with contradictory creative agendas do,[47] an intentionality about what, exactly, one wishes to gain from role-playing — self-exploration, world exploration, and connectivity — and in which degree, may serve to enrich the role-playing experience. I hope this study serves to initiate conversations within gaming groups about what we ultimately get out of the practice of role-playing, and welcome comments and critiques about how these conversations play out in actuality.

Finally, this research is ongoing, and there remains much more possibility for future work. Ethnographic observation of different gaming groups could show these processes or reveal additional processes I have not yet picked up on. The work in this study dovetails nicely with recent work by Thomas and Brown, Malaby, and Bowman. Bowman's work in this volume on the Jungian concept of "active imagination" provides a useful psychological counterpoint to the primarily sociological concepts I outline in this chapter. Much work on gaming, additionally, emerges out of the fields of literary criticism, cultural studies, and media studies. Interdisciplinary work in which the concepts and methods of various approaches to gaming were combined may be able to further strengthen our otherwise too-often disconnected analyses and provide a more holistic view of role-playing.

Notes

1. Mead, *Mind, Self, and Society* 150–162.
2. See Henricks, *Play Reconsidered* 3; Malaby, "Beyond Play" 95; Myers, "Glossary" 47.
3. Wright, Embrick, and Lucács, *Utopic Dreams* 3–4.
4. TRPGs, see Cover, *Creation* 5–7.
5. Bowman, *Functions of Role-Playing Games* 11; Cover 9; Fine, *Shared Fantasy* 14; Hitchens and Drachen, "The Many Faces" 3.
6. Arjoranta "Defining Role-Playing Games" 3; Hitchens and Drachen 3; Malaby 96.
7. This focus, of course, leaves out Massively Multiplayer Online games such as *World of Warcraft*, and other video game RPGs, board games, live action role-playing, and minimally narrative miniatures games or board games. This is not a value judgment on these games, merely a methodological/theoretical one.
8. See Cover 47–53.
9. See Malaby 105–109.
10. Fine 194.
11. See also, Bowman 12; Montola, "Invisible Rules" 23; Raessens, "Playful Identities" 53; Simkins and Steinkuehler, "Critical Ethical Reasoning" 351–352.
12. Montola, "Invisible Rules" 23.
13. Huizinga, *Homo Ludens* 10–12.
14. See Young, *Theory 101*.
15. Bowman 8.
16. Thomas and Brown, "Play of Imagination" 149.
17. See Cover (2010) and MacKay, *The Fantasy Role-Playing Game* (2001).
18. Pearce, "Productive Play" 18.
19. MacKay 122.
20. See Edwards "Provisional Glossary"; Fine 181–204; MacKay.
21. Stryker, "Identity Competition" 21–22.
22. Erikson, *Identity* 154–161.
23. Tajfel, *Human Groups* 255.
24. Goffman, *The Presentation of Self* 106–140; Stryker 23–24; Wenger, *Communities* 152.
25. Richard Jenkins, *Social Identity* 17; Lawler, *Identity* 5–8; Melucci, *Challenging Codes* 70–77; Wenger 175–177.
26. Giddens, *Modernity* 8–9.

27. Wenger 178.

28. Polletta and Jasper, "Collective Identity" 285; Stryker 23.

29. Kiecolt, "Self-Change" 121–123; Lamont and Molnar, "The Study of Boundaries" 167; Polletta, "It Was Like a Fever" 137.

30. See Hindmarch, *The Bones*.

31. By "community" I mean something very broad. A community may be, on the one hand, a subculture in which people share many things but do not all know each other or interact with each other on a regular basis as well as a small group who see each other regularly and are involved in each other's personal lives. The second, more intimate variation of community is often embedded within the larger, more diffuse variation of community. To continue the subculture metaphor, imagine a group of young people into hip-hop from a particular neighborhood who are all friends and how that small group is connected to the wide culture, networks, and collective identity of hip-hop. See Snow and McAdam, "Identity Work" 46–54.

32. Rhys Williams, "Social Movements" 954.

33. Geertz, *Interpretation of Cultures* 11–13.

34. Henry Jenkins, *Textual Poaching* 23.

35. Ibid.

36. Pearce 18.

37. See Bowman, in this volume.

38. Swidler, "Culture in Action" 273–274.

39. Swidler 284.

40. This fits with anecdotal evidence of the demographics of gamers more generally, see Cover 161; Fine 238.

41. Bowman 8.

42. Balzer, "Immersion" 33.

43. See Bowman, in this volume, "Jungian," 37.

44. See also, Balzer 32; Simkins and Steinkuehler 351–352.

45. Putnam 15–28.

46. Dmitri Williams, "Why Study Games Now?" 13–15.

47. See Edwards, "Narrativism."

Kid Nation: Television, Systemic Violence and Game Design

EVAN TORNER

At the conclusion of William Golding's parable *Lord of the Flies*, there is a moment when the entire novel's narrative is framed as a game. The protagonist Ralph finds himself mercilessly pursued by his former classmates, who have become hostile savages. When he stumbles upon a naval officer on the beach, however, the chase abruptly concludes as the officer peruses the "semicircle of little boys, their bodies streaked with coloured clay, sharp sticks in their hands" with a revolver at his side.[1] "Fun and games," are his words of dismissal, and with them he disenchants the life-and-death struggle among the children that is the substance of the book. "Reality" sets in, as the grown man and his holstered revolver abrutly introduce the adult world, bracketing off the events of the novel as part of one massive Huizingan *magic circle* of play that nevertheless caused the boys to forget their identities and to kill two of their own. Authentic danger is dismissed as merely ludic. The readers following the emotional roller coaster of the fiction up until this point are suddenly confronted with Golding's cold, deadpan fiat. Should the reader interpret the officer's statement on a metatextual level, they face two aporias: (1) whether or not Golding's fiction was itself simply a didactic game played with the reader, and (2) if there is not some fundamental brutality and transgression already inscribed into the very notion of "fun and games." For if an outsider to any human activity attributes a "lusory attitude"—a willing psychological subservience to a game, defined by Bernard Suits as a "voluntary attempt to overcome unnecessary obstacles"[2]— to its participants' behavior, then what is to stop *any* observable human behavior, including torture and suffering, from becoming perceived as a game given the proper context?

On the other hand, reality itself can easily become abjected from a proposed gamespace, despite the all-too-real consequences of its persistent influence. For example, in the fifth episode of the 2007 CBS reality show *Kid Nation*, council member Anjay confronts Markelle, who just tore down the posters of Taylor, a council candidate whom he dislikes. Markelle's justification for his deed is to trivialize the object of discussion: "Why not? It's a poster." Anjay responds by waxing philosophical about the disenchantment of their space: "Is this what Bonanza City was supposed to be? People ripping down other people's posters? This is everything the real world is. We do not want the real world." The gamespace of *Kid Nation* is conceived of as a sacred, positive space — a place where symbolic conflict must be banished in order to preserve the lusory attitude presumably held by all. In dialog with Golding, children's resolution of conflict in situations without adults somehow cannot be simultaneously *serious* and *real*; it is assumed that only the game's unnecessary obstacles hold authority over their actions, and Anjay's comment above concludes that games themselves embody a kind of administrative ideal. But Peter Firchow's commentary on *Lord of the Flies* may apply here: "Golding's intention is to establish, even at the cost of a drastic lack of realism, something like a laboratory situation.... The very lack of realism, the very extremity of the situation, calls attention to the 'experiment' that is being conducted in the novel."[3] In contrast, however, *Kid Nation* seems neither equally conscious of its own artificiality nor particularly interested in exploring the ways in which its forty child participants are, in fact, *powerless* over their fate due to unnecessary obstacles arrayed before them by the producers. The show does not ask whether a game is actually being played before or with the viewer, and categorically refuses the primacy of diverse game logics over its content.

A reality show about children's survival, *Kid Nation* inevitably invokes the discourse of children's' independence and, with it, Golding's famous parable. Indeed, Mike Meloy writes that "the show seemed to have a *Lord of the Flies* air about it: forty kids tribalized into competing factions without adults or clear rules governing their behavior in an abandoned town [Bonanza City] in the middle of the New Mexico desert."[4] Certainly the Golding analogy and that of the John Ford western are so overdetermined as to be the show's primary *architexts*, self-designated generic references that correspondingly shape the arc of a textual narrative, as formulated by Gérard Genette.[5] *Qua* Golding: there is a group of kids, assembled as an impromptu nation outside of direct contact with outside civilization, who inevitably descend into "madness" and decrepitude. Yet *qua* Ford: through their actions and inner moral character, the kids establish some semblance of ordered "civilization" against all odds.[6] Naturally, this somewhat cynically idealist scenario was created as controversial link bait, the show itself an imaginative spin-off of CBS' popular *Survivor* reality format that inherently begged questions of how conscionable it was to submit children to both the elements *and* to the whims of reality TV producers.[7] The question this essay seeks to answer, however, is not so much about the show's generic overtones,[8] courting of controversy,[9] presumptions about class mobility,[10] or wider transmedia interactions.[11] Rather, it is: to what extent is a reality show such as *Kid Nation* best parsed as a dramaturgical meeting point between a live-action *game* and a television *show*? That is to say, how might a failed TV program point to failures in game design, as well as the parapraxis inherent in reality itself when subjected to these game rules?

Reality Shows — More Game Than Reality

Reality shows are, in fact, barely conceivable without a competitive element facilitated by game rules. As Olaf Hoerschelmann writes, "audience members perform [in these shows] as individuals and participate in a form of mediated public life, yet at the same time, specific rules govern their participation and the authority of a host supervises them."[12] Yet little work has been done on the impact those rules have had on the shows' dramaturgy. This fact is especially surprising considering the two reality *game* shows *Survivor* (2000) and *American Idol* (2002) became, as Henry Jenkins notes, "the first killer [applications] of media convergence — the big new thing that demonstrated the power that lies at the intersection of old and new media."[13] Dominant scholarship instead focuses on its documentary heritage,[14] generic codes and stereotypes,[15] and its overall pre-packaged banality.[16] In other words, methodologies focus on those aspects of reality television most emphasized in mainstream critical discourse: reality shows as cheap exploitation of both the documentary tradition and the gullible participants themselves in order to emphasize suspenseful elements of a given scenario for the sake of selling viewers' audited eyeballs to advertisers. This limited approach is, on a pragmatic level, due in no small part to television studies' fairly recent assertion of legitimacy as a field, and an attempt to distinguish "quality" television from the trash. By contrast, game studies has only recently become academicized, and is understandably more preoccupied with the symbolic dissection of triple–A video game titles rather than the application of its formidable methods on other media such as reality shows.

But one could make the overarching argument that game rules are so integral to the structures of modern television — from the demands of televised football plays to game shows that impose artificial choices on their contestants for the sake of viewers at home — that the medium itself has arguably become a mere delivery technology for the playing and depiction of games, whether they be sports, machinima, or reality programming. Sheila Murphy sees television as a key centerpiece even of a digital media culture: "TV continues to provide a framework for digital media experience in an era when we are told, once again, to engage with 'smart TV.'"[17] And certainly media scholar Jason Mittel seeks a non-trivial answer to the question: "How might we conceive of [a TV series] as a video game?"[18] Games unleash their participants into dynamic digital and/or social systems, which can then be documented and retooled to engage viewers' expectations about how those systems play out. The systems by their very nature transmit ideology, or a series of expectations about how social reality functions. Mutually exclusive clichés like "working hard to get ahead" or "opportunity knocks but once" are more easily (pre-)scripted through footage of confrontations with unnecessary obstacles than with the messy, uneven business of humans laboring (or not) to survive.

The "reality" evident in a reality show thus corresponds more with the obvious, real-life stakes of preconceived contests and tournaments than the faithful representation of processes that affect our day-to-day lives. It likely comes as no shock to the modern viewer that games increasingly determine television, and the television as a medium determines what games are suitable to perpetuate its content flow. Staged contests, the illusion of chance, the suspense of variable reward systems; these patterns of game design all garner attention from fan communities eager to see the effects of imposed strictures on contestants. By watching a show such as *Kid Nation*, the viewer tacitly consumes dramaturgy of events that straddles somewhere between a psychology experiment, *bourgeois* melodrama, sports coverage and a documentary. At the same time, however, *Kid Nation* lets the promise linger that one might see the televisual evocation of "'the state of nature,' that hypothetical utopian/dystopian condition postulated by seventeenth- and eighteenth century philosophers from Hobbes to Rousseau."[19] It promised the audience a scenario in dialog with films like *Battle Royale* (2000), only without the battle, or *The Hunger Games* (2012) without the hunger. So if it does not deliver on this promise, is the show then a failed allegory? Or might one profitably interpret it as heavily augmented documentation of *non-fictional immersive play*, in which the forty child participants played their public and private "selves" for television, both of which were subsumed under the strictures of a game. I argue here that *Kid Nation*'s immersed subjects are not so much dealing with the exigencies of an existence without adults as they are navigating elaborate systems of control erected *in place of* the adults. For if the Lord of the Flies did not exist, television producers would have him invented, or at least stage his appearance for the sake of next week's ratings.

Game / Logic

What is meant by "game" anyway? Bernard Suits' definition of a game as the "voluntary overcoming of unnecessary obstacles" forms a worthy theoretical foundation. But the contemporary scholar who most productively articulates the concept for broader analysis is undoubtedly Jane McGonigal. She identifies four traits that inhere within all games: "a *goal, rules,* a *feedback system,* and *voluntary participation.*"[20] Goals are attainable outcomes that provide the players with a "sense of purpose," rules are the agreed-upon limitations in attaining this outcome, the feedback system tells one how close one is to the outcome and encourages achievement, and voluntary participation of the participants accedes to all of the above. By manipulating each individual element, a game designer structures the efforts, rewards and perceptions of efforts/rewards that guide human behavior toward modes of action and communication. Every game, well-designed or not, has its participants enact some form of ideology, a way of viewing the role of individual behavior within societal systems.

The primary preoccupation of every game designer is how to incentivize or discourage certain behaviors to achieve their design goals. Progress through these incentives creates narrative itself, and this progress is usually framed via media embedded into the game's aesthetic.[21] Gary Genosko argues that any media form, including games, accrues symbolic potency as it encounters other media flows: "The meeting of flows creates, in other words, meanings."[22] Through game design, one re/produces conditioned processes of signification and epistemology using the vehicle of the player, who maneuvers through symbolic reward systems.

A simple example of the above is in basketball's court design. With the *goal* being to amass the greatest number of points through baskets scored, the very spatiality of the court is centered on the polar opposite midpoints of a rectangle, with the box and the three-point line primarily delineating distance from the target. Both court markers serve as a feedback system to inform the player how far they are from the basket, and foreclose certain strategic approaches to the basket: one cannot, for example, slam dunk from the 3-point line. Gradually, a strategy develops that involves the basketball players moving the most efficiently to chart effective vectors to the basket. These strategies then take on heightened meaning when observed and commented upon by a sports program, or receive literary attention like in Carl Deuker's novel *On the Devil's Court,* another work similar to Golding's about the power of a game over children's lives. By observing the way basketball players negotiate a single game logic, we learn lessons about how to navigate other situations involving imaginary obstacles.

Like a game, television itself is a controlled feedback system that updates its users on (1) the progress of any given team toward a goal, (2) the rules and the players' adherence to them, and (3) the visible strategies the players deploy to maneuver toward the goal with or without breaking the rules. But the game feedback that television provides is also highly suspect in forming a *coherent* meaning; commercial breaks interrupt the flow of feedback (though never catastrophically) and insert other agendas into the viewers' consciousness. Television programmers often hedge their bets by offering contradictory incentive systems to as wide a possible demographic, in which the overall reward for continued viewing of a game — namely, knowledge of who won — is paralleled or even outstripped by the audio-visual rewards of high-budget commercials, the color commentators' mastery of the arbitrary aside, the cheerleaders, fan antics, and so on. The simplicity of the court is televisually replaced by a glut of different short-, medium- and long-term reward systems, all of which are designed to emotionally reconfigure the story arc of a game played to the advantage of the game's stakeholders. When this meeting of flows works for a program's producers, the result is intense viewer involvement; when it malfunctions, it results in noticeably incoherent and uncomfortable narratives that reveal the structures underpinning them. In any case, it is nigh impossible for the television viewer to be able to simply observe the game strategies used without an editor intervening and mediating these strategies. Television itself becomes part of the game.

Game elements and televisual tropes combined together — smiling hosts, leader boards, high-key lighting and post-competition interviews — often call attention to a television program's openly artificial qualities. Forged primarily in the editing room, reality television shows exhibit gaps in narrative and visual logic that constantly risk cognitive or emotional alienation from its constructed "reality." One of the reality show format's chief critics, Bill Nichols, intuits why this is:

> There is no "Aha!" on reality TV. A subsuming "logic" absorbs all incommensurate juxtapositions. It denies contradiction by refusing to propose any frame from which more local gaps, disturbances, or incompatibilities could be rearranged coherently.[23]

Nichols' critique is that the feedback reality television provides is *too* controlled, the gamespace[24] so all-encompassing as to stifle the very interest the show is designed to elicit for the advertisers. He accuses reality television of standing "in an antithetical relationship to the project of an existential phenomenology."[25] Rather than exposing the viewer to untold facets of existence, reality TV instead has the viewer play the pre-scripted *voyeur* in a tightly controlled game environment designed to not only engulf the narrative but even the potential possibilities of interpretation itself. The thought aligns with

Jonathan Beller's notion of the "cinematic mode of production," a specific subjective regime which captures the consumer's attention itself for the sake of hyper-accumulation by a financial elite.[26] Should a reality game show's producers attempt to relax their control over the documentation of a given reality game, as social advertising guru Billee Howard advises,[27] a medium so thoroughly entrenched within these logics such as television may very well disallow them from doing so. Despite the risk of losing active viewer involvement, reality television shows usually use game elements as ornamentation of an otherwise purely emotional spectacle engineered for the sake of capital.

Kid Nation is therefore a reality show under the thumb of multiple different masters whose interest does not lie in the documentation of children attempting to build their own society. The totalitarian logic of the social and material systems that underwrite television programming forbids an actual, non-fictional, immersive *Lord of the Flies* scenario filmed by an adult camera crew, if only for what it might have revealed about children. The show might have depicted children overcoming necessary obstacles without their parents by adopting what psychologist Michael Tomasello calls a "shared intentionality"[28] to combat looming threats to their survival. Instead the show resorts to unnecessary obstacles — Voice of God suggestions from the producers, arbitrary social stratification, physical challenges, extrinsic rewards, constrained options — to railroad[29] the 40 children's group narrative into an easily manipulable object at the expense of spontaneity and interest. Game rules take the place of active adults controlling the children's' lives, but an adult presence is still very palpable. These rules constitute not only failures in the production's vision, but also notional failures in game design.

Cynical Design for Systemic Violence

Immersive live-action gameplay can and should be stimulating to watch,[30] with its inherent goals, rules, strategies and participant enthusiasm all on display for the viewers to explore. To design a scenario that would immerse its subjects in the tasks of survival the way that *Kid Nation* promised, we might refer to the patterns of game design articulated by Staffan Björk and Jussi Holopainen. A designer seeking player immersion within a scenario, like for the kids within Bonanza City, wants the players to have a parallel awareness of both the game and the reality that contextualizes it. "[Immersion] does not mean that players are unaware of their surroundings or that they are playing a game," Björk and Holopainen argue, "but rather that they are deeply focused on the interaction they are having within the game."[31] This state of being is instantiated by the characteristics of "Narrative Structures, Characters, Avatars, Game Worlds, [Overcoming] Goals and the presence of Freedom of Choice."[32] The players can recognize, but are deeply involved with, story arcs, protagonists and their representations, and agency to effect progress toward their goals. Immersion is in many cases a particularly persuasive prompting of a participant's imagination. Note that most of Björk and Holopainen's structures are based on around the construction of a fictional persona within a fictional gameworld, rather than playing oneself in a live-action game show. The key idea in documenting such a game would be to keep those fictional elements the players find immersive in view without losing sight of the corporeal realities of the unnecessary obstacles posed by these elements.

By contrast, *Kid Nation* is a documentation of psychological stress under the totalitarian regime of reality television game strictures. *Kid Nation* as a game — the rules of which I describe in the section below — seeks to convince its participants that the show is actually not a game, nor even a summer camp; both contexts most American kids would otherwise find socially intelligible. Writer Tom Forman and CBS executive Ghen Maynard, the two major creative forces behind the show, saw it no less than an existential test that let children "prove to adults that they were capable of doing more than anyone thought they could ever do."[33] In doing so, they transform a potentially ludic or creative space into a competitive rat maze predetermined entirely by adults.[34] The children's "test" does not even begin with their own standards for survival, but with those of an adult reality show such as *Survivor*. In a contemporary review of the show in *USA Today*, for example, Marilyn Elias writes that "*Kid Nation* emphasizes some of the worst aspects of society, such as group inequalities and fighting for limited resources."[35] Institutional structures such as school or summer camp are the generally accepted basis for arbitrary groups of children to gather around labor and meals. But the direct competition Elias describes as emerging from the show's artificially imposed class hierarchies — competition which Björk and Holopainen describe as antithetical to "Experimentation"— emerges from the game rules, replacing institutional structures with diffuse *systemic violence*.

Systemic violence, as Slavoj Žižek defines it, "is no longer attributable to concrete individuals and their 'evil' intentions, but is purely 'objective,' systemic, anonymous."[36] It is the violence imposed not by individuals, but by cultures and systems: racism, resource extraction, fundamentalist crusades, and institutional indifference to human need are all manifestations of it. No one can be held responsible for it, which is what allows it to flourish. Systemic violence allows capital losses to be socialized, failures to be personalized, and individuals to be hierarchized[37] within an apparently classless society.

The game of *Kid Nation* engages most obviously in systemic violence through a four-rank caste system. The "upper class" makes the most money and has no assigned tasks, the "merchant class" gets half as much and runs the general store, the "cooks class" gets a meager salary and run the kitchens, and the "laborer class" gets almost no money and has to perform the unwanted tasks (i.e., cleaning the outhouses, fetching water). This system of rule is enforced by the presence of the show's host and crew, and is symbolized by a jobs board overlooking the town (and which burns to the ground in Episode 13). In his essay "From *Kid Nation* to Caste Nation," Mike Meloy argues that *Kid Nation*'s class antagonisms rest partially on the American glorification of unfettered social mobility and conspicuous consumption.[38] The "caste" game mechanic increases pressure on the physical challenges, which are the true gatekeepers of social mobility, while also providing a moral standard by which to judge the protagonists between said challenges. It allows viewers to indulge in a fantasy of a society that rewards winners, punishes losers, and gives a notional chance to let the losers become winners. The children are meanwhile subjected to the threefold consequences of a caste system based on arbitrary challenges injected into a community out to preserve and cultivate its resources: (1) children must endure a miniature form of class oppression, (2) talent and experience with regard to the game environment are *not* factors for appointing labor,[39] and (3) patriarchal authority outside of the children's social sphere robs them of their overall autonomy. That is to say, there were suspected "lasting emotional injuries to some children involved,"[40] not to mention the painful viewing experience of watching children contort them-selves to expectations of absent adults.

Debbie Clare Olson laments the adult realities imposed on the children of *Kid Nation*, calling the resultant systemic violence a result of the "death of play."[41] Her theory is that *Kid Nation* places children in a proto-capitalist space that meanwhile deprives them of the "natural" imaginary space of most children. She sees the game rules of *Kid Nation* as "insidiously [manipulating children] into creating the illusion of a paradise that, in reality, is a glorification of ... childhood's demise."[42] She frames the social mechanisms of the show (i.e. the unstated game rules) as the means to a cult built around consumerism and reductive thinking. In fact, the mechanisms appear only to provide a conflict motivation outside of the human factors already inherent in a chil-dren's survival scenario:

> The cult of the child is not just misplaced; it is missing in *Kid Nation*. Instead, the series structures a replica of the adult world: a cult of consumerism that inserts desirable products (and the children are encouraged to desire them) and infects their budding society with adult prejudices (groupings by color and class), intol-erances (religion), social Darwinism (showdowns), and capitalist exploitation (wage hierarchies and labor exploitation). What *Kid Nation* does not give the viewer is

the vision of play, make-believe, creativity, imagination, and the general joy of experiencing the world through a child's eyes, the very things idealized by those adults who search for a return to youth.[43]

This critique of the show more or less sums up the chief impositions made on the children by the producers: the children are not confronting some kind of frontier reality, but an invented game of adulthood in line with generic conventions of *Survivor* or other competitive reality shows. The show's participants are not only denied much of their comforts of home, but they are also denied the ability to play and imagine as a collective. Olson certainly keeps the cult of childhood — the adult worship of children as innocent and playful — in perspective in her piece, but she still abjects the negotiations of the adult world in favor of her own idealized form of play. This comes across as Huizingan thinking, much like Golding's dismissive officer: children are free to create powerful "magic circles" of play that adults nevertheless retain the authority to dispel. Nevertheless, the danger remains of what Huizinga calls "false play," the co-opting of play by organizations that manage it for their own ends.[44] What Olson's argument lacks is a recuperative notion of *game design*: that not all manipulation of human behavior is inherently bad, and that games could impart some serious shared intentionality unto the children by tuning incentives to fit their needs and providing the tools necessary to create shared bonds of experience. The fact that the *Kid Nation* game produces toxic competition has to do with how few incentives there are for cooperation within the reality show's unspoken game rules.

The Game Rules of Kid Nation

What then are the master rules of the game called *Kid Nation*? Here is an attempt at an answer. To set up the game, first gather 40 children between the ages of 8 and 15 to a location isolated enough to preclude travel of over a mile away. Then transport said 40 children to just outside the ghost town and charge them the task of building a community and surviving for 40 days. Provisions for these children for 40 days must be provided, as well as the bare minimum facilities (outhouses, water pump, kitchen, etc.), which are conspicuous in their insufficiency for the comfort of all. Divide the 40 children up into four teams, distinguished with bandanas: green, red, yellow, blue. Arbitrarily choose a child from each team to be one of the first four council members. Tell those four that they are in charge of the town, which means serving as a leader for one's own team, reading the producer-created pioneer's journal for the stakes of a given "episode," periodically deciding who deserves an out-of-game financial award (the gold star) for good behavior, and choosing which in-game prize the whole town gets if every team completes a physical challenge, usually a choice between a practical comfort (i.e. more outhouses) and an impractical luxury (i.e. a water slide). Next, pre-determine a narrative: create a script, if you will. To make sure the pre-determined narrative is being followed, have a moderator (Jonathan Karsh) occasionally shout "Pioneers, gather up!" and introduce the next big plot point, such as the job board.

Plan to assign castes to the children as a result of the first physical challenge, and create a job board. This is a completely arbitrary game show task that has nothing to do with long-term survival needs. The job board will serve as a symbol that maintains the caste order. The highest caste gets the most money (in town credit to buy frivolous supplies at the merchant store) and the least work, while the lowest caste gets the least money and the most work, etc. Keep changing the rules using the pioneer journal, and be prepared to dismantle and reconfigure these systems as needed to "add interest" for television viewers.

In principle then, there are multiple minigames and outside actors that have major influence on this purportedly self-contained *Lord of the Flies* scenario. Using the McGonigal definition of a game mentioned earlier, here are the parallel games running within the scenario:

- **Game 1: Survival**— The goal is to incur no health problems. The rules are to cooperate with the other children to survive. The feedback system is one's own body, and voluntary participation is, as with all the games, mandatory.
  Scale: Collective vs. Environment

- **Game 2: Good Sport**— The goal is to win a gold star to boost one's own family income. The rules revolve around an appearance of compassion and leadership at the right moments while council members are nearby. The feedback system is based on the behavior of past winners of gold stars and otherwise withheld for suspense purposes.
  Scale: Individual vs. Expectation[45]

- **Game 3: Caste System** —The goal is to win the assignment of any caste on the job board except the "laborer class" for the team. The rules are dictated by the individual challenge, usually a time-sensitive obstacle requiring group problem solving to overcome. If one team cannot complete the challenge before the time runs out, the collective loses the possible reward. The feedback system is clearest here: measurable progress toward the challenge's ostensible finish line. Other teams' progress also provides feedback.
  Scale: Team vs. Team, Collective vs. Challenge

- **Game 4: Producer's Fiat** —The goal is to satisfy the demands of producers by producing dramatic action that conforms to expectation. The rules are based on the whim of the production crew's expectations of the moment. The feedback system is opaque, given the lack of knowledge of how the footage will be edited.
  Scale: Individual and Collective vs. Producer Expectation

Though the stated goal of a *Lord of the Flies* simulation might be to play Game 1, Games 2–4 are *Kid Nation*'s emphasis by far. In confessionals, protagonists such as Greg and Mike emote about potentially attaining a gold star, Laurel waxes about finally leaving the laborer class,[46] and no council member ever seeks to interrogate the "wisdom" passed down by the early settlers. Obviously the editing prioritizes the elements that the show's producers introduced into the scenario to give the 40 days an episodic arc for the season. Nevertheless, the four games listed above compete for priority in such a way as to highlight both the constructedness of the program and its consequent dissimilitude with anything resembling a place where kids reign supreme. The health of the collective should naturally remain the top priority, but extrinsic rewards (gold stars) are given only to individuals who stand out as helpers of the collective. The scenario pits individualism against collectivism, the desire for survival against physical violence against the desire to live an existence of leisure supported by systemic violence, and the producers' gameplay narratives against the evolving story of children having to manage on their own.

There is some degree to which the ideology lying behind this game is best exposed by contrasting it with an earlier ideology about games for children. Consider for example the "Nineteen Principles" set out by Howard Braucher, Secretary of the National Recreation Association in the 1930s, that are to underpin children's game activities (paraphrased here): a broad range of said activities, personal satisfaction, small spaces and small amounts of time, memorability, the encouragement of positive reading habits, a few songs, artistry, exposure to sunlight, hobby formation, rhythm, ceremonial eating, time for repose, immersion, personal achievement, employment of seldom-used skills, play that can transfer to adulthood, citizen formation, and formation of a community to continue this recreation. The thirteenth principle, immersion, is actually framed as "those recreation activities ... which most completely command the individual so that he loses himself in them and gives all that he has and is to them."[47] These principles, including that of immersive recreation, are each gainsaid to some degree by the implicit principles of *Kid Nation*: televisual activities mixed with the daily grind, inherent caste-based dissatisfaction, lots of space and a 40 day duration, digital memorability, reading as not really a priority, no music or rhythm, few crafts, exposure to sunlight, idleness, mess-hall eating, camera confessionals, immersion in game constructions over survival concerns, personal financial gain, employment of seldom-used skills, rehearsal of adulthood, desiring subject formation, and clique formation.

The game of *Kid Nation* is also that of media exposure, or how to ignore the camera and production crew while nevertheless getting them to follow one around. When Sophia takes to the streets to dance her way into some extra money for a bike in Episode 2, for example, there appears to be an agreement between her and the crew that she would do something appropriately televisual to get other citizens to donate some of the fruits of their labor power to her. And 10-year-old Taylor virtually models for the camera each time she cries or imposes order. She looks like an archetypal female child fashion model, and takes on the archetype of the soulless hedonist multiple times in the series to provide a suitable antagonist for the children who otherwise abide by the system. The meta-game of television — its slots, minutes of airtime, and fickle audiences — guide the very footsteps the *Kid Nation* subjects take, the words uttered before the camera, and the society they choose to erect.

Another function of these competing game logics is to posit, via the imposition of false choices, the radical equivalency of *all* objects. Systemic violence acts by way of rendering all accessible in the symbolic and material realms as commodities. No better object lesson of this can be found than in the choices the town council must make at the end of a physical challenge. For example in Episode 5, the council must choose between steak for all and 40 toothbrushes as a town reward. They get one option and, though out in the desert, have to decide to "discard" the other. Let us unpack the situation for a moment: the town council won this privilege of choice based on the fact that all four teams manage to pop balloons with presidents' faces and put them in the right chronological order. This achievement gives them the right to at least choose between dental hygiene/wasting food and rotten teeth/full bellies. The town, having been atomized into selfish beings through the caste system, cries hungrily for the steak. "Council members," Jonathan Karsh says with his high-school track coach tenor, "It's pretty clear what your town wants, but you are the politicians.... It's time to ... talk it out and let us know what you're going to do." A costly item such as steak is suddenly in the same camp as the virtually worthless toothbrushes.

Does Karsh want to help teach them a lesson about the indispensability of mundane, cheap objects over luxury items that are expensive to haul out into the desert? This choice depicts the *Kid Nation*'s producers' power over the council rather than *vice versa*. Either choice will elicit a certain televisually desirable discontentment within the ranks of the children. If they had chosen the steak, then the camera crew would have the added pleasure of documenting the kids' hedonistic joy of consuming it. Since they chose the toothbrushes, however, an orchestra and timpani declares their right/pragmatic choice on behalf of the collective. The cycle repeats a dozen more times over the course of Season 1: daily labor then leads to a completely unrelated challenge that then offers a completely unrelated reward that may or may not impact the long-term health of the community. The game choice smacks of inauthenticity when serving as an assessment of the children's' capacity to distinguish between needs and wants. True, they reached this point thanks to collective performance, but the labor on the challenge is completely divorced from the reward. The message taught to the players is not "hard work will be rewarded in kind," but the more conditional "hard work will be rewarded by the miracles of finance capital (via the commodified labor relations necessary to deliver steak to their doorstep in the desert), but not in a way related to your work." As a *caveat* to those who would argue that at least the children received toothbrushes: the general store run by the merchants serves tooth enamel-eroding soda. That is to say, the 40 toothbrushes constitute the conjured solution to the problem the producers themselves created. The issues are thus not between need and want, but about the ability of television to profile consumer goods as so desirable that their mere presence nearby would overwhelm practical needs required for a healthy sustained existence (i.e., toothbrushes).

As a game, *Kid Nation* is then potentially in dialog with two others: Will Wright's computer simulation *The Sims* and Vincent Baker's tabletop role-playing game *Apocalypse World*. In the former, players adopt a God-like role in manipulating representations of lowly humans as they go about their day-to-day lives within limited material and psychic economies. In the latter, players play humans in an isolated community called a "holding" 50 years after the end of the world and, thanks to the help of character-based rule-altering Moves, can substantially affect this new world around them. Both games are about pioneering new human relations within spaces of scarcity, much like *Kid Nation*. What reveals the reality show's incoherent game design, however, are the alternate reward systems for story-related action. *The Sims* rewards players for *constant vigilance* over their Sims, ensuring that they are well-fed and trained in how to make themselves happy. It uses a bird's-eye camera to monitor them, much like the frequent flyover shots in *Kid Nation* used to convey the viewer's mastery over these children and their town. Stories in *The Sims* emerge from sheer attention paid to an individual or group of Sims and resources allocated to them. *Apocalypse World* rewards players for *constant interventions in the story* based on the aspects of their characters that other players highlight. The world and its rules are literally determined by the alternating Moves between the players and the MC[48] to enhance the gut-level power of the emergent fiction. Stories in *Apocalypse World* emerge from Moves characters make in light of the scarcity of resources, but not as a sheer expression of them. Characters determine their own path, and the world follows behind to accommodate them. *Kid Nation* certainly keeps constant vigilance over its children participants, but the children are more or less powerless to generate new resources without the help of the producers. And though the children in *Kid Nation* may make bold decisions within their own holding, they cannot alter the pioneer guidebook, the physical challenges, the caste system or the council structure; all instruments of their own class oppression. Whereas both *The Sims* and *Apocalypse World* provide game vehicles for scarcity-based storytelling, *Kid Nation* provides a vehicle for dealing with nothing but the game show's logic itself.

Naturally, the children eventually conform to the gamespace that surrounds them. Mia Consalvo affirms that players play games to reflexively adjust themselves to their challenges within their context:

> There is no innocent gaming.... Players also have real lives, with real commitments, expectations, hopes, and desires.... Games are created through the act of gameplay, which is contingent on acts by players. Those acts are always, already, contextual and dynamic."[49]

Take, for example, 9-year-old Emily of Nevada in Episode 2 who protests the chickens being killed by 15-year-old Greg, who ostensibly is doing it only for the extrinsic reward.[50] The episode centers in on her conflict between putting up her symbolic protest of the chickens or letting the town walk all over her. But the game found here is not so much whether or not she resists, but whether or not she leaves. Despite town peer pressure that silences her protest, she decides to stay with the village once she realizes the whole *Kid Nation* project is a game about staying power: "When my mom told me to come here, she told me to be a rough and tough cowgirl. So, I'm going to stay." On the one hand, players like Greg watch the importance of the game's extrinsic rewards supersede Game 1— Survival in terms of motivation. On the other hand, players like Emily have become aware of the incentivization systems at play and want to show they can withstand them. Both types of players can be easily incorporated into the logic of *Kid Nation*, though neither will ever quite find the level of autonomy they both apparently seek through the means of money and freedom.

The show's apparent breakdown in order after the job board is lit on fire by the production crew in the last episode (Episode 13) also shows the level to which the participants have adjusted to the producers' arbitrary game rules. Recall Jonathan Karsh's promises from Episode 2, resonating with Meloy's class mobility-based argument about the show: "It's time for the next showdown, where you guys can change your place in society, your job, and your salary. And if you *really* try hard, the Council will give you that gold star." The game reality appeals to both notions of continuous rebirth within society and the virtue's reward. The destruction of the job board, which otherwise allowed the children to say "That's her job, not mine," actually prompts a run on the general food store, namely the candy section. This has been portrayed as the ultimate *Lord of the Flies* moment: the breakdown of the societal order leading to utter chaos. But the viewer should be skeptical that this is the children's inherent/natural state. Indeed, Karsh again frames a false choice, as with all the objects before: "You can keep working as you have been, or you can do ... whatever you want." Well, the first thing the children want is to have the journal — the producers' master discourse about the town — set on fire. After that, they then endeavor to produce their own narrative by raiding the candy store and reallocating themselves to the bunks that they see fit. DK reminds his fellow participants to "use your brain! The job board is not the freakin' town!" But the extent to which the job board determined social realities for the residents of *Kid Nation* for so long that the playful, imaginative sphere of childhood bursts forth into Dionysian violence. Karsh intervenes and has the children perform one final challenge — the cleaning up of the town for their parents — before conducting the final town hall meeting and advising the participants as they go to go forth and make "a better world."

The "better world" the children might create, however, would benefit greatly from cooperative game mechanics such as those of Jane McGonigal,[51] who is famous for re-tooling incentive systems to get game players to break down social barriers and produce active knowledge about their environment. If the show's goal was to prove how tough and smart children can be, it erred in the favor of proving how cunning they were in order to work within the interlinked structures of an equally cunning game that would — any way one looks at it — produce supposedly high-quality reality TV. The neoliberal relocation of an entire community of young people to an artificial clime and the expectation of innovation amidst an environment of absolute institutional and financial control both seem like dubious scenarios in which to expect children to produce moral behavior. Instead, the game design has these little adults play out a reward system that dictates one must compete among artificially imposed classes in order to survive as the financial elite decide what two choices this child proletariat should be given at the end of every Sisyphus-like challenge.

Conclusion

This essay has dealt briefly with the mechanics of a show teasing viewers with the possibility of viewing a radical form of freedom expressed through children on their own, and instead using multiple systems of control to make them conform to very specific societal and reality television standards. This fact is due in no small part to television itself framing imposed restraints that benefit neoliberal capitalism as "reality." 13-year-old Natasha's mother, Isa Goenaga, suggests an even more disturbing connection between "fun" and "reality," namely: "Competition made it more fun for them.... [*Kid Nation*] is an accurate depiction of our society. You have to work hard, and you have to work harder than the next guy to move up in life."[52] In her paradigm, "fun" is perceived as the reward of hard work and winning against competitors. But hard work in *Kid Nation* is perversely rewarded with either total lack of responsibility (i.e., upper class privileges from the physical challenges) or a gold star that's inherently worthless within the game itself. That hard work does not necessarily guarantee comfort or security is indeed a fact of life. But that hard work is actively discouraged by the caste system reveals much more about the mechanisms of reality television and its motivating game logic[53] than it does about what children would do when left to their own devices in such a scenario. *Kid Nation*'s portrayal of a hardscrabble existence against multiple arbitrary structures may indeed be more a self-reflexive expression of the show's own navigation of the social Darwinian environment of 21st century television production. Reality shows have flourished because they are cheap products, and as cheap products they are disposable and interchangeable. As one NBC executive once put it: "There is a little survival-of-the-fittest thing [reality programming] ends up creating."[54]

Thus the frontier at which both the kids on *Kid Nation* and its viewers find themselves is not between the wilderness and civilization, but between a reality governed by conventional means of socio-political power — charisma, bureaucracy and/or fear — and one governed by an ever-expanding game world, hastily designed for the sake of short-term television ratings and containing mutually contradictory incentive systems (i.e., desire to survive vs. desire to do nothing to ensure that survival). This author joins with Olson and Meloy in deploring the results of a television experiment gone awry: the influx of television's easily tapped logics of class conflict and zero-sum competition into *Kid Nation* was what drove viewers away. Perhaps the audience wished to discover that American children in *Kid Nation* would not fall into the same delusions of power as in *Lord of the Flies*, but would rather work out a shaky collective through long-term trial and error. The crew could have silently observed as events unfolded. As Jacques Rancière reminds us, "television broadcasting has its Other: the effective performance of the set."[55] One might have seen these children play, interact, form relationships and negotiate the strange new situation in which they found themselves. "Fantasy, imagination and a joyful technology of foolishness" are what some French poststructuralists would recommend in encounters with "mapping unknown terrain,"[56] rather than solely emphasizing dull hard work, obedience and the American disciplines of competitive personnel management built into reality television.

Games are their own medium, and thus can be designed in alignment with any given program's overall goals. As with television, games constrain, allow for, and reinforce certain types of play.[57] Any reality television activity that imposes unnecessary obstacles beyond those of accepted society is inherently a game, and therefore can be studied as an object of game design. In fact, a certain playfulness is actively encouraged within the design of reality shows. James Poniewozik defends the medium on the grounds of its potential for play: "A great reality–TV concept takes some commonplace piety of polite society and gives it a wedgie." Reality television enacts blank parodies of human affairs, rather than serving as serious meditation on human existence. That being said, however, both reality television and games share the characteristic of enacting *ideology* through the users' interactions with their content. *Kid Nation* is a perfect example of a bad object that rendered both its televisual and game ideologies all too clearly. The compromised feedback mechanisms of the show made it too freeform to be a game show and too constrained to be a documentation of the *Lord of the Flies* state of nature that viewers perhaps hoped for with more than a little *schadenfreude*.

I wish to end by returning to the Golding analogy at the beginning of this essay. In the novel, the officer with his revolver reinstates patriarchal authority by dismissing the activities of Ralph and the rest as "fun and games." The description presumes the existence of a magic circle formed by the children that then is dissected by the entry of an adult viewpoint. This dismissal of the children's fight for survival as a ludic experience is reversed in the context of *Kid Nation*; the ludic transforms into the authentic during the latter half of Episode 13 "We've All Decided to Go Mad!" After participating in a mini-orgy of consumption in the candy store, the pioneers are then "gathered up" for a challenge to clean up Bonanza City for some special guests. Sweeping music introduces those special guests as their parents — the adult intervention — and they come running into town to embrace their children. After a shared meal, the parents then visit the children's homes, only to be relatively underwhelmed by the filth and mediocrity of the children's existence, thanks to the moralizing editing. Anjay was right in that respect: Bonanza City prior to the arrival of the adults was not really the "real world," but a series of games orchestrated by the producers that nevertheless promoted the idea that the kids were somehow in charge. The gaze of the concerned parents trained on the children's spaces, not insignificantly shaped by what producers were willing to provide, suddenly brings reality home to the viewer. Games now played within global economic realities are serious, but perhaps the liminal gamespace of reality television is the most serious and real of all.

Notes

1. Golding, *Lord of the Flies* 246.
2. Suits, *The Grasshoper* 54.
3. Firchow, *Modern Utopian Fictions* 142.
4. Meloy, "From *Kid Nation* to Cast Nation" 1.
5. Summarized in Stam, Burgoyne and Flitterman-Lewis, *New Vocabularies* 212.
6. Gallagher, *John Ford* 417.
7. Throughout this essay, I use the "children" to denote the *Kid Nation* participants and the "producers" to include the host, crew and financiers responsible for the show. They are almost always referred to as antagonists within the scenario, given the power differential between one and the other.
8. See Olson, "Babes in Bonanzaland."
9. See Masters, "Kid Nation."
10. See Meloy.
11. Olson.
12. Hoerschelmann, *Rules* 46.
13. Henry Jenkins, *Convergence Culture* 59.
14. See Kilborn, *Staging the Real*.
15. Cf Andrejevic, *Reality TV*. See also Dulick in this volume.
16. See Taylor and Harris, *Theories*.
17. Murphy, *How Television* 58.
18. Mittel, "All in the Game" 431. The show he is referring to is HBO's *The Wire* (2002–2007).
19. Firchow 145.
20. McGonigal, *Reality Is Broken* 21.
21. Think of tabletop role-playing games without character sheets or baseball games without scoreboards. Without the help of other media's frames, player engagement with game algorithims not so readily assumes the form of narrative.
22. Genosko, *McLuhan* 49.
23. Nichols, "Reality TV" 402.
24. See the Introduction of this volume for a discussion of gamespace, a description of reality as a series of framed games.
25. Nichols 401.
26. See Beller, *Cinematic Mode* 19. Beller's nuanced argument, though primarily applied to the cinema, can unproblematically be applied to television as well.
27. According to Howard: "You appear to let go.... But in fact you have more control than ever.... Advertising used to interrupt life's programming. Now advertising *is* the programming. And if you're actually being marketed to successfully, you have no idea." Quoted from Rose, *Art of Immersion* 242.
28. See Tomasello, *Why We Cooperate*.
29. "Railroading" is a role-playing game term for the Gamemaster's act of forcing the player-characters down a linear, narrow plotline.
30. As I have noted in another essay, larp does not lend itself well to film documentation unless the filmmakers understand the specific exigencies of larp as a medium. Arousing interest from the viewer necessitates giving voice to its inherent spontaneity and first-person character. Pervasive games like *Kid Nation* require a similar kind of understanding of the game medium for a crew to successfully document them.
31. Björk and Holopainen, *Patterns* 205.
32. Björk and Holopainen 207. Capitalization is theirs.
33. Littleton, "Eye."

34. See Goodman, "Barbarians" for the most scathing critique of this cultural framing.

35. Elias, "One."

36. Žižek, *Violence* 13.

37. Kornberger, et al., point out to good effect that hierarchies within the West are derived from Judeo-Christian orders of angels in relation between their closeness to God and "the inevitable sin of humanity" ("The Others of Hierarchy" 64). The contemplative angels (Seraphim) sit at the top, and the active laborers among humans (Cherubim) are ranked at the bottom. The notion that inactivity and pontification are a sign of privilege and purity, whereas activity and filthy labor are a sign of lowliness and contamination. Of course, this has less to do with the running of a successful institution than with an establishment of a moral order.

38. Meloy.

39. This is with the exception of Sophia, whose cooking skills were so vital that she was allocated cooks' duties regardless of her caste.

40. Elias. According to Maria Elena Fernandez, the most dramatic adjustment the children had to make was apparently getting used to being filmed all the time, suggesting that the psychological violence committed by the omniscient cameras outweighed that of the scenario.

41. See Olson.

42. Olson 192.

43. Olson 191.

44. Huizinga as paraphrased by Henricks, *Play Revisited* 217.

45. In theory, this game should promote the Kantian categorical imperative, in that every *Kid Nation* player would then be on their best behavior at all times. The rules reflect the actual implementation in the television show.

46. For Greg and Laurel's confessionals, see Episode 5 "1Viva La Revolución!"

47. Smith, *Games* 10–11.

48. Master of Ceremonies, or Game Master.

49. Consalvo, *Cheating* 415.

50. Greg's justification for killing the chicken is obviously *not* the nutrition it will provide the town-dwellers, but rather: "20 grand is ... amazing."

51. McGonigal 270.

52. Elias.

53. For the way in which viewing reality television's own complicity in marketplace forces becomes in itself a game for the viewers, see Jenkins, *Convergence Culture* 88.

54. Poniewozik, "Why Reality TV."

55. Ranciere, *Future* 6.

56. Kornberger, et al. 73.

57. As per Caldwell, *Televisuality* 262.

Survivor Meets the Hero's Journey: Connecting Mythic Structures to Reality Television

ERIK DULICK

Based on an examination of the "reality show" *Survivor*, which as of January 2011 has aired twenty-one seasons over the course of a decade, I argue that the contestants' roles in the game (show) are structurally similar to characteristics found in archetypes in general and the Hero's Journey described by Joseph Campbell in particular. This argument is grounded in the idea that regardless of whether or not Campbellian structures are self-consciously drawn upon by the creators of long-term immersive narratives such as reality television, they serve as a powerful analytical tool for making sense of those narratives because the dramaturgical logic embedded in *Survivor* and similar fictions taps into long-standing conceptions about how stories should work. In other words, reality television — rather than being an unvarnished and unscripted depiction of "how real people act" — involves stories built out of the recorded interactions of those it depicts according to conventions of storytelling that focus on developing "character arcs" that happen to reproduce archetypical functions and their concomitant narrative structures. The mythologically based narrative logic employed by reality television producers is recognized and accepted by audiences because of how it enables vicarious identification with characters via the dramatization of contestants' interactions as heroes, villains, and supporting characters.

Previous efforts to make sense of the popularity of *Survivor* emphasize its sporting quality. For example, Richard Crew argues that viewers watch *Survivor* to see real people engaging in challenging situations.[1] Contestants must battle the elements and harsh conditions for thirty-nine days. More than mere endurance contest, however, *Survivor* is also billed as a long-term "game" that involves using strategic thinking and logic to win. The strategy involved entails elements of cooperation and competition, as success requires both

147

team-based action and coordination of efforts but also lying and manipulation in order to gain advantage over others. The presence of "strategic masterminds"— contestants who are particularly adept at playing others off against each other to their own advantage — highlights the balancing of self-interest and teamwork needed to do well. The resulting dynamics of group behavior are ostensibly compelling for viewers to follow. Crew also suggests because "real" people are on the show, the unscripted nature of reality shows is another major attraction for viewers. The resulting sense of unpredictability means that the audience cannot predict exactly what will come next, which engages them to watch more. Audience members may also picture themselves in these fantasy situations and imagine what they would do if they were on the show.

Because the audience's engagement with the show is thus mediated via viewers' identification with one or more contestants, character development plays a primary role in the success of these programs. The remote and exotic locations at which the *Survivor* contests are located notwithstanding, it is the characters that audiences fundamentally care about. Without well-developed characters, the drama and complexity would be absent. The shows would devolve into anticlimactic episodes and not give the audience anyone to root for or against. Well-developed characters competing in rival camps provide the audience with initial teams or individual players to support. Even though the audience is aware of the similar setup each season, they continue to tune in because the characters are nevertheless compelling to watch throughout their endless struggles in the game.

The Structure of Survivor

Survivor is a competition-based reality show that features ordinary Americans competing to win a $1 million prize. The overall process of competing on *Survivor* is often viewed as a "game" with a very large cash prize. However, only one contestant can win despite the tribal configuration at the start of the game. The contestants' demographics vary by season. For example, many casts have been relatively young with few contestants over the age of 40. An exception to this is when *Survivor: Nicaragua* divided contestants by age, putting ten contestants under thirty on one tribe and ten contestants over forty on the other.[2] There are normally an equal number of men and women in the game, and most of the contestants on the show are white.

The starting number of the cast has also varied by season. Earlier seasons started with sixteen contestants and ended with two finalists. As seasons progressed, the number eventually reached twenty starting contestants and three finalists. These contestants are split into tribes at the beginning of the game.

Survivor has started every season with two, three, or four tribes. The tribes compete in team challenges and the losing tribe votes out a member of the tribe in every episode. Halfway through the season, the tribes merge and then individuals begin to vote each other "off the island." Former teammates eventually turn on each other in order to progress and ultimately win the million-dollar cash prize. This process continues until only the finalists remain. A jury of the most recent individuals voted off decide who is worthy of the prize.

Even so, there is more to the show than competitions and eliminations. From the beginning of a season, the survivors have to battle nature and learn to live together as a very primitive society. They are given very little supplies and must build a shelter, make fire, gather water, and survive the elements together on an otherwise deserted beach. *Survivor* adds the elements of starvation and poor living conditions to test the contestants physically and mentally. Most are able to weather this part of the game of human vs. nature, but there have been several who have quit because the harsh living conditions were too overwhelming.

Finally, in addition to the standard game, the show's producers have often thrown in twists to keep both the audience engaged and the contestants scrambling. Common twists used in a given season are swapping tribe members midway through the first stage of the game, sending contestants to an island of exile, and hidden individual immunity idols that can save a contestant from elimination. These twists are meant to add excitement to a season and make sure the outcome is not predictable. Twists ensure that the season's overall narrative is unique and therefore more important to the producers than a consistent and fair game structure.

Surviving the Hero's Journey

Christopher Vogler describes the hero's journey as "a set of principles that govern the conduct of life and the world of storytelling."[3] These established set of parameters are themes that continuously reappear in mythical stories. This framework has also been discovered and incorporated into movies such as *Star Wars, Casablanca,* and *The Godfather*. Voytilla also states that it is important to note that the Hero's Journey is flexible and that different stages may be "avoided, repeated, or shifted about depending upon the needs of the individual story."[4]

After analyzing 30 randomly selected episodes across different seasons of *Survivor*, I conclude that the show embodies the hero's journey and its corresponding archetypes in many different ways. Regardless of their intent, producers knowingly or unknowingly incorporate aspects of the hero's journey because audience members relate to and identify with past experiences, giving them "real" people to root for in a fictional or "Special World." It manifests in behavior to which most audiences relate. I argue that each stage of the journey can be found in the twenty-one completed seasons of *Survivor*. I have included many examples throughout my analysis, but it is important to note that these are not all of the examples. Instead, these are just a small sampling to help illustrate the presence of the hero's journey and archetypes. It is important to consider that the stages of the hero's journey can be applied to the arc of each season of *Survivor*, as well as individual players' narratives throughout *Survivor*. In other words, each season of *Survivor* can be thought of as a complete hero's journey narrative wherein one or more heroes are either victorious or vanquished by one or more villains, and each contestant has his or her own individual hero's journey narrative that involves a "Call to Adventure," a "Crossing of the Threshold," and some more or less successful engagement with the perils of the underworld before returning to the "Fields We Know" (i.e., everyday life) as winner, loser, or runner-up in the game.

The first stage is the glimpse of the "Ordinary World." For the survivors, this is the everyday life they lived before entering the reality game show. Viewing the normality of the ordinary world at the start of the tale sets up several important aspects of the story. First, it provides a comparison to the special world to which the hero will soon travel. The special world is only unique when compared to the bland commonplace lifestyles that exist only in the ordinary world. It also provides the reader with background information and a way to get information and make perceptions about the Hero before the story really begins.[5] Stuart Voytilla also argues that this phase gives viewers the opportunity to potentially see the motivations, urges, and other characteristics that may aid the viewer to see how the individual may play the game. Normally the best way for fans to view the survivors in the ordinary world is to research the contestant bios on the *Survivor* website or do research on *Survivor* forums. This preliminary research allows viewers to identify and make comparisons among the castaways before the adventure even begins. These brief descriptions often emphasize to fans that these are real people with real jobs, just like them.

After background information is gathered, the Call to Adventure stage begins. The call to adventure essentially presents a challenge or quest to the hero that must be completed. Vogler states that "the call to adventure establishes the stakes of the game, and makes clear the hero's goal: to win the treasure or the lover, to get revenge or right a wrong, to achieve a dream, confront a challenge, or change a life."[6] Voytilla argues that the ordinary world is thrown off balance by the delivering of this news, and peace can only be restored once the challenge has been completed. Examples of a call to adventure include a message being delivered, storm, death of a loved one, or kidnapping. Every show begins with a call to adventure by presenting the game of *Survivor* as the challenge or quest that must be completed. This segment occurs right at the start of a season premiere as the contestants get out of the boat and are welcomed to the show. Host Jeff Probst welcomes everyone to the island, establishes the stakes—1 million dollars—and makes clear that everyone's ultimate goal should be to win that prize. The call to adventure may also highlight the achievement of dreams and life-changing experiences that are set up during the first few days of life on the island. Contestants may feel more drawn to the adventure side of the game once they begin working together to build a shelter, make fire, and live in an environment with very limited supplies. Some Survivors may not see the cash prize as the only reward of the experience, but are instead motivated by the adventure of living in and conquering nature. The establishment of a new society and the creation of an effective team have been very important elements of the call to adventure to past contestants, highlighting tests of personal strength other than the cash prize.

In most cases there is some hesitation from the hero, bringing forth the Refusal of the Call stage. The Hero may not immediately accept the quest because of fears and insecurities, and even may provide excuses or try to avoid the potentially dangerous adventure completely. Vogler supports this claim by stating this hesitation "serves as an important dramatic function of signaling the audience that the adventure is risky."[7] The intensity surrounding the adventure's risks helps to heighten the audience's emotional commitment to both the hero and the journey at hand. As a result, the emotional commitment deepens both the immersion and investment into the Journey.

Not every survivor passes through this phase, but often times there are survivors who do not think they are up for the adventure. These contestants are "not willing to make changes" and prefer the ordinary world's safety and familiarity. Their fear of directly battling the elements causes many survivors to question their place and whether they should quit the show. A perfect example comes from the most recent installment *Survivor: Nicaragua*. On day five, Holly decides that she wants to quit because she does not think that her body could battle the physical, mental, and emotional aspects of the *Survivor* adventure. She refuses the call and wants to turn back.[8] Other seasons have faced other forms of hesitation (see list on page 152).

Notice how the refusal of the call on the part of some contestants highlights the heroic commitment of other contestants to the adventure and to the hero's journey while at the same time completing the heroic narrative of the refusing contestant, albeit in a negative way: he or she returns to the ordinary world as a failed hero because of some character flaw that prevented commitment to the adventure: self-doubt, diffidence, lack of competitive drive, failure of physical stamina or psychological grit, or other unheroic trait. Meanwhile, the other contestants are by contrast endowed with (that is to say, characterized by) confidence, determination, competitiveness, athleticism, or resolve inasmuch as they do not share the refusing hero's flaw. In this way, the individual contestant's character arc as hero serves as a commentary upon those of other contestants as well as a constituent of the larger story arc of the *Survivor* season as a whole.

REFUSAL OF THE CALL

- *Survivor: Guatemala*
- Contestants: Blake, Judd, Bobby Jon
- Episode(s): 1–2
- Description: Three men sick and exhausted after an 11 mile hike on the first day. Their tribe mate Margaret helped nurse them all back into good health. Blake and Judd ended up being heroes in a Reward and Immunity Challenge (respectively) in episode two, each thereby committing himself to the adventure.

- *Survivor: Pearl Islands*
- Contestant(s): Osten
- Episode(s): 2–3, 7
- Description: Osten wanted to quit the game on day six. His tribe convinced him to stay and kept him in the game. Osten then committed to the journey in episode three and made it through the next few episodes. However, he refused the call again in episode seven because he was worried about his health and did in fact quit the game at this point.

Refusing to participate often leads in to the next stage, which is the "Meeting of the Mentor." In myth, Vogler argues that the Mentor helps the hero prepare for the unknown through advice, guidance, or magical equipment. The mentor is often an older authoritative figure that provides the hero with some sort of advice or wisdom to convince the hero to progress and accept the challenge. Mentors may also possess special training or equipment to help the hero prepare for the journey ahead. The mentor can also appear in nonhuman forms such as a map, compass, letter, or logbook. The mentor in *Survivor* can take different forms, such as host Jeff Probst or other members from the tribe.

For example, Holly's tribemate Jimmy Johnson helped coach her to remain in the game. Thanks to his guidance, Holly decided to remain in the game and made it to the final four contestants. In addition to tribe mates, the list below provides evidence that host Jeff Probst has also acted as a mentor in many cases by providing the castaways with extra equipment available though reward challenges.

MEETING THE MENTOR

- *Survivor: Australian Outback*
- Contestant(s): Remaining seven castaways
- Episode(s): 10
- Description: When the tribe ran out of rice and fishing hooks, they had no way to catch or make food. Host Jeff Probst offered the tribe rice and hooks in exchange for the tarps from their shelter.

- *Survivor: Palau*
- Contestant(s): Winning tribe
- Episode(s): 2
- Description: Jeff reveals the winners of the Reward Challenge will receive fishing supplies, equipment that will help contestants in the game.

- *Survivor: Samoa*
- Contestant(s): Winning tribe
- Episode(s): 1
- Description: Jeff provides the initial challenge winners with flint, which is essential for making fire. This flint is extremely important and is necessary for the contestants to survive the adventure.

The next stage in the hero's journey is Crossing the Threshold. This stage signifies the hero's commitment to the journey and gains him access to the guardian that separates the ordinary world from the special world. There is no turning back for the hero from this point on, and the journey can truly begin at this point. The hero must start identifying with the new ways of life present in the special world or perish. On *Survivor,* this stage is reached when physical, mental, and emotional aspects of the game are all in full throttle. Now the strategizing can truly begin. This is important to note because strategizing is arguably the most important aspect of moving forward in the adventure. Without carefully planned tactics, a contestant will most likely be voted out quickly.

From here, the hero enters the Tests, Allies, and Enemies stage of the adventure. It is here that the hero is challenged with many minor tasks that help prepare the hero for the greater ordeals ahead. Along the way, the hero will learn who to trust and may form teams filled with Allies to help her along the way. This is also the stage that the hero learns about the culture and rules that govern the Special World. The hero must adapt to these rules in order to learn the lay of the land and progress further into the adventure. This stage is in a majority of the episodes because survivors are constantly making allies and forming alliances, testing their strength in challenges, and voting off enemies to progress further in the game. Vogler adds that "scenes like these allow for character development as we watch the hero and his companions react under stress."[9] This is played out in the tests and interactions with other contestants, which helps develop individual personalities of each player and reveal secrets to the viewing audience. There are many different types of strategizing in the game of *Survivor*, as evidenced in the list below. Strategies are crucial in this stage as the contestants slowly start to play the game.

TESTS, ALLIES AND ENEMIES

- *Survivor: Gabon*
- Contestant(s): Bob
- Episode(s): 10
- Description: Bob creates a fake immunity idol in an attempt to deceive his tribe that he was dangerous. He uses this idol as leverage in an attempt to get opponents voted out before him.

- *Survivor: Gabon*
- Contestant(s): Fang Tribe
- Episode(s): 6
- Description: The tribe strategizes and tries to figure out who should be voted out.

- *Survivor: Cook Islands*
- Contestant(s): Jenny
- Episode(s): 9
- Description: Jenny questions the loyalty of her allies wonders if new tribe mates Candice and Jonathan have manipulated themselves ahead of her, keeping them safe and putting her in danger.

- *Survivor: Australian Outback*
- Contestant(s): Remaining castaways
- Episode(s): 12
- Description: When a flood wipes out most of their camp, including their

rice, the remaining contestants must regroup and find the energy to move on from this devastating test.

The hero then enters the next stage, which is the Approach to the Inmost Cave. This stage prepares the hero for the most difficult point of the journey. Here, the hero may plan his attack, review his strategy, or thin out the army in order to prepare him to conquer the hardest enemies. The hero has survived the preliminary descent into the special world and now must prepare himself to defeat what he came to vanquish. In the game, this is the step in which the remaining survivors plan and prepare for the final stages of the adventure or, in this case, a final episode of *Survivor*. "The inmost cave" of the show usually occurs when the survivors merge into one tribe and the battle to advance to the finals can begin. This is the point in the game where focus shifts from a team effort to an individual effort. Contestants must outwit and manipulate each other to progress further into the endgame represented by the inmost cave. This complexity is another point in the game where the tests, allies, and enemies aspect is revisited once the approach is complete.

This stage can also appear for different contestants at earlier points in the game. If a contestant feels that she is in danger of being eliminated, then she is going to readjust her tactics and strategy to make sure that she survives and move on to the next stage of the adventure. Individual tribe members must reaffirm their strategy at this point in order to ensure that they survive a potentially disastrous tribal council.

APPROACH TO THE INMOST CAVE

- *Survivor: Gabon*
- Contestant(s): Dan, Susie, Ace, Crystal
- Episode(s): 7
- Description: These four contestants were all shown as being in danger of being voted out. We observe each person's strategy to remain in the game. Only Susie and Crystal survive the Ordeal of Tribal Council.

- *Survivor: Cook Islands*
- Contestant(s): Jonathan
- Episode(s): 9
- Description: Jonathan fears that his tribe will vote him out next, so he works hard and catches a lot of fish in order to gain respect and prove that he is a worthy tribe member.

The Ordeal stage comes next. This is the central crisis that the hero must defeat. It is here that the hero is in "direct confrontation with his greatest fear."[10]

Often times this is the stage where the hero faces off with the primary villain for the first time, and the result of this battle may determine the level of success on the Journey. In *Survivor*, a contestant's greatest challenge or fear is to be voted out and thus eliminated from the game. When contestants face this challenge, they must fight to remain in the game. Vogler adds that the ordeal is a "black moment for the audience, as we are held in suspension and tension, not knowing if the hero will live or die."[11] The producers of *Survivor* will often develop episodes in which the audience is not sure of who is being voted off, creating the necessary tension and excitement of wondering if our hero survives the episode.

The climactic ordeal in a season of *Survivor* is when the final part of the game has been reached and only the two, three, or four finalists remain in contention for the $1 million prize. Vogler: "The hero begins to deal with the consequences of confronting the dark forces of the ordeal. If she has not yet managed to reconcile with the parent, god, or the hostile forces, they may come raging after her."[12] The finalists of *Survivor* must confront the jury, comprised of contestants they had a hand in eliminating from the game. The jury is given the opportunity to address the finalists — which allows us the audience to complete the narratives of these fallen or failed heroes as well as continue the story of the final heroes, who must explain themselves to the jury and plead to be rewarded with the elixir of one million dollars.

Once the hero has overcome the ordeal, he receives the Reward that he has been seeking. The reward stage is a time for a hero to celebrate his triumph over his enemies and claim the elixir he sought. The reward may come in many different forms, such as a sword, potion, or even a loved one being reunited with the hero. On *Survivor*, the most obvious reward is the million-dollar prize at the end for the winner of the game, but other contestants may pronounce themselves on web sites, in post-show interviews, and in other epitextual venues to be satisfied with their own rewards — greater notoriety or fame, the personal satisfaction of having been in the game and played their best, the self-development and self-knowledge engendered by the experience, and so forth.

The hero may then begin The Road Back. This stage begins a slow transition back into the Ordinary World, with the Reward in hand (for a successful hero) or empty-handed (for a fallen one). On *Survivor*, the road back is signified *inter alia*, when we see contestants again at the live finale and listen to their accounts of their post-game experience.

The Resurrection stage indicates that the story is almost complete. Voytilla explains that this "final life and death ordeal shows that the hero has maintained and can apply all that he has brought back to the ordinary world."[13] In this stage, the hero may face off with the villain in one final battle, or the resurrection can be represented by a cleansing moment that occurs when the

Hero rises from the dead around him. The Resurrection aspect of *Survivor* comes into play when the contestants transition back into the ordinary world. When reentering the ordinary world, the hero is "reborn or transformed with the attributes of his ordinary self in addition to the lessons and insights from the characters that he has met along the road."[14] There is a significant amount of time in between when the show is filmed and aired on television, so contestants have time to transform and readjust to the ordinary world before the final prize is awarded at the finale months after the experience. Contestants have the opportunity to talk about lessons learned and experiences when they attend the reunion at the live finale. This time also gives the contestants time to explain themselves and address any unanswered questions that may still be lingering at the conclusion of the season.

The final stage is the return with the elixir. This stage sets up the resolution of the story and depicts the hero returning to the ordinary world with the elixir in hand. This stage also tends to resolve any unsolved issues and brings closure to the tale. The final stage of the hero's journey is the return with the elixir stage. This elixir is the $1 million awarded to the survivor that has outwitted, outplayed, and outlasted all other opponents. The winner takes this money home to the ordinary world to show what was achieved through the experience of the game.

Survivors as Mythological Archetypes

Another main component of mythic structure is the use and recurrence of mythological archetypes, or personality patterns instantiated across multiple cultures' narratives over time. The use of archetypes in storytelling is intended to make characters universal and recognizable. These characters become familiar to the audience and help them relate the present narrative to similar narrative experiences in the past. Eight primary archetypes are discernible across many different works, and any one character can manifest more than one of the archetypes throughout the story. This way, the characters are not limited to one role, but can have multiple roles to add complexity to the story and thus further the character's development. Goffman also supports this and claims that people often act as though the character that they are currently performing is the only or most essential aspect of their identity. However, there are many different sides of our identities, and we choose wear these different "masks" of our identities in different situations.

At the same time, the mythological archetypes are also extremely flexible. Different characters may embody or wear different masks at different points throughout the Journey. Vogler argues that these archetypes "offer a way to understand what function a character is performing at a given moment in a story."[15]

A key point to consider is that we as viewers are able to see every contestant's private confessionals when watching each episode, giving us insight into how that contestant is attempting to play the game. We construct and make connections in our minds as to who is the hero, who is the shadow, and who we think will survive the entire hero's journey. However, this is not how the contestants view themselves or the other contestants on the show. They are not able to see the edits being made and the strategies of each contestant. Instead, each one protagonizes his/herself: they all believe they are the hero of their own journey. Many contestants have little idea as to how they will be portrayed after editing. A perfect example of this is Jerri Manthey originally from *Survivor: Australian Outback*. Jerri has been dubbed the first "Black Widow Villainess" to play *Survivor*. However, she had no idea that this would be how her character was edited, and was shocked when she saw all of her flaws and weaknesses aired on national television.[16]

On the flip side, some contestants are perfectly aware of the role that the producers expect them to embody. Russell Hantz from *Survivor: Samoa* knew from the beginning that he was going to play the villain of the season. Hantz happily embodied the shadow and the trickster on many different occasions. He claims his motivation behind his actions was to control the mental state of his tribe, but many feel he did these things to gain camera time and be molded into one of the biggest *Survivor* villains ever.

Archetypes can be seen as masks or different elements of a character's identity and overall development. In addition, contestants can embody more than one archetype in different situations, and these archetypes can be used interchangeably. Therefore, different contestants may embody or wear different masks at different points throughout the journey. Vogler argues that these archetypes "offer a way to understand what function a character is performing at a given moment in a story."[17] In the next few pages I discuss the most common archetypes found in *Survivor*: the hero, mentor, herald, shapeshifter, ally, shadow, and trickster. I will also introduce two additional character type unique to *Survivor*, which I have named the lunatic and the pawn. These mythological archetypes are without a doubt present in every season of *Survivor*, with montage framing such archetypes when simple observable behaviors do not suffice.

The Good Guys: Heroes, Mentors and Allies

The most common archetype is the Hero. The hero is the protagonist of the story whom the audience is supposed to support, in particular because they want to recognize his/her traits within themselves, such as the desire to be loved or understood. Vogler elaborates that they "should have universal qualities, emotions, and motivations that everyone has experienced at one time or another."[18] These traits could be things such as loyalty, patriotism, honesty, nobility, or even competitiveness. Obviously the producers want to include heroes to give viewers someone to root for. However, the tricky part is that producers have a large audience to please. Different people may value and identify with different qualities of a hero. Essentially, not everyone will view the same people as Heroes and the same people as villains. For example, some people view contestants that win the majority of the challenges, such as *Survivor: Palau's* Tom Westmann, as Heroes because they are extremely competitive and physically superior over their competitors. Other fans enjoy watching more subtle Heroes such as *Survivor: Australian Outback's* Elisabeth Filarski (now Hasselbeck), who was an underdog and played a superior social game. Therefore, the producers strategically edit the season in a way so that there are many different types of contestants that make it far into the game. This way, a majority of the audience has a hero to cheer on for most of the season. This is evident because the most exciting or controversial players are typically not eliminated early. Below are other examples of heroic qualities demonstrated by contestants.

HERO

- *Survivor: Nicaragua*
- Contestant: Jane
- Episode(s): 7
- Description: Having already won immunity from the women's challenge, Jane opted to stay in the challenge and beat the men too. This shows her competitive side and is an admirable feat.

- *Survivor: Cook Islands*
- Contestant: Yul
- Episode(s): 6,11
- Description: Yul describes in confessionals how he wants to play this game with as much honesty and integrity as possible.

- *Survivor: Tocantins*
- Contestant: J.T.
- Episode(s): 12
- Description: J.T. says he hates lying to anyone, doesn't want to lie in the game but realizes that he must in order to get further.

The Mentor is another recurring archetype present in many different works. In most fiction, the mentor is often a wise old man or woman that provides advice or magical equipment for the hero in order to prepare for the journey. On *Survivor*, mentors are infrequent, but several do appear on different occasions in order to encourage survivors to remain in the game. As mentioned previously, the host Jeff Probst serves as a gift-giving mentor early in each season. The mentor appears early on in the season when the game is still a team effort, and contestants want their tribe members to be strong. Mentors in *Survivor* are often the ones who have basic survival skills and can motivate people to remain positive even in the bleakest circumstances.

MENTOR

- *Survivor: Guatemala*
- Contestant(s): Bobby Jon, Stephanie
- Episode(s): 1
- Description: Bobby Jon and Stephanie were both a part of *Survivor: Palau*, and returned this season to compete again. They were seen as mentors because they had already played the game and helped the newer players adjust to the game.

- *Survivor: Nicaragua*
- Contestant(s): Jimmy Johnson
- Episode(s): 2
- Description: Jimmy mentored Holly and motivated her to remain in the game.

An Ally is an easily identified archetype present in many stories. This character serves as the hero's assistant that the hero can trust. Allies are often companions throughout the journey that keep the hero company, provide assistance, deliver messages, or even battle alongside of the hero. Allies are also extremely visible in the game of *Survivor*. Alliances have to be formed and trusted in order to vote off your opponents. Survivors typically do not make it to the end of the game unless they had help from their allies. Of course, alliances can shift throughout the game in order to benefit the individual, tying back in with the fact that different contestants wear different masks at different times.

In the overall story depicted by the producers, there are often characters that we as the audience are supposed to like, but know that the character is merely there to support a main protagonist or villain. These players serve primarily as Allies. They do not have as much character development and are often voted off before the conclusion of the game. One typical example would be from *Survivor: Panama Exile Island.* Sally, Austin, and Nick were all portrayed as allies of the season's main hero: Terry. They were not given much of a storyline, and were solely there to act as votes and support for Terry. They were voted off one by one until only Terry remained to compete against the majority alliance.[19]

ALLY

- *Survivor: Samoa*
- Contestant(s): Mick, Natalie, Jaison
- Episode(s): 8
- Description: These three are seen as allies of Russell Hantz. They do not get their own plot in this episode and merely exist to prop up Hantz's storyline.

- *Survivor: Cook Islands*
- Contestant(s): Becky
- Episode(s): 11
- Description: Becky is seen as Yul's Ally. They are seen strategizing and planning the vote together, with Yul being the "ringleader" and Becky following his instructions.

A sub-type of ally specific to *Survivor* and derived from its ensemble nature may be the Pawn. Not every contestant may be granted the same amount of airtime. Many contestants, often those eliminated early on, have a minimal impact in the game. Therefore, those contestants do not get elaborate story arcs to which principal characters are entitled. Like pawns in the game of chess, they play a minimal role in the scheme of the game, and are eliminated in a nonchalant manner. Viewers are not supposed to care when pawns are voted off because we as viewers are not supposed to get attached to these characters. Pawns exist to advance the storylines of the major players in the game. The show would become too complex and confusing for viewers if everyone was a major player in the game. Pawns are essential to enrich the overall scope and story the producers have in mind for the season.

The Bad Guys: Shapeshifters, Shadows and Tricksters

The Shapeshifter is a manipulative archetype occasionally manifested in the hero or the villain himself or herself. The shapeshifter's primary method is to deceive opponents by instilling doubt or escaping scrutiny. This archetype is the most prevalent on *Survivor*, and just about all contestants must embody this archetype at some point in the adventure. Similar to the shapeshifer, contestants must often be cunning and elusive in order to outsmart their opponents. This is an archetype that many *Survivor* contestants must incorporate into their strategy at some point. Many contestants have to manipulate their rivals to advance further in the game, as evidenced by many surprise eliminations. Shapeshifters have many different tactics to choose from when formulating a strategy. One method is through being aggressive and bullying your opponents into doing what you want them to do. Russell Hantz of *Survivor: Samoa* was known for doing this. He manipulated others by bullying and threatening them into doing exactly what he wanted. Despite his aggressive nature, his strategy worked and he made it to the end of both *Survivor: Samoa* and *Survivor: Heroes vs. Villains.* Other examples can be seen below.

SHAPESHIFTER

- *Survivor: Gabon*
- Contestant(s): Kenny
- Episode(s): 7
- Description: Kenny lies to Sugar in order to convince her to vote with his alliance.

- *Survivor: Nicaragua*
- Contestant(s): Sash
- Episode(s): 7
- Description: Sash claims in a confessional: "Let everyone else do work and enjoy the fruits of their labor, but then vote them off when time comes."

On the other end of the spectrum, some shapeshifters use physical attraction and flirtation to get themselves further. By using physical appeal, shapeshifters can often distract an opponent and use their charm to convince opponents to keep them around. A contestant that has fit this description in the past is Parvati Shallow, originally from *Survivor: Cook Islands.* On *Cook Islands*, Shallow used her flirtation to convince all the men on her tribe to keep her over some of the weaker women on the tribe. This strategy helped her get far into the season, and the attention she received resulted in her being cast in two future seasons of *Survivor.*

The most effective shapeshifters manipulate their opponents in a number of ways. By combining effective word choice and persuasive skills, an alliance of shapeshifters can be dangerous to opponents. One instance that exemplified this is the all-woman alliance led by Shallow in *Survivor: Micronesia*. This group of five women orchestrated the eliminations of the entire second half of the game through manipulation and deceit, including toward one of their own members. The women dominated the game in this fashion by blindsiding their opponents and the four that ran the show ended up being the final four of the game.

The Shadow often represents the dark side of characters and reveals their greatest fears and desires. Shadows "create conflict and bring out the best in a hero by putting her in a life-threatening situation."[20] Aspects of the shadow are often used for villains, antagonists, and other enemies. Carl Jung also suggests that the shadow is what we "hate, fear, and disown, and therefore repress into the personal/cultural unconscious."[21] A dark side to any *Survivor* character would include the shadow. The shadow is often worn as a mask or acts as a supplement to some of the show's most villainous cast members. Contestants use this darkness against the rest of the cast members. Manipulation certainly has shadow characteristics, but it is the malicious acts that survivors commit that I find the shadow to exist.

There are many instances in which the shadow has been present on *Survivor*. One example would be NaOnka from *Survivor: Nicaragua*, who pushed a woman with a prosthetic leg to the ground in order to receive a clue for a hidden immunity idol.[22] Although this idol brings power in the game, aggressive behavior against another teammate, especially one with a prosthetic leg, definitely qualifies NaOnka as a shadow archetype. Another example would be Russell Hantz from *Survivor: Samoa*. Hantz embodied the shadow on many instances when bullying his tribe mates to stick to his plans, but he most notoriously dumped all of the water from his tribemate's canteens in an attempt to control their mental well being.[23] Finally, Corinne of *Survivor: Gabon* showed off her dark side in the final episode when she attacked a contestant's character and claimed the contestant was insincere when crying about a deceased loved one.[24]

Tricksters embody mischief and manipulation in order to change or disrupt the situation. Often times the jokesters or the comic relief characters embody this archetype. There have been a number of tricksters to play on *Survivor*. Many survivors have turned to mischief, causing confusion and disruption to camp life. Some have played tricksters as a comic relief, such as Greg in *Survivor: Borneo* talking into a coconut phone, or Tyson from *Survivor: Tocantins* dancing around in a homemade loin cloth.[25] However, other tricksters have been out to cause more serious damage to camp life. Examples of this type of trickster were embodied in Sandra from *Survivor: Pearl Islands* when she dumped the tribe's fish bucket after a vote that hurt her strategy, and Russell Hantz from *Survivor: Samoa* emptied water canteens and burned socks in order to mess with his tribe's mental state.[26]

Survivor also uses an extreme version of the trickster which I call the Lunatic. The lunatic is quite literally a media contrivance. These are the characters that producers cast to generate excitement and unpredictability. While they don't always play jokes on their tribe mates, they do odd things that cause both the contestants and the viewing audience to question their sanity. For example, *Survivor: Tocantins* Ben "Coach" Wade referred to himself as "the Dragon Slayer," which would cause viewers to question if his actions were sincere or not.[27] Shane from *Survivor: Panama Exile Island* also displayed the antics of the lunatic. One example comes from when Shane's erratic mood swings caused him to name a rock his "Thinking Seat" and screamed at his tribe that nobody could sit on that rock except for him.[28] The audience is aware that the lunatics typically don't make it to the end, but will be around long enough to keep us off balance and to make the show unpredictable for enhanced audience interest. It is unclear as to whether or not these contestants actually carry themselves like this in the ordinary world, or if it is exaggerated for television. It could also be a strategy to attain more airtime and be a primary focus of the season. Although a good strategy to gain airtime, a Lunatic has never won in any season of *Survivor*.

A mixture of the cunning shapeshifter, the dark shadow, and the mischievous trickster constitutes the basic framework of a typical villain, both in fiction generally and on *Survivor*. For example, when Jon lies about the death of his grandmother in order to manipulate his tribemates into letting him win a family reward,[29] he is both shapeshifter (because he is engaging in manipulation) and shadow (because he is behaving dishonorably). Later, his fellow contestants would chastise Jon for his villainy, characterizing him as "one of the biggest liars to ever play *Survivor*."[30]

The Bit Players: Heralds and Threshold Guardians

A Herald exists primarily to "issue challenges and announce the coming of significant change."[31] Heralds often have a great impact on the story because it is their message or challenge to the hero that advances the story and makes the adventure really begin. This is probably the easiest universal *Survivor* archetype to identify, because the herald is host Jeff Probst. Probst often acts as a messenger by explaining each challenge, sending the contestants a message to indicate when it is time for these challenges via Treemail, and runs Tribal Council where members are voted off. Probst also communicates other important messages that bring significant change to the game, such as the Merge and other tribal twists.

The Threshold Guardian is any sort of obstacle that separates the Hero and ordinary world from the quest or special world. The guardian is not the main villain, but instead acts as a test to see if the hero is ready to face the villain. The guardian could be something as simple as an enchanted door or a force of nature such as a tornado in the *Wizard of Oz*. However, the threshold guardian is not an archetype that has a strong presence on *Survivor,* occurring off-screen via the producers' act of selection via the casting process.

Conclusion

Executive Producer Mark Burnett says that *"Survivor* is based on real life. We've all met people like this; we've all experienced workplace politics. We've all dealt with situations like this — people befriending you, people stabbing you in the back."[32] But the show also differs from real life in that the presence of a million-dollar cash prize creates an atmosphere that gives the contestants permission to exhibit behaviors such as lying, cheating, manipulating the loyalty of others, bullying teammates, and other questionable ethical actions.[33] *Survivor: Samoa* contestant Jaison Robinson highlights the disconnect:

> This game is a lot like real life. I mean, everyone works in an office, on a team, working on projects like our challenges, trying to get individual distinction so that they can move forward while at the same time winning the games and challenges. I think everyone who works in an office also has a [guy like Russell] there, who says "I didn't come to work, I came to play." And I think it's interesting that people really seem to be valuing his negative contributions ... so it's interesting to me that people HATE "Russell" in real life. They go to work every day and go "I hate that guy!" But then you come on *Survivor* and then all of a sudden all the backstabbing and pouring out water and burning socks is gameplay?[34]

Robinson's complaint underscores the fundamental thematic tension of *Survivor* as a narrative. The structure of *Survivor* as a game is such that aggressive and competitive behavior gets contestants further toward the end, a "procedural rhetoric"[35] that valorizes deceit, manipulation, and selfishness as instrumental tools for success. Players who are unwilling use those tools, who demonstrate honesty, loyalty, and friendship (for example) are punished in the context of the game. For example, Colby of *Survivor: Australian Outback* had to make the decision as to whether or not to eliminate his closest ally and jury favorite Tina, or the less-liked Keith in the final three. Even though Colby knew he could win against Keith, he chose to be loyal to his friend and eliminated Keith because he thought Tina was more deserving of being a finalist.[36] Despite his honor and loyalty, this decision ultimately cost Colby the million dollars. A similar example occurred in *Survivor: Pearl Islands* in which Lil had to make a decision between jury favorite Sandra and the unpopular Jon. Lil made the decision to eliminate Jon because she was not comfortable letting a man she viewed as vile get anywhere close to winning the money. Lil also appreciated Sandra's motivation to win for her family and felt that was more deserving of the money than Jon's manipulation tactics. Lil essentially gave up $900,000 because she was not morally prepared to help a deceitful man win the money.[37]

One function of heroic narratives is to establish an ordering of the world in terms of positive attributes or virtues (usually attributed to the hero) and negative attributes or vices (usually attributed to the villain), which then help explain the victory of one character or the defeat of the other. In simplest form, the good guys win because they are good. On *Survivor*, however, this moral ordering is inverted: vicious (i.e., villainous) players often win the game. Just as in Greek tragedy, it is possible to be a hero and be defeated — except that the tragic flaw of a survivor is an unwillingness or inability to embrace one's own dark side (to coin a phrase).

So if *Survivor* is just "like the real world," as some assert, the only lesson that can be taken away is that the moral virtues displayed by heroes are in fact obstacles to "survival," that success requires the true survivor to divest himself or herself of such weaknesses. Like Robinson, we should be unsatisfied with this conclusion. However, the hero's journey provides an alternate understanding that relies for its force on the idea that contestants cross a threshold into a Campbellian underworld that is at the same time the "magic circle"[38] of the game. The million-dollar prize becomes a *temptation*—an obstacle that is the crux of the heroic ordeal — that must be faced down in order to preserve one's identity. The elixir with which the defeated but triumphant survivor returns to the ordinary world is then his or her tested personal integrity of character. It remains to be seen, of course, which lesson the audience takes away from the show, but it may be comforting to regard the victory of the villain as hollow.

Notes

1. See Crew, "Viewer Interpretations."
2. *Survivor: Nicaragua* Episode 1.
3. Vogler, *Writer's Journey*, Preface.
4. Vogler 5.
5. See Voytilla, *Myth and the Movies*.
6. Vogler 11.
7. Vogler 107.
8. *Survivor: Nicaragua* Episode 2.
9. Vogler 13.
10. Vogler 15.

11. Ibid.
12. Vogler 17.
13. Vogler 12.
14. Voytilla 12.
15. Vogler 79.
16. See "Exclusive Interview."
17. Vogler 79.
18. Vogler 30.
19. In *Survivor: Panama Exile Island* Episodes 7–9.
20. Vogler 66.
21. Rushing and Frentz, *Projecting* 39.
22. *Survivor: Nicaragua* Episode 3.
23. *Survivor: Samoa* Episode 1.
24. *Survivor: Gabon* Episode 13.
25. *Survivor: Borneo, Survivor: Tocantins* Episode 4.
26. *Survivor: Pearl Islands* Episode 11, *Survivor: Samoa* Episode 1.
27. *Survivor: Tocantins* Episode 7.
28. *Survivor: Panama Exile Island* Episode 3.
29. *Survivor: Pearl Islands* Episode 11.
30. *Survivor: Pearl Islands* Episode 15.
31. Vogler 55.
32. Andrejevic, *Reality TV* 203.
33. Crew 67.
34. *Survivor: Samoa* Episode 14.
35. As per Ian Bogost, *Persuasive Games.*
36. *Survivor: Australian Outback* Episode 14.
37. *Survivor: Pearl Islands* Episode 14.
38. See Huizinga, *Homo Ludens.*

A Game About Killing:
Role-Playing in the Liminal
Spaces of Social Network Games

Eric Newsom

The social game takes place in a liminal, or in-between, space that is not quite the fiction of the game, and not quite the reality of social interaction. A study of one such game, *Spymaster*, reveals a group of players comfortable enough in the space of the game to push a button marked "Assassinate," with few qualms, but immersed enough in the social network of the game to feel betrayal and sadness when a former comrade does the same after defecting to the enemy. Tensions between social norms about following rules and the genre-derived expectation that spies will break them yielded numerous conflicts about whether rule-breakers were players committing to the game's fiction or just cheaters. Constantly negotiated boundaries of gameplay and reality yield a player experience that traverses both, but is comfortable in neither.

Unlike traditional role-playing games — where players assume a character and participate in an *in-character* narrative — in social games, users are often playing as themselves, through their own social networking accounts, often with their own photograph as their avatar. And unlike computer-based role-playing games, their communications, choices, and actions are not enacted or detached through a separate gaming program that would offer, however tenuous, the buffer of a fictional persona or avatar. Interaction with the social game occurs in a digital environment where numerous other social interactions are concurrently taking place. Notifications of achievements and actions in social games are intermingled among personal status updates, communication with family and friends, exchange of links and media, and advertising of personal businesses. These are not games intended to provide a full immersive experience, in the sense of allowing the player to occupy a secondary world the details of which are supposed to substitute for the primary one.

168

Indeed, social games are often corralled into the larger genre of casual games, those that can be played and put down without specialized skills or commitment. But as my study of *Spymaster* revealed, even in the social gaming genre, players can find ways to immerse themselves in the fiction of the game. Because these games utilize social networks as a primary cornerstone of their interface, their fictions inform and shape the social interactions of those who play them.

Over the past half-decade, social games have become a multi-million dollar industry, and are now played by tens of millions worldwide. Game publishing company Playfish defines social gaming as, "games designed to be played together with friends," specifically games that are created to use the infrastructure of already existing social network programs, such as Facebook, to allow people to play together with real-world friends. They are similar to massively multi-player online role-playing games (MMORPGs), such as *World of Warcraft* in that they allow for the potential of many users to play simultaneously, but are less graphically intense and do not require an initial purchase or subscription.[1] Some of the more popular titles include *Farmville, Mafia Wars, (Lil) Green Patch, Bejeweled* and *Café World.* Anyone who has used Facebook since mid–2008 has inevitably received an invitation from a "friend" to participate in one of these games, or observed their friends' in-game accomplishments listed in the status feed on the Facebook index page. Through these social games, players can cultivate virtual farms, train hitmen for a virtual crime syndicate, or sit down at a virtual high stakes poker table. An August 2010 study by marketing firm The NPD Group estimates that over 56.8 million Americans aged six and up, or 20 percent of the United States population, have played games on a social network, with ten percent having spent real money on virtual goods, and 35 percent never having played a video game before.[2]

In his book *Homo Ludens: A Study of the Play Element in Culture,* Johan Huizinga coined the term "magic circle," in discussing the space in which play takes place. He writes, "All play moves and has its being within a playground marked off beforehand either materially or ideally, deliberately or as a matter of course."[3] The term was later utilized by Katie Salen and Eric Zimmerman in *Rules of Play: Game Design Fundamentals,* to describe a discrete time and place that a player enters during gameplay: "As a closed circle, the space it circumscribes is enclosed and separate from the real world."[4]

The concept of the magic circle as an enclosed and separate space downplays the continuing contexts and pressures of the world outside. For instance, games scholar Jesper Juul, in his 2005 book *Half-Real: Video Games Between Real Rules and Fictional Worlds,* asserts that video games are made of two distinct elements: the fictional world, and the real rules that guide exploration of those worlds.[5] Thus, for instance, *Super Mario Bros.* consists of both the fictional world (the brightly colored mushrooms and castles, the princesses in need of rescue, the spiky lizards that live in underground, lava-filled castles) and a system of rules from outside the fictional world (extra lives, limitations of linear side-scrolling, pressing the "A" button to jump) that the player utilizes in achieving the goals of the game.

Juul complicates the notion of the magic circle, by suggesting that an interaction of real world rules and game world fiction is at the very core of gameplay: "The fictional world of a game strongly depends on the real world in order to exist, and the fictional world cues the player into making assumptions about the real world in which the player plays the game."[6] Social games complicate the half-realness of video games further, as they take place in an incomplete or imperfect magic circle. Players do not enter a completely separate space when social gaming, but rather play takes place as one part of the larger activity of social networking. Thus, the social game presents a medium in which the nature of social network interactions impacts the fictional world of the game, and the nature of the game's fictional world shapes players' social interactions.

Spymaster

My observations on liminal spaces in social games came as a result of ethnographic observation of players in a social game called *Spymaster* over a period from October to December of 2009. The game was created as a side project by Irata Labs, then known as the programmers of iList, a web application that spread classified ads amongst "friends" at various social network sites.[7] He made a joke at one point about calling down airstrikes on his Spymaster enemies, then became momentarily serious as he noted that he actually works with the military. In *Spymaster*, players took on the role of the titular spook in attempting to assassinate other users while amassing espionage-related in-game goods and money for themselves. *Spymaster* was launched in April 2009 and situated at the website PlaySpymaster.com, but players registered through a Facebook or Twitter username that was then tethered to their *Spymaster* account. I first encountered *Spymaster* through media bloggers I followed on Twitter. Short tweets describing accomplishments, for instance, "I just collected a dead drop. #spymaster," or "I just assassinated a head of state. #spymaster," began appearing a few at a time, increasing in number across Twitter until #spymaster was a trending topic, one of five most-discussed phrases listed on the Twitter front page. The Twitter updates were a shrewd part of the game's infrastructure, combining advertising with gameplay. But, as thousands of players joined the game, sending hundreds of tweets a day, this aspect of the game angered non-players who considered the constant flow of updates from the game to be unwarranted and uncontrollable spam, leading to write-ups at high-profile sites like TechCrunch and cnet, whose article on the subject was simply titled, "Why are you ruining Twitter?" Here was a tension between the game and the social networks through which it was played right off the bat: players could opt out of notifying friends of their progress, but there was a consequence in that players earned less in-game currency for each task accomplished silently. Players had to leverage fictional game rewards against alienating real world relationships. Aptly-named *Spymaster* programmer Eston Bond wrote an essay defending the notifications on his personal website, shortly following the game's launch in May, 2009, in which he avowed that the main goal of the notifications was to fully integrate the game with the social sphere. But he also said that the decision was the player's to make, and that it would be improper for the developers to remove a potential avenue of play:

> There are so many ways to play Spymaster that the heavy notification route is one of them, your friends be damned. I was actually surprised at the psychological effect of this; some people have outwardly defended their notification-increasing actions as part of the game's strategy. If that's the way people want to play, I'm not going to stop them; they're having fun and it's the player's user experience I am controlling. They can alienate themselves if they feel it is worth the reward.[8]

Players chose at the start whether to affiliate themselves with one of three spy agencies, the American CIA, British MI6, or Soviet KGB, but this choice had limited consequence within the game aside from establishing the Cold War theme. Players could complete tasks through the website, the success of which depended on a mixture of a player's in-game assets and level as well as the number of agents in a player's "spy ring," or the number of other *Spymaster* players directly followed by the player on each social network. These tasks were completed in order to gain in-game currency that could then be spent on items like super spy cars or sniper rifles that bolstered the level of attack or defense. Once a player had passed a certain level, these tasks became less meaningful or valuable, and, having accumulated a substantial amount of assets to back their attack and defense numbers, players shifted their focus to attempting to assassinate other players. Players had a profile on the website, with a "wall" where other players could leave messages, as well as a listing of the player's level and cell affiliation. Most communication, however, took place outside of the *Spymaster* website, through the social networks of Twitter and Facebook, or through external sites set up by "cells." Originally, cells were communities of players created independently of the *Spymaster* game, but were later added to the infrastructure by the developers. Each cell had their own chat space, or website, or method of recruiting and organizing multiple members, and some cells had, counting splinter cells, over 300 members.

This study primarily followed one such cell, Zone (short for "Zombie Network"). Following the example set by ethnographers such as Tom Boellstorff in his 2008 book, *Coming of Age in Second Life: An Anthropologist Explores the Virtually Human*, and Mark Chen, in his 2009 paper, "Communication, Coordination and Camaraderie in World of Warcraft," I became a participant-observer, joining the game to learn its mechanics and to interact with other players.[9] I adopted the username "ethno007" and introduced myself to other players with the following information on my Spymaster dossier page:

> [Ethno007] ... Is a Ph.D. student in communication/rhetoric at Rensselaer Polytechnic in upstate New York. I'm here as part of an ethnographic study of digital communities / social network-based games, and am interested in your opinions and experiences. Feel free to contact me through my connected Twitter account or by posting here on my dossier.

Following an invitation to join the Zone cell, I also became a member at their website, SpymasterZombie.com which continued to be in development throughout my study. I was also invited to join Zone members on a chat space where they hosted what they referred to as "hunts," and it was through observing and communicating with Zone players during these hunts that I gathered much of the information for this study. Participants in the chat sessions were always made aware that I was an ethnographer and of the nature of the work I was doing, and given the opportunity to opt out of the study if they so chose. Some players chose not to discuss the game with me because they simply did not want to take part in my research, others made clear that they did not trust me and suspected I was a member of a rival cell pretending to be a researcher to ferret out secrets of their gameplay, their cells, or their targets. Many of those who did talk to me consented to follow-up discussions via email, Skype, or instant messenger for clarification purposes. In addition, I observed interactions on public websites like Twitter, GetSatisfaction.com (the complaint/player-developer interaction site for the *Spymaster* development team), and the official *Spymaster* site itself. Player names have been reduced to initials, and personal information has been kept to a minimum to obscure player identities.

The Hunt

They met at 10 P.M., coordinating through a site called the "Advanced Intel and Tracking System," aka AITS, and pronounced by my host, P, as "Aida's." It was a small group that night, but one that had worked together enough times before to get the job done quickly and efficiently. I had arrived to observe only, though the initial invitation invited me to participate, darkly: "Come kill with us Wednesday night," the email read. I explained in the chat the scope of my research, and said that I wanted to see how they function as a community. One of the assembled typed back, "Think *Lord of the Flies*. LOL."

These players had gathered to carry out what is known as "the hunt," an organized assertion of communal power. The ultimate consequence in *Spymaster* was assassination. In the asynchronous game system, players could take a digital bullet from an opponent when they were not looking, or, as often happened, when they were offline. The price of assassination was the loss of all in-game goods and money that were not safely squared away in a fictional Swiss bank account, and a temporary 15-minute inability to play. But even a missed attempt, should it wound, meant virtual money lost. A player could attempt to ward off death by bolstering their stats, via in-game purchases of defense items from laser watches, to claymore mines, to stealth-armored supercars. But the best protection the game offered was in the amount of actual hits it took to be assassinated. Wounds were one thing, but they were survivable. It took more than that to bring a spymaster down.

This is where the hunt came into play. Coordinated attacks from multiple assassins meant more wounds, a better chance at assassination success. As I watched them take out a chosen target in what seemed like mere seconds, I realized that these Zone spymasters had the art of virtual killing down to a science. They typed brief, enigmatic nuggets of information: "4 attacks and 4 wounds," "I've got EOS," "2/2." I asked why the sharing of information was necessary, thinking that time would be better spent pushing the button that would start the next attack.

"We know it takes about 7 hits to kill someone," typed one of the cyber-assassins, D, "So by knowing how many are successful, we know when the target will die."

The targets dropped like flies. As soon as one was assassinated, one of the hunters typed the name of the next victim. I asked how they chose their targets, and D responded with numbered points:

1. People who have attacked or killed our cell members recently
2. People with bounty
3. People with stupid names

I understood the first, as D had already told me that one of the basic functions of the cell was protection. I was also familiar with the *Spymaster* bounty system, where players could monetize their grievances against others by placing an in-game cash bounty on their enemies' heads. But the third? As if to answer my question, the next target was chosen: "CAT SHIT EATER!" types another player, G, and a link was provided to a player whose username is only a few mispronounced words away from that unique epithet. This target too, was quickly vanquished.

After awhile, I began to see the group as real hunters, like the early men who ritualistically drove mammoth off cliffs by closing in on them with Clovis spear points. Their answers to my questions came in short, clipped sentences, perhaps befitting players of a game spread through the limited character counts of Twitter, or perhaps because answering my questions was interrupting valuable hunting time. More targets were vanquished, but I'd given up counting. By this time, I felt I'd developed a clear portrait of the spymasters of Zone: methodical and, aside from the occasional "LOL," mostly emotionless. They seemed to me to be virtual killing machines, gunning down all enemies in their path. P drew my attention to a column on the left side of the website: "You see the column that says 'Top 20 Spies'? The people there are big time addicted to *Spymaster*." P's username was third on the list, after the names of two of the game's developers. Another target assassinated. Lord of the Flies. LOL.

Somewhere around thirty minutes into the hunt the chat room ran silent, or, I suppose, blank. At first, I feared that I had crossed some boundary with my most recent question, but it was by far the most innocuous thing I had asked, a follow up about secret alternate accounts. D broke the silence/blankness by commenting that it's a shame I wasn't getting the audio, because they'd just had a funny argument that I would have appreciated.

"Audio?" I asked.

Within a minute, I was connected to the Skype conference call where almost everyone I'd been chatting with was assembled. Perhaps they had forgotten to mention this mode of communication to me earlier, perhaps they didn't consider it important to my observations, or perhaps they simply did not trust me — earlier in the chat after explaining my research, one of the players commented, "Sounds like a SPY to me. Hehe." — a suspicion that prior game experience may have instilled.

J, then #6 and rising on that list of top 20 spymasters, introduced the group: "Basically, what you've got ... P is the head of the clan, and you have three Zone officers here — myself, G, and D — and M is one of our strongest players." He described his compatriots as "people who are just brilliant ... we take in everyone, look at their skills, and try to utilize them." D was a social media expert who got into *Spymaster* as a result of a conversation at the South by Southwest Festival (SXSW), and who took pride that she was assassinated for the first time in the game by famed Silicon Valley blogger and technology commentator Louis Gray. She told me chunks of the history of the game and the Zone cell, in a cheery, playful voice that acknowledged both recognition of the game as a grand social media experiment and as something personal into which she had put a good bit of time and emotion. Chiming in occasionally from the background of D's Skype connection was G, whom J described as a "software guru-genius." It was he who was the subject of the funny argument, because he had just remained mum while being systematically assassinated himself.

P was also a social media wiz, organizing YouTube gatherings when not busy leading Zone. M was the oldest of the gathered group in her late 50s, narrowly beating P, in his early 50s. She was a divorce attorney who said she'd never even participated in a chat room before playing *Spymaster*—her perception was colored by chat room logs that were often entered as evidence in her cases. M was one of the 35 percent who was new to online gaming. She told me her technical prowess had grown in leaps and bounds from playing the game, and that now she considered herself to be "tech-savvy." Her desire to be a better fictional spy had informed her progress with data analytics at the AITS site. Her membership in the Zone community had yielded efficiency with communications technologies like the Zone forum, chat spaces, and Skype.

J, the Skype host, was a bit of an enigma, a self-admittedly aggressive military man,[10] who still went out of his way to be a congenial host, chatting with old friends. He alternated between taking the game quite seriously, citing "tactics" as the skill he provides, and finding it humorous how seriously others take it. In the real world of espionage, he told me, most people who play the game would be dead as dirt within minutes.

They chatted about the history of the game, about the formation of the Zone from the earlier cell Zombies & Ninjas, about general relationship dynamics across social networks, about the latest gossip regarding the affairs of rival cells. They talked about the scandals, the watershed moments that marked the development of *Spymaster* over the last six months, and the conflict, which they saw as inevitable.

"This game breeds conflict," P said. When I asked him why, he told me, "It's a game about killing."

Killing, P said, was at the very core of the game, and there was no getting around that fact: "It takes some people a long time ... you know, some people never figure out that you get killed, yeah, you die, but you're going to come back 15 minutes later. Who cares? They get all bent out of shape, start calling people names, and it starts a lot of drama."

P's choice of words is apt. The game is about killing, not about death. The conflict came from questioning why one was being targeted, not from the actual killing blow. D recalled the early days of the game, when almost every spymaster played through their regular Twitter account, how difficult it was to separate the in-game act of assassination from something more personal: "When we were first playing, people didn't attack each other, and it was really shocking the first time you got attacked by somebody. 'Why are they attacking me? What I did do wrong to them? Whose feelings have I hurt?'"

In the early, pre-cell *Spymaster* days, D told me, options in the game ran out pretty quickly, because there were no dossier pages and no organized means of selecting potential assassination targets aside from a list of "Worthy Adversaries," that often displayed the same names over and over again. Through Twitter, players began to share information with each other about viable targets, their statistics, their previous actions, and so small groups of players began banding together on a regular basis to trade names and information. From these regular exchanges and team-ups were formed the first communities, who created their own names and identities, and then these communities began to merge together to form larger groups.

Around that same time, P set up the Advanced Intel Tracking System as a way to share these statistics and as a central meeting place for *Spymaster* players. Though it was run by the head of Zone, AITS was open to any player who cared to join. Here, users could download a Firefox extension that reported their kills to the website, which then displayed stats on how many had been assassinated or wounded for each cell over the past 24, eight, two, and one hours. Within the official game system, the sum of each user's defense and attack properties were not seen by the would-be assassin until the attempt had already commenced, and so users posted this information, once revealed, on the dossier pages of each spymaster so that future assassins could calculate their percentage of success. Later, with the cell system in place, and group hunts the norm, such information was more easily obtained and distributed through the community. Social rules drove the process of decision making that went into choosing a viable assassination target. The first consideration was, of course, the intended victim's cell association. For the most part, players did not attack other players who were in their cell, and there was a sort of unspoken system in place that allowed for losses from "friendly fire" to be repaid. The procedure was defined differently by each cell, but generally involved a direct message apology through the Twitter or Facebook interface, and a return of any in-game money or goods taken in the attack. Friendly fire incidents were fairly common, owing to the amount of players in some of the cells and the difficulty in recognizing the name of each cell comrade. Most players abided by the general ethic of friendly fire recompense, but there were consequences for those who did not. Within some cells, this meant a general decrease in prestige or respect within the community, leading to rescinded invitations to join others in hunts and limited protection from the cell. In other cells, the penalty was defined more clearly. For instance, the Zone Code of Conduct stipulated that, "If attacker has no good explanation and won't give $ back, Zone will compensate victim and banish the attacker."

Friendly fire could also mean assassinating members of a cell with which the assassin's cell had a truce, or strategic alignment. And, as there were truces, there were also rivalries. The two superpower groups of *Spymaster,* based on sheer number of members, were Zone and PUMA (Predatory Underground Mafia Alliance, which began as a sort of diaspora of players from a similar social game, Mafia Wars), who, in the Cold War iconography of *Spymaster,* might be seen as the United States and Soviet Union, the big two whose conflict provides context for all other cell relationships. Smaller cells could align with one of these two super groups to procure protection for their members, and the larger clans sought alliances with the smaller cells to build their reputation and presence in the game. This could lead to some tricky issues on the battlefield. During one hunt, the Zone members were joined by the leader of a cell with which they had a fairly neutral relationship — they were free to attack members of this cell, but did not consider them enemies in war as they did the rival PUMA cell. To allow this cell leader to participate, the Zone hunters did their best to avoid targets from the leader's cell, or cells with which the leader's cell had alliances. Occasionally, such a target would slip through, and the cell leader would simply and calmly abstain from participating while Zone members attacked her comrades and allies, saying "I can't do that one. Maybe next one." However, it should be noted that shortly after this cell leader left the chat, she assassinated a few of the Zone hunters, perhaps as a sort of delayed retaliation.

A look at a series of posts by J on the AITS site further demonstrate this strange quandary in making digital attempts on a person's life, while still showing respect. On November 13: "Hi all Its Friday the 13th November 2009 and this is going to be nightmare weekend for The 'Princess' so please all click below link to participate in her nightmare" (link goes to page where would-be assassins are able to target the user in question). On November 22: "Well I must always give credit when credit is due. Well its due! The "Princess" is a fine example of a warrior! No question! Brave, resilient & above all tenacious, truly qualities required of a warrior. She is awesome in my book! A worthy adversary and a great friend! :)" This relationship was further identified by mention of the concept of "frienemies" [sic] in the Zone Code of Conduct: "Friendship with non-zone members is highly encouraged (we love our Frienemies!) but should not interfere with the execution of zone strategies." During one hunt, J seemingly contradicted this aspect of the Code of Conduct by telling me, "We all have friends that we will not hit irrespective of cells," discussing ex–Zone members who have moved on to form other cells. However, later during that same hunt, J targeted one such former Zoner who was attacking current Zone members. "[That player] is a friend, but he was in the wrong place at the wrong time," J said after the kill.

Ari-Pekka Lappi, discussing the nature of ethics in gameplay, points out that often times in gameplay, "Things that are normally immoral or bad may suddenly become not only acceptable, but also expected behavior." He cites the board game *Diplomacy* as an example, noting that the act of betraying one's friends in the separate space of the game was, "not fully commensurable with betraying in the 'real' world."[11] And yet, in the liminal space of *Spymaster*, "traitors" — referring to those who were a member of a cell who left to join, or *defected* to, another cell — caused real difficulties for those they left behind. Sometimes they were chosen as a regular target by their former cell, and other times, as J described above, they were excluded from consideration as targets because of feelings of friendship that still remained. Such players were often considered actual traitors in the social sphere, though they had defected while pursuing the goals of the game, within the rules of the game. D said that this could become problematic for players who have different perceptions of the boundaries of the game: "Some people think it's real life and some think it's RPG. Lots of bad drama comes from that. A lot of people use 'game friendships' as tactic, while the people they are befriending view it as real social interaction."

Many of the tensions in the game came from the undefined boundaries of gameplay and social reality constantly being negotiated among players, and between players and developers. *Spymaster* was, as P noted, a game where one of the winning conditions was the fictional assassination of others, but it was also a taking place in a social space where the sting of being targeted and having one's virtual death broadcast across the network caused hurt feelings or even a sense of betrayal outside the supposed enclosure of the magic circle.

Can Spies Cheat?

In his *The Grasshopper: Games, Life and Utopia*, Bernard Suits defines the classes of those who participates in games: the triflers, the cheats, the players, and the spoilsports:

> Triflers recognize rules, but not goals, cheats recognize goals, but not rules, players recognize both rules and goals, and spoilsports recognize neither rules nor goals ... while players acknowledge the claims of both the game and its institution, triflers and cheats acknowledge only institutional claims, and spoilsports acknowledge neither.[12]

The question of what made one a cheat or a spoilsport created constant tension among *Spymaster* players, and most times, the answer was debatable based on where each player personally wanted to draw the boundaries of game-play.

Some instances of spoilsports were obvious, such as aforementioned players with names unbefitting spymasters. Others were not so clear cut. For instance, J declared, the most cowardly way to assassinate someone in *Spymaster* was the kamikaze method. Through the *Spymaster* system, a player could purchase a one-time pass that guaranteed them an assassination on the first attempt. The only catch was that the attempt also killed the assassin. J pointed out one of the recently targeted victims and told me that particular player's perception of the game until recently had meant getting liquored up on Friday, then drunkenly spending the weekend buying up "suicide attacks," and taking out rival spymasters. Kamikaze assassination was widely seen as a spoilsport activity, although it was fully sanctioned and enabled by the official *Spymaster* rules and infrastructure. The kamikaze method violated social rules of what was sportsmanlike.

Early in her *Spymaster* career, M was shunned and nearly kicked out of the cell due to a reputation as a frequent kamikaze: "It got around that I had suicided [sic] dozens of people," she said, but maintained that it only happened three times in a five month period. "I was tired of having some of these people kill me, and it was the only way I could kill them." Still, word got around through the cells that M was a *Spymaster* deviant, and she found herself the subject of waves of assassinations, not allowing her to respawn and effectively preventing her from playing the game for days at a time. M's public dossier page at the time of our discussion still bore retaliation threats from the incident: "Suicide to get a bounty??" wrote another player, "Wrong cell to do it too [sic], well I guess you won't be playing a lot this weekend." Despite the fact that it was a part of the game rules sanctioned by the developers themselves, the perception of the suicide attack among *Spymaster* players led to community-driven social punishments for those who acted as spoilsports. Said M: "Needless to say I never kamikaze'd anyone ever again."

As a class of *Spymaster* player, cheats were harder to define, especially in a game set in a fictional espionage world. Mia Consalvo, in her 2007 book *Cheating*, discusses the ability of players to circumvent the game system via cheat codes, and argues that most players cheat while playing online games, but that there exists a general acceptance because cheat codes and glitches are commonly shared throughout the gaming community.[13] Because of the espionage nature of *Spymaster*, however, these shortcuts become valuable "intel" that, when kept secret, can be powerful for the player and the community in which that player is a member. Players only discussed their specific intel with me in explicitly off-the-record circumstances, or were reluctant to share the "good stuff with a potential mole" as a player from one of the smaller cells put it. That same player jokingly said that I should try back in 20 years, after the intel had been "declassified." Alternate or "alt" characters are sometimes used to infiltrate cells, gather "intel," and report back to their own community, or perhaps even to the developers about a player exploit that violates the terms of service. Alternate characters were frowned upon by *Spymaster* developers, and the use of alts for collusion purposes (striking with a low level character to find out the stats of a would-be target, for the purposes of calculating the risk for a higher-level character) was against the terms of service. But D said that the use of alts was rampant: "It is against terms of service to COLLUDE with alts. But you can use different alts for different situations / levels of targets / etc. Anyone who is anyone has an alt for SOME reason. It's more suspicious if you are a big player and DON'T admit to having an alt somewhere."[14] The use of alt characters as a sort of spy disguise for infiltration purposes leads to suspicion and uncertainty about who the other players are. One of the most notorious users of alts reportedly had dozens of other identities, and in sending my initial requests to potential interviewees, one player quite blatantly accused me of being this master of disguise, just to mess with them.

Early in the game, developers gave mixed signals when players figured out ways to cheat the system, sometimes intimating that such activities would naturally come from players immersing themselves into the role of spy in the fictional game world. For example, responding to a question about whether an exploit that allowed players to dodge attacks by changing their Twitter username was cheating or being stealthy, Irata employee Brent responded on the Get Satisfaction forum that, "There's no official stance on that. We're working on a workaround and future changes [might] fix this. In my opinion ... it's kind of being stealthy." Posts further down the page debate the subject both from within the allowances of the fictional world of the game and from the external system of rules. The comment, "I have to agree with [Brent] ... it's being stealthy and conniving but it's part of the spy game," is met with a response of, "The person who strikes then changes screen name momentarily to thwart revenge is introducing something akin to teleportation to the game. Since this is espionage and not sci-fi, I would think this would fall well outside the parameters of this game." Again, the unclear boundaries of the game and validity of playing the role of spy created different expectations for fair play among players.

Further glitches and exploits threatened the viability of the game. One such glitch involved the merging of accounts. A *Spymaster* player reported on the complaints page for *Spymaster* developers that merging multiple accounts produced a glitch that left the player with trillions of in-game dollars.[15] In reporting this publicly, this player acknowledged that this was being circulated as a sort of intelligence and that some players were taking advantage of the bug. In his closing statement, the player who leaked the information wrote that, "It was fun for a while, but we need to put an end to it, as it is not fair to other users. I know who took profit of this glitch, but I assume that everyone feels the same as I do, and will report it themselves." Yet again, the trouble was that everyone did not feel the same, particularly the user U, who posited that, in a game about espionage, why follow any rules at all? (text unchanged):

> Has anyone even considered that this is a built in premeditated part of the game,..and because it makes us feel as if we are doing something wrong,.that it adds a much needed level of excitment and intruige...? The people who created this great game seem to be pretty on top of things and very smart cookies,..I think that as "Spy's," it is our duty to push the boundries, and test the rules, as in true spygames,..there are no rules,..its kill or be killed ... and now what we have here is a situation, were it is a war of points,..and a war of perception, a battle to win over the hearts and minds of the thousands upon thousands of players , new and old alike, who are not members of any cell,. and to whom, a few million dollars would change there whole game forever.

Here again was an example of the fictional world informing the real-world rules and interactions. U's perception was that spies fight dirty, and that in a spy role-playing game, dirty fighting should be celebrated, not frowned upon. In a later post, he re-asserted this view: "I personally think that this is the best thing that could be happening for it,..and should it continue, intentionally or not, officially condoned or not,..it mimics the real life spy world, in which money is no object, weapons are temporary and disposable, and stats are irrelevant, and frankly embarrassing because as spy's our goal should be to be invisible and go along with our business as undetected as possible."[16] Still, others perceived the game as one with different boundaries and set rules and resented the violation of those rules. In response to the above, another user wrote to the game developers, "Please put a stop to this blatant cheating and vindictive twisting of the game's intent. We want to play, and have some fun, but this person has destroyed not only the monetary system, but also the points system."

Spymaster developers, who were eager earlier not to tread on player experience after outrage over Twitter spam, took action this time.[17] At first, they banned accounts that seemed to have benefited from the glitch. But, because of the game's infrastructure and multiple ways in which money could be transferred, the across-the-board banning of accounts was ineffective and punished some who weren't even aware of the exploit. The developers reinstated most accounts, many of whom still possessed large amounts of in-game currency from the glitch. Retribution was instead served through the social network, where accusations of cheating continued to fly, and in the game, where glitch beneficiaries were routinely the target of mass assassination efforts.

Conclusion

Throughout my observation, I found numerous examples where the espionage nature of the fictional *Spymaster* game, and rules that emphasized push-button assassinations and purchasing of commodities, were influential on the communication, socialization, ethics, and infrastructure of the *Spymaster* player community. In, as P put it, "A game about killing," tensions often ran high, and because this was a social game, not completely bound by the magic circle, people felt distrust, aversion, or camaraderie toward other players. These feelings were not mediated through avatars, and condemnations of players as cheats and traitors often bypassed aliases in favor of real first names when posted on Facebook and Twitter. By immersing themselves in a game that crossed over with their social sphere, players opened themselves to interactions that at first transcended the game, but later became part of it. Clan politics were systemized by players to have consequences within the game. The cloak-and-dagger nature of the fictional world defined the nature of relationships that players could have with each other outside of the game: could one still be friends with a traitor, and should one be on the lookout for moles? The game world was inextricable from the social sphere, and tensions between the expectations of the fictional world and the rules of the social network continued to simmer until the game was closed just before the News Corp purchase in April 2010.

I cannot extrapolate whether the situation would be the same for other social games. *Spymaster* may be an extreme case, due to the content and function of the game. *Spymaster* players, as seen in comments above, seemed to be aware of how the nature of an espionage game influenced their interactions within it. Some also discussed how those interactions, if playing a different game, would differ. One player responded in an email, "If I were playing *FarmVille* right now, I'd be inviting you down to the co-op and asking to borrow your tractor or something. But instead I'm trying to figure out if you're somebody's alt account trying to mess around with me." In any case, with numbers of social games players increasing daily across a wide demographic, future research into the social implications of those games is warranted.

Notes

1. Some social games are "freemium" games, which means they allow for the purchase of in-game items or points through transfer of actual money or completion of surveys for mar-

keting partners. This enables players to progress more quickly through game levels, gain special achievements, or acquire more in-game wealth. Such purchases are typically an optional, but advantageous, part of an otherwise free game.

2. See Riley, "20 Percent."

3. Huizinga, *Homo Ludens* 10.

4. Salen and Zimmerman, *Rules of Play* 95.

5. See Juul, *Half-Real.*

6. Juul 168.

7. Irata Labs was later purchased by Rupert Murdoch's News Corp. in April 2010.

8. See Eston Bond, "On Spymaster's virality."

9. See Boellstorff, *Coming of Age*; Chen, "Communication."

10. He made a joke at one point about calling down airstrikes on his Spymaster enemies, then became momentarily serious as he noted that he actually works with the military.

11. Lappi, "Contra-Moral" 193.

12. Suits, *Grasshopper* 60.

13. Consalvo, *Cheating.*

14. "Ucana's Alts."

15. "Mayor Glitch."

16. "Merging Multiple Accounts."

17. "Working on Updates."

Deleting Memory Space:
The Gaming of History and
the Absence of the Holocaust

M.-NICLAS HECKNER

In this chapter, I investigate the relationship between immersion and the construction of historical memory in mass culture retellings of Nazi Germany. As I demonstrate, it is the bodies of the audience/gamers and the intensity of their involvement that define appropriate historical spaces via an immersive experience. Visceral involvement limits the field of history that mainstream media can respectably address and determines its particular contribution to historical memory.

As shown by genre films and fictionalized games like *Wolfenstein* as well as allegedly historically accurate video games such as *Brothers in Arms: Road to Hill 30*, pop cultural forms associated with a high presence of the body generally detach Nazi Germany from historical events and the horrors of the Shoah. Similar to what Frederic Jameson calls a "well-nigh libidinal historicism,"[1] these pieces turn Nazi Germany into an ensemble of aesthetic and narrative codes, overwriting their connection to history with a generic connection to Fantasy, Science Fiction and Horror.

Departing from Vivian Sobchack's chapter "What My Fingers Knew," in which the author describes a relationship between the viewer's body and the film,[2] I will first take a closer look at the act of immersion in video games. Here, paratexts such as marketing and gaming extras address the player in less bodily-involved situations to create a consciousness of the games' historical accuracy, while different mechanisms during gameplay let the player, as body, experience this alleged authenticity. After this examination of immersive experience and its mechanics, I will examine the treatment of history in *Wolfenstein* through a close reading of some of its visuals. These games immerse the player in an "experience" of history triggered by visual cues, symbols and aesthetic tropes that are isolated from a broader historical context, a result of the medium's low cultural capital. I will then examine how decidedly fictional genres, such as horror and science fiction, appropriate these free-floating signifiers and recode them as narrative, generic and ludic cues.

Nazi Nostalgia and the Experience of Authenticity

In Sung-Hyung's 2006 documentary *Full Metal Village*, Ann-Kathrin Schaak, a teenage girl obsessed with World War II and Nazi Germany, innocently states that one of her greatest wishes would be to travel back in time and experience this fascinating chapter of history herself:

> I also watch the films on TV, whenever documentaries are on, or buy them on DVD and watch it all the time, again and again, until I know every scene by heart. I'd like to spend an hour in World War II.... Like, I don't know, to stand with the Hitler Youth and just look at it as an outside observer, to really experience it with them.... To see how my grandfather stood there back then and then how that all was in reality, because you only ever read all that in stories, but to really be a part of it once, that would be great.

Her naive view of German history, clearly informed by the perspective of her German refugee grandmother, is one of a romanticized and abstracted accumulation of events that does not become 'real' enough through source materials, and that she yearns to experience through physical presence, the underlying assumption being that there exists a hierarchy of knowledge organized by its potential to immerse her. She constructs her ideal experience of history as a seemingly contradictory amalgam of being an "outside observer" for a limited time and to "really experience it with them" and "really be a part of it."

The idea that knowledge is first and foremost a physical process is not a new one. One can look as far back as the Bible to find examples of the conflation of knowledge with physical contact. The Hebrew euphemism for physicality/sexuality as "knowing" (e.g., Genesis 4:1) is as revealing here as the later example of Doubting Thomas, who would only believe in the resurrection of Jesus if he could "see in his hands the print of the nails, and put my finger into the print of the nails, and thrust my hand into his side."[3] Similarly, Siegfried Kracauer asserts that all abstract knowledge needs to be grounded in experience to become relevant: for him, the street grid of Manhattan "becomes concrete only if we realize, for instance, that all the cross streets end in the nothingness of the blank sky."[4] In other words, the pattern makes sense only when its context — its physical limits and its domain of application — is understood.

So it would seem that a physical experience of history could approximate the 19th century German historian Leopold von Ranke's wishful thinking for a historiography capable of knowing and passing on "what actually happened," and that a video game, with its half-observing, half-participating subject position would be ideal for someone like Schaak, who wishes to be engaged viscerally while nonetheless keeping a safe distance.

In spite of this long tradition of embodied knowledge, immersive media such as action movies and video games have had to shy away from formulating a narrative of traumatic historical events, leaving the field to more respected or respectable intellectual approximations. That this is at least partly a result of outside pressures becomes clear whenever immersive media overstep this line and attempt to physically mediate the experience of historical trauma.

For example, Jens M. Stober attempted, in his modification of the game *Half-Life 2: Death Match* called *1378 km*, to confront the player with the ethical dilemmas of the armed guards on the East German wall. Either as fugitives that attempted to dodge bullets during their escape, or as soldiers making decisions of whether to fire at or run after them, its players would reenact history in an online multiplayer setting. The outrage in the German press and political discourse long before the online release of this student project revealed that there are historical spaces held to be inviolable by physical experience. The tabloid paper *Bild* headlined a story on the mod "So disgusting! The murders on the death strip as online game"[5]; elsewhere, socialist politician Gesine Lötzsch called it "tasteless and dumb," while conservative Helmut Rau deemed it "a mockery of the victims."[6] The most direct connection between video game genre and inappropriate content was made by Rainer Wagner, chairman of the Union of the Alliances of Victims of Communist Tyranny (UOKG) when he said: "As is common to all shooters, it tends to lowest human instincts. One aspect of this game, however, makes it even worse than other first person shooters. Because usually one shoots at armed opponents in such games — here it is unarmed civilians."[7]

Immersive media are therefore in a problematic position. While there may exist a wish to use them to understand, to physically approach, and to experience Germany under communism, for example, or under the Nazis, attempts to address historical trauma with immersive media are castigated as trivializations of human suffering — as a kind of "misery tourism" motivated by designers' desire for public attention and catering to a base and unworthy attraction to visceral stimulation.

Here I look at the effects of this tension on the representations of history in video games. I suggest that a reduction of historical events to their fetishized tropes and iconography is the problematic outcome of this moralizing censorship. The isolation of formerly historical markers and their transformation into generic and aesthetic cues potentially hampers and discourages the pursuit of historical interests by offering the titillation cued by tabooed iconography with the generic excitement of horror and science fiction, resulting in the pleasure of historic play because of, rather than in spite of, history's very absence.

Immersive Play: What My Fingers Said

Film Studies offers a phenomenological model to explain the immersive effects of media, made most famous by the work of Vivian Sobchack. She explains how the body is one that "in experience, lives vision always in cooperation and significant exchange with other sensorial means of access to the world, a body that makes meaning before it makes conscious, reflective thought."[8] She suggests that the body subverts notions of "onscreen" and "offscreen," and dissolving fixed subject positions, the body of the viewer becomes one with the bodies on the screen by literally sharing their senses. She introduces the concept of the "cinesthetic subject,"[9] linguistically alluding to the terms synaesthesia and coenaesthesia. While the former describes both the involuntary experience of one sense caused by the stimulation of others (e.g. smelling colors) and the deliberate linguistic exchange of the senses as a stylistic device, the latter describes:

> the potential and perception of one's whole sensorial being. Thus, the name is used to describe the general and open sensual condition of the child at birth. The term also refers to a certain prelogical and nonhierarchical unity of the sensorium that exists as the carnal foundation for the later hierarchical arrangement of the senses achieved through cultural immersion and practice.[10]

This and the former term are combined into the notion of the "cinesthetic subject," that is, "the film viewer (or, for that matter, the film maker) who, through an embodied vision informed by the knowledge of the other senses, 'makes sense' of what it is to 'see' a movie — both 'in the flesh' and as it 'matters.'"[11] The act of watching is thus a coming-together of viewer and medium via the body.

While Sobchack describes a relationship between a spectator who is constructing meaning out of a medium that he/she is actively interpreting, or one that is between a film maker and the medium she is giving meaning to, video games set up a different relationship between player and medium in that the player fulfills both positions to a larger extent constructing the given game's generic and narrative fabric during the act of play[12] and making visceral and cognitive sense of it during an interactivity that transcend that of spectatorship. Mark J.P. Wolf describes a game's "real" narrative as player-determined:

The very "rules" and cause-and-effect logic that dictate the events of the video game's diegetic world contain an imbedded worldview which matches actions with consequences and determines outcomes.... Goals and obstacles, choices and their consequences, and the means and ends with which the player is provided; these become the tools that shape narrative experience, and the real narrative becomes the player's own passage though the narrative maze of branching storylines and events.[13]

According to Wolf, one might therefore think of a video game as an extensive tool kit from which the player constructs play, with author and consumer forming a unity. To be sure, this is a general argument that was made about literature and film as much as about video games. In games, however, the player not only viscerally and cognitively constructs meaning from cues on-screen, but he or she triggers these cues with a physical interaction via gamepad, keyboard, mouse, or other device. Now, with the help of translating devices such as Kinect, one can even heighten the illusion of unmediatedness, as the player's whole body becomes the game controller. The body is not only understanding, but also constructing, what is to be understood. Or to put it in Sobchack's language, it is more about what one's fingers *wrote* than about what one's fingers knew. The construction of meaning on the part of the player influences the player's experience at least as strongly as the reception of its results, which in itself serves as a trigger for player actions, i.e. for the construction of meaning. The mechanics of play thus transcend those of spectatorship and bring about a different relationship between offscreen and onscreen. For one, the unity between the player's body and the body onscreen is an even more intense one, especially when the act of controlling remains in the background and the translation between pad and action/movement happens intuitively. This stronger unity causes the medium's immersion to feel more natural, which is, apart from practical considerations, the reason first-person-perspective has become a cliché in gaming, while film has, after the failed attempt of *The Lady in the Lake* in 1947, largely abandoned the idea of immersing the audience by restricting itself to one point of view. It is a fair guess that the medium of the video game would be ideal to not only critically analyze historical events, but also to open up emotional spaces of history, leading to a visceral, pre-conscious understanding of events, rather than an allegedly reflected rational knowledge of detail. However, in traumatic historic settings such as the Third Reich and World War II, today's video games explicitly focus on the replication of war's materiality, rather than on an emotionally (and immersively) driven affective understanding. Relying on material culture, iconography and tropes to simulate accuracy, they detach those from history and, by passing them on to non-historic genres, deprive them of productive insight.

How They Prove It's Real and Why It's Not: Experiencing History in Video Games

Actively witnessing the "reality" of the past is a paradox, given that once one has become part of it, one necessarily participates and thus changes it. Frank Cushing bears witness to this as much as *Back to the Future's* Marty McFly does. So would video games, with a code discrete from and not able to be changed by gameplay, not be an ideal way of immersing oneself in history "as it was" without distorting what happened through the player's presence?

As much as German historian Leopold von Ranke might have believed in the possibility of portraying an unmediated "as-it-was" of the past, rare is the historian who still holds this to be true. Video games like *Brothers in Arms*, however, pursue this ideal with such factographic obsession that events are reduced to their materiality and iconography. In her fascinating readings of video games in "Immersive Historicity in World War II Digital Games," Eva Kingsepp claims that allegedly historically accurate games set in World War II are not based on original footage as much as on filmic representation of these documents, such as *Saving Private Ryan*. She is struck by this "remediation of certain specific visual material and how this might lead the viewer's association to another source than the original. In [her] view, this adds important aspects to be considered about our perception of historic events, as original footage here actually becomes secondary to simulacra."[14]

While I concur that the feeling of immersion in historic reality is largely grounded in the intertextual imitation of filmic representation, I suggest that the game seems to open a different channel for a far less embodied, rather than visceral and emotional immersion. Kingsepp quotes the manual of *Medal of Honor: Underground* that states: "You unlock each Mission Gallery after successfully completing the previous mission. The best OSS agents are the best-educated OSS agents. Enter the Gallery to view actual footage from World War II, highlighting events mirrored in each of *Medal of Honor Underground's* missions, as well as a slide show on the making of *Medal of Honor Underground*."[15]

This description implies that the game's distributors envisioned the relationship between game and reality to be more complicated than an imitation of the fictionalized war tropes in Hollywood movies. It suggests a unity between player and avatar during gameplay by connecting the player's education via historical documents to the soldier's performance in the battlefield ("The best OSS agents..."). At the same time it emphasizes the game's textuality by addressing both the game's making of and the gallery's "actual footage"—as opposed to the missions that merely "mirror" these images that "highlight" what was real. So while the battle scenes' simulacra of Hollywood create an effectual immersion of the body, the mind seems to be able to operate outside of this mechanism with the alleged indexicality of photographs. Similarly, the back of the game's box cover invites the player to experience "Real soldiers. Authentic battlefields. True combat."[16] Next to this caption, a black-and-white photograph flanks a gradual translation of this photograph into game graphics. Hence, there seems to be a different conception of what is real, dependent on how much the player's body is involved, the extreme points being the inspection of the game's box in the store on one end and the physical stress of gameplay on the other.

Brian Rejack suggests that the documents accompanying the game do indeed serve a visceral function when he describes the emotional relationship between player and player-avatar Sergeant Matthew Baker: "The extras suggest that if one cannot feel for Baker's loss, perhaps the introduction of a historical document will entice an emotional reaction. *Brothers in Arms* attempts to use history as a means for sympathetic identification precisely because gaming struggles to achieve such a goal on its own."[17] While I strongly disagree that gaming is in a bad position to entice emotions, the emotional relevance of the characters is certainly greater if they are being connected to the fate of real soldiers, and the emotionally charged position we are used to taking when we look at photographs of the deceased also helps by providing the player with an affective template. However, if the player enters this mode, it still happens outside and often quite separated from gameplay: in order to view the extras, one has to end the game and return to the title screen, or do so before one starts playing. The physical investment is thus lower and temporally discrete from that of gameplay, and functions as a cognitive guarantee of authenticity, heightening the visceral immersion during 'combat' with the pre-acquired (alleged) knowledge that what the player participates in matches historical fact.

Beneath this double-address lies the idea that bodily experienced Hollywood representation and authentic time documents (or rather, their virtual representation on the screen) are different ways of approaching the same truth: via the documents, because of the alleged indexicality of photography; and via gameplay, because it "mirrors" the events represented by these photographs.

What do players learn from these "authentic," fact-obsessed war games? Stephanie Fisher claims that World War II FPS video games can provide an engaging, immersive historical experience and can be appropriated by players to learn about World War II history. These games could be used to dispel historical myths and misinterpretations or scrutinized for historical accuracy, in turn promoting the development of critical inquiry, comparative analysis, and other disciplinary skills. Moreover, as demonstrated in this study, World War II FPS video games can function as a gateway to learning about the event, providing players with an interesting "hook" that encourages self-directed learning and also potentially shape how some players conceptualize World War II history.[18]

Fisher makes a distinction between "immersive historical experience" and "to learn about history," as the game needs to be appropriated by players to achieve the latter, critically using the game as a potentially inaccurate account of the events. Fisher comes to this conclusion, because their familiarity with First Person Shooters allowed them to question the authenticity of aspects that fell along the lines of genre conventions all to neatly:

> For instance, while the participant's [sic] agreed that hand-to-hand combat could have been a plausible experience for a soldier, they viewed the inclusion of this as a game play feature meant to give the player a break from the predictable shoot-em-up scenario, and not necessarily historically accurate.[19]

The knowledge they have extracted from the parts of the game that were subject to less suspicion led to its application in the classroom, as the students were able to define *blitzkrieg* and explain how the military introduced the flamethrower. While I appreciate Fisher's defense of games, and I agree that recognizing the textuality of the game and questioning its content due to the genre's conventions is a valuable skill, I have difficulty inferring from her data that "the domain of history-themed video games anticipates historical questioning and scrutiny, thus positioning these games as excellent facilitators for practicing historical inquiry skills."[20] Her presentation of the students' frustration with their high school history class rather highlights a preoccupation with the mechanics of warfare and an ideologically motivated interest in World War II history: they criticized their teacher for (1) not discussing the exceptional (e.g. secret missions, contributions made by brave individuals or "heroes"), and (2) learning about World War II at the macro level of nations and leaders, not the micro level everyday experiences of citizens and soldiers. These complaints describe a World War II historical experience that is strikingly similar to the delivery style and content of World War II FPS video games.[21]

So rather than encouraging self-directed learning, the games seem to spawn or reinforce a perspective of history as a narrative of conflict and sub-narratives of technological innovation (the game series primarily discussed in her article, *Medal of Honor*, *Call of Duty* and *Brothers in Arms* do not highlight the lives of civilians). When I taught a history class on the origins of Nazism, I frequently found that those — often very smart and articulate — students whose interests were informed by the materiality-obsessed heroic narratives of video gaming and The History Channel had trouble mustering up enthusiasm for learning about the cultural and social environment from which the crimes of Nazism originated. In the light of these developments, it would seem that "authentic" World War II games in their current state are not only not teaching us anything helpful, but they distract from what is really to learn from these events in Germany, since neither heroic deeds of those soldiers that shot so many enemies by themselves, nor any intimate knowledge of flame throwers will help us understand what we can do to prevent as horrific a system as Nazi Germany from happening again. Rather, it will focus our collective memory on "relatively unknown individuals who 'did something cool or heroic.'"[22]

While gamers generally are certainly clever enough to differentiate between fiction and reality, particularly given their own investment in the suspension of disbelief, by concentrating their interest in the National Socialist regime and World War II on guns and war heroes, they run the danger of satisfying their productive interest with the Nazi-ness of the fictionalized battles, enjoying the often brilliantly designed games and the simplicity of coherent, familiar narratives. Moreover, by disconnecting iconography and tropes from their historic context, such factographic games enable generically unhistoric games (horror, fantasy, etc.) to use historical markers for dramatic effect. While the technically brilliant *Call of Duty: Black Ops*, possibly in a self-aware move, added a horror-driven multiplayer game full of Nazi zombies to its own largely factographic franchise, other video game franchises like the *Wolfenstein* series are entirely based in this fictionalizing reframing of Nazi tropes.

Claiming the Swastika: Secret Agents and Nazi Magic

The simplification of history and the act of condensing it into easily accessible tropes, which can be observed in video games as much as in television shows, novels, graphic novels, film and other forms of narrative, allowed other, decidedly non-historic (or alternative-historic) genres like horror, fantasy and science fiction to integrate them into their collection of tropes. They bound the now free-floating signifier of, for example, the swastika to these genres and turned them into narrative, generic or ludic cues, which then no longer stood for Nazi Germany, but served as tools for hypervillainization.

As much as Seinfeld's "Soup Nazi" is not really a National Socialist, but a *proverbial* Nazi for his totalitarian and arbitrary rule of his restaurant, the games connect Nazi tropes to legends about the Thule Society, mystical Nazi gold and other myths that borrow from fictionalized history and conspiracy theories as well as from other fictional media and Nazi aesthetics, rather than the historical Nazis. As such, they function as *narrative cues*, pointing to a pool of narrative inventory filled by pulp fiction like Mike Mignola's *Hellboy* comics and films like *Raiders of the Lost Ark* and *Dead Snow*. Nazi tropes also function as *generic codes*, as one can expect a non-"historical" game (i.e. a game unlike those discussed above) that features Nazis to include genre elements of horror and science fiction.

Thirdly, they function as *ludic cues*, as someone wearing a swastika is most likely to be one of the protagonist's antagonists, and it is a pretty safe bet that the player should fire at them in order to advance. These cues are often embedded in other, non-history related tropes, taken from well known video games or movie genres, such as the spy movie. All this situates the player within a narrative pre-inscribed with a tradition of other narratives and their markers, superimposing the game onto a "notion" of a genre. When it succeeds, the narrative texture is presumably richer, appealing to the player's experiences *outside* of the particular game and establishing a strong connection between the player's life and the fictional space of the game. On top of this, the experience of play becomes more intuitive, as the player can draw on her experience from other games and different media to establish appropriate ways of engaging with the game.

One fairly recent example is the 2009 FPS *Wolfenstein*. As part of the franchise that was spawned with *Wolfenstein 3D* in 1992, it is set during World War II, with an American soldier called B.J. Blazkowicz fighting the Nazi regime. In particular, he faces the supernatural powers of the SS Paranormal Division. This is loosely based on the *Ahnenerbe*, a Nazi think tank associated with Heinrich Himmler, whose obsession with the occult awarded him a part in an earlier installment of the game series, 2001's *Return to Castle Wolfenstein*. Set mostly in the fictional town of Isenstadt, which harbors a major branch of the resistance, Blazkowicz investigates the Nazis' interest in crystals (named "*Nachtsonne*") that are only available in the area of the town, and that give their owner magic powers if combined with the 'Thule Medallion.' More precisely, the crystals make it possible to enter the "Veil," a limbo dimension between the "real" dimension and a dimension called "The Black Sun." The Veil also allows disguised creatures to be seen as what they "really" are. General Zetta, for example, who is likely modeled after Hermann Göring, turns out to be a mixture between a slug and an insect with gigantic muscular arms. In the course of the game, it is revealed that the Nazis attempt to wipe out the city and the resistance with a weapon powered by the Black Sun. Blazkowicz follows a Nazi military official and a scientist into the Black Sun through a portal that was excavated and rebuilt by the scientist and his unknowing students and that is now located on a Zeppelin. Defeating the major villains and destroying all the opportunities to access this dimension, Blazkowicz saves the day.

The game itself is permeated by traditions of spy, horror and science fiction narratives, as well as by the tradition of the Wolfenstein game series itself. In its opening, the game largely follows conventions of spy action movies, such as the James Bond series. Blazkowicz secretly sneaks on the German battleship Tirpitz that is about to attack London. He is discovered and as he is about to be executed, unknowingly activates the Thule Medallion he just found on the ship, killing everyone on board, destroying the ship with its own rockets, and escaping on a Nazi airplane. He is then shown at the Office of Secret Actions in London. The dialogue that takes place there between two officials (A and C) and Blazkowicz (Bl) in the office of the director of the "Office for Secret Actions" in London very openly plays on James Bond tropes:

A: Agent Blazkowicz, come in.

C: Your mission on the Tirpitz was a success, B.J. She's at the bottom of the ocean.

Bl: Thanks, but I'm more concerned about that medallion I found.

C: So are we. Dozens of specialists are studying it right now.

Bl: What have they found out?

A: Very little, but enough for us to move forward.

C: The medallion's a symbol that was used by an obscure clan of mystics; they worshipped something called the Black Sun ... [J]ust a few decades ago, the symbol was adopted by The Thule society, a German occult group that has a number of high ranking Nazis among its members.

Bl: No doubt some of them are part of the SS Paranormal Division.

A (surprised): They are indeed. But even more intriguing than that are the crystals the medallion contains.

C: They can only be found in one place on earth; a City in Germany called Isenstadt.

A: We made contact with resistance fighters of the Kreisau Circle there. They had some very interesting information.

C: This is General Victor Zetta, a rising star in Himmler's Paranormal Division. In the last few weeks, he established a large operation in Isenstadt — but what they're doing there is unknown.

Bl: So you think the medallion there was the result of Zetta's work?

A: That's what we need you to find out, Agent Blazkowicz. Your orders are to travel to Isenstadt, rendezvous with the resistance fighters and assess the situation.

C: Sorry to send you back into the field so soon, B.J., but you've dealt with this kind of thing before. You're the only man for the job.

Bl: Not a problem. When do I get started?

A: Immediately. Travel arrangements have already been made. The best of luck to you, Agent Blazkowicz.

Bl: Thank you, sir.

The opening sequence and this conversation recall a central cliché of James Bond movies. The setting is nearly identical to M's office, the British accent and the location of London certainly contribute to this, and the deliberate decision to have the American Blazkowicz work for the British is likely motivated to support the scene's Bond theme. Apart from that, the conversation follows the typical pattern:

• Greeting
• Praise about successful mission (or criticism for his carelessness)
• Briefing
• Bond/Blazkowicz surprising with his knowledge
• Immediate begin of mission (often Moneypenny hands Bond the ticket right away)

The beginning, with its one-agent-against-an-army story, and the flight from the exploding ship in an airplane, already anticipate this accumulation of James Bond tropes (even though we are not granted a gun barrel sequence). Along with the briefing mentioned above, it sets itself within a familiar narrative tradition and thus allows the player to follow pre-established decoding strategies, making the suspension of disbelief, and hence immersive play, easier to achieve. In this way, cutscenes can function along the lines of the paratexts discussed above, such as *Medal of Honor: Underground*'s gaming manual, and the "historical documents" in *Brothers in Arms*. Similarly, horror and sci-fi genre convention, such as graphic gore and monstrous creatures (e.g., living skeletons and supersized animal-human hybrids) establish further immersive generic frameworks.

This generic background, a common set of generic associations with Nazis, is then combined with iconography and aesthetics that materially invoke the Third Reich. These now have lost their original signification and trigger, as mentioned, narrative, generic or ludic cues. Let us look at two Nazi posters in the streets of *Wolfenstein*'s Isenstadt that narratively integrate the game into the series' good-vs.-evil plotlines, reinforce the connection between the game's generic cocktail and Nazi iconography, and on a ludic level rekindle player motivation to fight the game's villains. One poster, a representation of a historical poster used by the Nazis, shows Hitler in front of a red and white background (referencing the swastika flag), with a map of post–World War I [sic] Germany before him. Big Gothic letters read: "Deutschland ist frei!" ("Germany is free!"). Since the setting of the game freely floats between different periods, one can assume that the posters do not establish a specific historic setting: some posters advertise the party rally of 1939, while others demonize the United States so specifically that one would assume this to take place at a later point in time, particularly after the USA had entered the war. The game's German money, which was only in circulation from 1990 to 2002, is even less helpful in marking out a specific period.

Why did the designer choose this picture with its pre–1939 German borders? In the context of the game, it serves a different function than constructing a coherent historical setting. It speaks to general ideas of and knowledge about Nazi Germany, creating immersive substance as a result that is similar to that triggered by generic clichés. First, the later territory, including the Protectorate of Bohemia and Moravia, and the "Ostmark," appears much more as a stable unity than that defined by the earlier borders. The earlier map is more ragged on the edges, rendering it unstable and ready to change its shape, and resembles a pair of claws attempting to reach out towards East Prussia. The extension towards the East and the "reaching out" towards East Prussia visually resonates with the expansionist concept of Germany's war for *Lebensraum*, living space for the racially "purified" German people. Second, the glowing map serves as Hitler's breastplate and left shoulder pad, suggesting a unity of the dictator and the German space/people that as a homogeneous mass protect him. This helps the player to distance herself from the entirety of the population outside of the resistance (all of which are, indeed, antagonists), and thus more fully enjoy defending the avatar from them.[23] Hence, the map, while disconnected from its original historic environment, in combination with Hitler's face and the aggressive gothic font with its exclamation point, serves its message on an emotional level better than an accurately historicizing map could have done. On the other hand, it unhinges its tropes them from their original context and connects them to narrative, generic and ludic cues in a fictionalized historic space.

Other posters are not replications of historic documents, but are entirely fabricated. One example is the "*Unterstütze unsere Truppen!*" poster, a clumsy translation of "Support our Troops!" and clearly taking off from post–Vietnam popular American rhetoric. Here, the game showcases that it is its obsession with symbols and tropes, rather than historical content, that functions as an immersive mechanism in the game. We see a uniformed man — whose face is invisibly dark — wearing a fictional variation of the SS-Einsatzgruppe's uniform: SS insignia on the helmet and the collar, black epaulets and a swastika armband. The symbols and insignia are clearly the stars of the picture: as they stand out from the dark uniform and the blacked-out face neither draws any attention to itself, but rather gives a demonizing effect. The faceless soldier does not conform to historical Nazi visual propaganda that generally emphasizes the face, but rather seems informed by American World War II propaganda, such as Grothe's famous "He's Watching You" poster and the animated short *Education for Death*. The symbols connect with the game's texture in a similar way as the "Deutschland ist frei!" poster, presenting the player with fake German propaganda based on American aesthetics of the time to create an immersive, subjective perception of historicity. By rendering the soldier faceless, this image also dehumanizes the game's antagonists, encouraging the player to fight them, just like the American propaganda had done. Opening them up to the American audience's experiences by using American slogans and 1940s American propaganda aesthetics, creating the illusion of historical accuracy, these symbols become connected to a different linguistic and aesthetic setting, determined less by their connection to Nazism than by their application in the game's world.

Instead of using the immense potential that video games have, their inability to meaningfully address historical trauma thus leaves them with the scraps of a history — the symbols, icons and aesthetics; empty signifiers that become recycled and disconnected from their original context.

Cultural Capital and Legitimacy of the Messenger: Why We Can't Play Anne Frank

So why is the serious engagement with this chapter of German history a taboo for video games, when it is permissible for other media to address it? For one, while graphic novels (and films and literature, for that matter) have also had to struggle to rise above the low cultural status of pulp for children or the "ignorant masses," ever since Art Spiegelman's *Maus* and its Pulitzer prize in 1992, an explicitly adult treatment of the Holocaust has been universally recognized as an artistic achievement. Similarly, the association of works of literature — including even comic books — and film with the creative agency an individual or a small circle of artistic minds[24] differs from the conception of video games as connected to a production company solely interested in profit, rather than an artistic vision or a respectful treatment of the subject matter. Moreover, the concept of play, games and toys is rarely seen as transcending the world of children. Thus, there is a direct, if tangled, line between the respectability of the medium of video games (in particular that of the genre First Person Shooter) and its inability to address history in a productive way in Adorno's sense.

Possibly one of the most illuminating examples of this is Germany's way of dealing with symbols of unconstitutional organizations (the swastika being one example) in different media. While the law permits using them to further "civic education, the defense against unconstitutional endeavors, art or science, research or teaching, the coverage of past events or history or similar ends,"[25] as of today, popular video games have never qualified as educational or artistic. As a result, video games are not allowed to use these symbols, bringing about alternative versions of games like *Wolfenstein* for the German market, in which the swastika is exchanged for the iron cross, and the SS runes are erased altogether. I believe that due to the heavy censorship that German gamers are generally faced with, they trust the games' iconography even less than Americans, knowing that they are not playing the game's "real" version. But whether this anachronistic mistrust of the medium is useful, leaving it to other media to decontextualize these symbols, or whether it only impedes the evolution of gaming into a effective new way of conveying knowledge is a question with an obvious answer — independent of whether such a restriction of free speech suits a country that calls itself a democracy. It is symptomatic of a wider phenomenon with which the not-yet-mature medium of the video game has to deal. While it is legitimate to turn Anne Frank's tragic fate into a sappy Hollywood drama, it is not socially acceptable for games to address the most meaningful questions of what many Germans refer to as their history's "darkest chapter." The medium is preoccupied with pulp tropes and iconography, detaching them from their original context and handing them over to genres that choose factographic fiction over the material representation of historical reality, depriving the images of their original meaning, thus contributing to the inevitable difficulty in understanding the past and the impossibility to see "what actually happened."

That Nazism has shifted into a set of signifiers deprived of significant ethical weight shows in the reactions to multiplayer scenarios in *Wolfenstein* and *Medal of Honor*. The latter originally intended to have the player reenact conflicts between the Taliban and the U.S. Army and caused such outrage by allowing the player to take the Taliban's side that Electronic Arts eventually renamed the foreign party to "Opposing Forces." *Wolfenstein*, however, offering both the side of the Nazis ("Axis") and that of their opponents ("Allies") to the player, failed to stir up any controversy. Apparently, we have come to accept that Nazis aren't really "the" Nazis, because those in our media are paradoxically just too perfect a villain to have caused the death of millions, and most of the current representations of Nazism are less likely to leave us with usable knowledge of Germany during the NSDAP's rule, than with an uncomfortable feeling about our own culture, in which these representations arose.

Notes

1. Jameson, *Postmodernism* 66.
2. See Sobchack, "What My Fingers Knew."

3. John 20:25, *King James Bible.*
4. Kracauer, *Theory of Film* 297.
5. "So widerwärtig!"
6. Schneider, "'Mauer-Shooter.'"
7. Ibid.
8. Sobchack 59.
9. Sobchack 67.
10. Sobchack 68–9.
11. Sobchack 70–1.
12. Heckner, "Choice and Freedom."
13. Wolf, *Medium* 109.
14. Kingsepp, "Immersive Historicity" 72.
15. Kingsepp 69.
16. Ibid.
17. Rejack, "Toward" 418.
18. Fisher, "Playing" 83.
19. Fisher 80.
20. Fisher 81.
21. Fisher 79.
22. Ibid.
23. Heckner "Constructive Carnage."
24. Cf. Truffaut.
25. See StGB §86 (3) in the Federal German Constitution.

Works Cited

Books and Articles

Advanced Intel Tracking System. <http://stats. spymasterzombie.com/node?page=92> Accessed 15 Mar. 2010.

Anderson, Leon, and Jimmy D. Taylor. "Standing Out While Fitting In: Serious Leisure Identities and Aligning Actions Among Skydivers and Gun Collectors." *Journal of Contemporary Ethnography* 39.34 (2010): 34–59.

Andrejevic, Mark. *Reality TV: The Work of Being Watched.* Lanham, MD: Rowman and Littlefield, 2004.

Ang, Ien. *Watching Dallas: Soap Opera and the Melodramatic Imagination.* London: Routledge, 1985.

Apter, Michael J. *Danger: Our Quest for Excitement.* London: Oneworld Publications, 2007.

_____. *The Dangerous Edge.* Mankato, MN: The Free Press, 1992.

_____. *Reversal Theory: The Dynamics of Motivation, Emotion and Personality.* London: Oneworld Publications, 2006.

Arjoranta, Jonne. "Defining Role-Playing Games as Language Games." *International Journal of Role-Playing* 2 (2011): 3–17.

Aronson, Elliot, Timothy Wilson and Robin Akert. *Social Psychology.* 6th ed. New York: Pearson, 2005.

Asch, Solomon. "Effects of Group Pressure Upon the Modification and Distortion of Judgements." H. Guetzkow, ed. *Groups, Leadership, and Men.* Pittsburgh: Carnegie Press, 1951.

Atkins, Barry. *More Than a Game: The Computer Game as Fictional Form.* Manchester, UK: Manchester University Press, 2003.

_____, and Tanya Krzywinska. *Videogame, Player, Text.* Manchester, UK: Manchester University Press, 2008.

Balsera, Leonard. "Do We Really Know GNS When We See It?" *Story Games.* (2009) <http://story-games.com/forums/comments.php? DiscussionID=9646& page=1#Item_52> Accessed 1 August 2011.

Balzer, Myriel. "Das Erzeugen Von Immersion Im Live-Rollenspiel." Dombroski, K., ed. *Larp: Einblicke. Aufsatzsammlung Zum Mittelpunkt 2010.* Brunswick, Germany: Zauberfeder, 2010. 17–33.

_____. "Immersion as a Prerequisite of the Didactical Potential of Role-Playing." *International Journal of Role-Playing* 2 (2011).

Bandura, A., B. Underwood, and M. E. Fromson. "Disinhibition of Aggression Through Diffusion of Responsibility and Dehumanization of Victims." *Journal of Research in Personality* 9 (1975): 253–269.

Bankov, K. "A Sociosemiotic Model of the Standards for Discourse Validation." R. S. Hatten, ed. *A Sounding of Signs.* Imatra, Finland: International Semiotic Institute, 2008: 253–74.

Barrowcliffe, Mark. *The Elfish Gene: Dungeons, Dragons, and Growing Up Strange.* New York: Soho, 2007.

Beller, Jonathan. *The Cinematic Mode of Production: Attention Economy and the Society of the Spectacle.* Hanover, NH: Darmouth University Press, 2006.

"The Bill W.— Carl Jung Letters." *The AA Grapevine. Silkworth.net's Project.* (January 1963). <http://www.silkworth.net>. Accessed 30 July 2011.

Björk, Staffan, and Jussi Holopainen. *Patterns in Game Design.* Boston: Charles River Media, 2004.

Boal, Augusto. *Games for Actors and Non-Actors.* London: Routledge, 2002.

Boellstorff, Tom. *Coming of Age in Second Life: An Anthropologist Explores the Virtually Human.* Princeton, NJ: Princeton University Press, 2008.

Bogost, Ian. *Persuasive Games: The Expressive*

Power of Videogames. Cambridge, MA: MIT Press, 2007.

Bond, E. J. "The Essential Nature of Art." *American Philosophical Quarterly* 12 (1975): 177–183.

Bond, Eston. "On Spymaster's Virality." *Eston Bond.com*. (29 May 2009) Accessed 15 July 2011.

Boss, Emily Care. "Thoughts on Why Immersion Is a Tar Baby." *The Forge Forums Read-Only Archives*. (2002) <http://indie-rpgs.com/archive/index.php?topic=4640> Accessed 1 August 2011.

_____. "Collaborative Role-Playing: Reframing the Game." *Push #1*. (2006) http://bleed ingplay.wordpress.com/push/collaborative-roleplaying

_____. "Key Concepts in Forge Theory." Markus Montola and Jaakko Stenros, eds. *Playground Worlds: Creating and Evaluating Experiences of Role-Playing Games*. Jyvaskyla, Finland: Ropecon ry, 2008: 232–47.

Bowman, Sarah Lynne. *The Functions of Role-Playing Games: How Participants Create Community, Solve Problems, and Explore Identity*. Jefferson, NC: McFarland, 2010.

Boyer, Pascal. *Religion Explained: The Evolutionary Origins of Religious Thought*. New York: Basic Books, 2001.

Brier, Søren. *Cybersemiotics: Why Information Is Not Enough!* Toronto: University of Toronto Press, 2008.

Caldwell, John Thornton. *Televisuality, Style, Crisis and Authority in American Television*. New Brunswick, NJ: Rutgers University Press, 1995.

Calleja, Gordon. *In-Game: From Immersion to Incorporation*. Cambridge, MA: MIT Press, 2011.

Campbell, Joseph. *The Hero with a Thousand Faces*. Princeton, NJ: Princeton University Press, 1973.

Carroll, Joseph. *Literary Darwinism: Evolution, Human Nature, and Literature*. New York: Routledge, 2004.

Carroll, Noël. *The Philosophy of Horror: Or, Paradoxes of the Heart*. New York: Routledge, 1990.

Casement, Patrick J. *Learning from the Patient*. New York: Guilford Press, 1992.

Charvill, Ian. "Invention as a Creative Agenda." *The Forge Forums Read-Only Archive*. (2003) <http://indie-rpgs.com/ar chive/index.php?topic=8108.0.> Accessed 1 August 2011.

Chen, Mark G. "Communication, Coordination, and Camaraderie in *World of War-craft*." *Games and Culture* 4.1 (2009): 47–73.

Chomsky, Noam. *Syntactic Structures*. Berlin, Germany: Walter de Gruyter, 1957.

Cohen, David, and Stephen A. MacKeith. *The Development of Imagination: The Private Worlds of Childhood*. London: Routledge, 1991.

Consalvo, Mia. *Cheating: Gaining Advantage in Videogames*. Cambridge, MA: MIT Press, 2007.

_____. "There Is No Magic Circle." *Games and Culture* 4.4 (2009): 408–417.

Costikiyan, Greg. "I Have No Words and I Must Design." (1994) <http://www.costik. com/nowords.html> Accessed 30 September 2011.

Cover, Jennifer Grouling. *The Creation of Narrative in Tabletop Role-Playing Games*. Jefferson, NC: McFarland, 2010.

Cox, Stephanie. *Lessons from the Stanford Prison Experiment*. (2008) <http://human-testing.suite101.com> Accessed. 20 November 2011.

Crew, Richard E. "Viewer Interpretations of Reality Television: How Real Is *Survivor* for Its Viewers?" David S. Escoffery, ed. *How Real Is Reality TV?* Jefferson, NC: McFarland, 2006.

Csikszentmihalyi, Mihaly. *Beyond Boredom and Anxiety: Experiencing Flow in Work and Play*. San Francisco: Jossey-Bass, 1975.

_____. *Flow: The Psychology of Optimal Experience*. New York: Harper & Row, 1990.

Daegmorgan, Ravenscrye Grey. "Immersion, Childishness, and Understanding." *The Forge Forums Read-Only Archives*. (2005) <http://indie-rpgs.com/archive/ index.php ?topic=16135.0>. Accessed 1 August 2011.

Daly, Kristen. "Cinema 3.0: The Interactive Image." *Cinema Journal* 50.1 (Fall 2010): 81–98.

Dawkins, Richard. "Memes: The New Replicators." *The Selfish Gene*. 30th Anniversary Edition. Oxford: Oxford University Press, 2006.

Day, David. *The World of Tolkien: Mythological Sources of* The Lord of the Rings. New York: Gramercy Books, 2003.

Deuker, Carl. *On the Devil's Court*. Burlington, VT: Paw Print Press, 2008.

Dinehart, Stephen. "Journey of Jin & Transmedial Play." MFA Thesis. University of Southern California, 2006.

Dissanayake, Ellen. *Homo Aestheticus: Where Art Comes From and Why*. Seattle: University of Washington Press, 1995.

Douglas, J.Y., and A. Hargadon. "The Pleasures of Immersion and Engagement: Schemas, Scripts, and the Fifth Business." *Digital Creativity* 12.3 (2001): 153–66.

drhoover. "[Fiasco] in a Nice Southern Town..." *Story Games*. (2010) <http://indie-rpgs.com/archive/index.php?topic=29240.0> Accessed 4 October 2011.

Durkheim, Emile. *The Elementary Forms of Religious Life*. Oxford, UK: Oxford University Press, 2001.

Dutton, Denis. *The Art Instinct: Beauty, Pleasure, and Human Evolution*. New York: Bloomsbury Press, 2009.

_____. "A Naturalist Definition of Art." *Journal of Aesthetics and Art Criticism* 64 (2006): 367–377.

Edwards, Ron. "All-Out Dissection (Long and Brutal)." *The Forge Forums Read-Only Archives*. (2001) <http://indie-rpgs.com/archive/index.php? topic=24.0> Accessed 1 August 2011.

_____. "Beating a Dead Horse." *The Forge Forums Read-Only Archives*. (2008) <http://indie-rpgs.com/archive/index.php?topic=25417.0> Accessed 1 August 2011.

_____. "Feeble Attempt at Defining Immersion." *The Forge Forums Read-Only Archives*. (2002) <http://www.indie-rpgs.com/archive/index.php?topic=3654> Accessed 10 September 2010.

_____. "GNS and Other Matters of Role-Playing Theory." *The Forge*. (2001) <www.indie-rpgs.com/articles/1/> Accessed 1 August 2011.

_____. "Narrativism: Story Now." *The Forge Forums Read-Only Archives*. (2003) <http://www.indie-rpgs.com/_articles/narr_essay.html> Accessed September 2011.

_____. "The Provisional Glossary." *The Forge*. (2004) <http://indie-rpgs.com/_articles/glossary.html> Accessed 29 September 2008.

_____. "System Does Matter." (1999) http://www.indie-rpgs.com/_articles/system_does_matter.html.

_____. "Understanding the Pool." *Adept Press*. (2010) <http://adept-press.com/ wordpress/wp-content/media/Understanding_The_Pool.pdf> Accessed 1 August 2011.

_____. "The Whole Model — This Is It." *The Forge Forums Read-Only Archives*. (2003) <http://indie-rpgs.com/archive/index.php?topic=8655> Accessed 1 August 2011.

Elias, Marilyn. "One *Kid Nation* Under Fire." *USA Today* (25 September 2007).

Ericsson, Martin. "Play to Love: Reading Victor Turner's 'Liminal to Liminoid in Play, Flow, and Ritual; an Essay in Comparative Symbology.'" Markus Montola and Jaakko Stenros, eds. *Beyond Role and Play: Tools, Toys, and Theory for Harnessing the Imagination*. Helsinki, Finland: Ropecon ry, 2004: 15–30.

Erikson, Erik H. *Identity and the Life Cycle*. New York: W.W. Norton, 1980.

Ermi, Laura, and Frans Mäyrä. "Fundamental Components of the Gameplay Experience: Analyzing Immersion." Suzanne De Castell and Jennifer Jenson, eds. *Worlds in Play: International Perspectives on Digital Games Research*. New York: Peter Lang, 2007: 37–53.

"Exclusive Interview with *Survivor*: Heroes vs. Villains' Jerri Manthey." *Buddytv.com*. (3 January 2010) <http://www.buddytv.com/articles/survivor/exclusive-interview-with-survi-33710.aspx> Accessed 4 April 2011.

Fatland, Erik. "Can Playing Games Teach Us About War?" Presentation at Nordic Larp Talks 2011. <http://www.nordiclarptalks.org> Accessed 1 August 2011.

_____. "1942 — Nåen å stole på? Role-Playing Living Memory." Jaakko Stenros and Markus Montola, eds. *Nordic Larp*. Stockholm: Fëa Livia, 2010.

Feagin, Susan L. "The Pleasures of Tragedy." *American Philosophical Quarterly* 20.1 (1983): 95–104.

Fernandez, Maria Elena. "Is Child Exploitation Legal in *Kid Nation*?" *Los Angeles Times*. (17 August 2007).

Festinger, L. *A Theory of Cognitive Dissonance*. Stanford, CA: Stanford University Press, 1985.

_____, A. Pepitone, and T. Newcomb. "Some Consequences of Deindividuation in a Group." *Journal of Abnormal and Social Psychology* 47 (1952).

Fine, Gary Alan. *Shared Fantasy: Role-Playing Games as Social Worlds*. Chicago: University of Chicago Press, 1983.

Firchow, Peter E. *Modern Utopian Fictions*. Washington, DC: Catholic University of America Press, 2007.

Fisher, Stephanie. "Playing with World War II: A Small-Scale Study of Learning in Video Games." *Loading...: The Journal of the Canadian Game Studies Association* 5.8 (2011): 71.

Frasca, Gonzalo. "Ludologists Love Stories, Too: Notes from a Debate That Never Took Place." *Digital Games Research Association (DIGRA)* (2003). Accessed February 12,

2009 <http://www.digra.org/dl/db/05163.01125>.

Frazer, James G. *The Golden Bough*. New York: Avenel Books, 1981.

Fromm, Erich. *The Sane Society*. New York: Macmillan, 1990.

Gallagher, Tag. *John Ford: The Man and His Movies*. Berkeley: University of California Press, 1988.

Galloway, Alexander R. *Gaming: Essays on Algorithmic Culture*. Electronic Mediations 18. Minneapolis: University of Minnesota Press, 2006.

Gaut, Berys. "Art as a Cluster Concept." Noël Carroll, ed. *Theories of Art Today*. Madison: University of Wisconsin Press, 2000.

_____. "The Enjoyment Theory of Horror: A Response to Carroll." *British Journal of Aesthetics* 35.3 (1995): 284–289.

Geertz, Clifford. *The Interpretation of Cultures*. New York: Basic Books, 1973.

Genette, Gérard. *Palimpsests: Literature in the Second Degree*. Lincoln: University of Nebraska Press, 1997.

Genosko, Gary. *McLuhan and Baudrillard: The Masters of Implosion*. London: Routledge, 1999.

Giddens, Anthony. *Modernity and Self-Identity: Self and Society in the Late Modern Age*. Stanford, CA: Stanford University Press, 1991.

Gillespie, D., A. Leffler, and E. Lerner. "If It Weren't for My Hobby, I'd Have a Life: Dog Sports, Serious Leisure, and Boundary Negotiation." *Leisure Studies* 21 (2002): 285–304.

Goffman, Erving. *The Presentation of Self in Everyday Life*. New York: Bantam Doubleday Dell, 1959.

Golding, William. *Lord of the Flies*. New York: Capricorn, 1959.

Goodman, Ellen. "Barbarians at the *Kid Nation* Gate." *Boston Globe* (28 September 2007): 15A.

Gotthard, Pavel, and Jiri Zlatohlávek. "Children of a Freedom Clock." Elge Larsson, ed. *Playing Reality*. Knutpunkt, 2010. <http://interactingarts.org/pdf/ Playing%20Reality%20(2010).pdf>

Gras, Vernon. "Myth and the Reconciliation of Opposites: Jung and Levi-Strauss." *Journal of the History of Ideas* 42.3 (July–Sept. 1981): 471–488.

Gräslund, Susanne. "Europa: Intimate Refugee Role Reversal." Jaakko Stenros and Markus Montola, eds. *Nordic Larp*. Stockholm: Fëa Livia, 2010.

Grodal, Torben. *Embodied Visions: Evolution, Emotion, Culture, and Film*. New York: Oxford University Press, 2009.

_____. *Moving Pictures: A New Theory of Film Genres, Feelings, and Cognition*. Gloucestershire, UK: Clarendon Press, 1999.

Grossman, Dave. *On Killing: The Psychological Cost of Learning to Kill in War and Society*. New York: Back Bay Books, 1997.

Hakkarainen, Henri, and Jaakko Stenros. "The Meilahti School: Thoughts on Role-Playing." Morten Gade, Line Thorup and Mikkel Sander, eds. *As Larp Grows Up*. Frederiksberg, Denmark: Knudepunkt, 2003. 54–64.

Hall, Stuart. "Minimal Selves." *ICA Documents* 6 (1988): 44–46.

Harding, Tobias. "Immersion Revisited: Role-Playing as Interpretation and Narrative." Jesper Donnis, Morten Gade and Line Thorup, eds. *Lifelike*. Frederiksberg, Denmark: Projektgruppen KP07, 2007: 24–33.

Harrigan, Pat, and Noah Wardrip-Fruin. *First Person: New Media as Story, Performance, and Game*. Cambridge, MA: MIT Press, 2006.

_____. *Second Person: Role-Playing and Story in Games and Playable Media*. Cambridge, MA: MIT Press, 2007.

_____. *Third Person: Authoring and Exploring Vast Narratives*. Cambridge, MA: MIT Press, 2009.

Harviainen, J. Tuomas. "Corresponding Expectations: Alternative Approaches to Enhanced Game Presence." *Dissecting Larp*. Petter Bøckmann and Ragnhild Hutchison, eds. Oslo, Norway: Knutepunkt, 2005: 71–79.

_____. "Information, Immersion, Identity: The Interplay of Multiple Selves During Live-Action Role-Play." *Journal of Interactive Drama* 1.2 (2006): 9–51.

_____. "The Larping That Is Not Larp." Thomas Duus Henriksen, et al., eds. *Think Larp: Academic Writings from KP2011*. Copenhagen, Denmark: Rollespilsakademiet, 2011: 172–193.

_____. "The Multi-Tier Game Immersion Theory." *As Larp Grows Up: Theory and Methods in Larp*. Morten Gade, Line Thorup and Mikkel Sander, eds. Frederiksberg, Denmark: Projektsgruppen KP03, 2003.

_____, and Andreas Lieberoth. "The Similarity of Social Information Processes in Games and Rituals: Magical Interfaces." *Simulation & Gaming* (10 April 2011).

Haslam, Alex, and Steve Reicher. "BBC

Prison Study Official Website." *BBC.* <http://www.bbcprisonstudy.org/> Accessed 20 November 2011.

Hassan, Robert, and Julian Thomas, eds. *The New Media Theory Reader.* New York: McGraw-Hill, 2006.

Heckner, M.-Niclas. "Choice and Freedom in Generic Conventions." *PCA/ACA.* San Antonio Marriott Rivercenter Hotel, San Antonio, TX. 22 April 2011. Conference Presentation.

_____. "Constructive Carnage: Violent Gameplay as Affective Ethical Instruction." Michigan State University. East Lansing, MI. 23 October 2010. Conference Presentation.

Hedges, Chris. *Empire of Illusion: The End of Literacy and the Triumph of the Spectacle.* New York: Nation Books, 2009.

Heliö, Satu. "Role-Playing: A Narrative Experience and a Mindset." Markus Montola and Jaakko Stenros, eds. *Beyond Role and Play.* Helsinki, Finland: Ropecon ry, 2004: 65–74.

Hendricks, Sean Q. "Incorporating Discourse Strategies in Tabletop Fantasy Role-Playing Gaming." J. Patrick Williams, Sean Q. Hendricks and W. Keith Winkler, eds. *Gaming as Culture: Essays on Reality, Identity, and Experience in Fantasy Games.* Jefferson, NC: McFarland, 2006: 39–56.

Henricks, Thomas S. *Play Reconsidered: Sociological Perspectives on Human Expression.* Champaign: University of Illinois Press, 2006.

Hill, Annette. *Reality TV: Audiences and Popular Factual Television.* New York: Routledge, 2005.

Hindmarch, Will, ed. *The Bones: Us and Our Dice.* Alexandria, VA: Atomic Overmind Press, 2010.

"History, Reliability and Validity of the Myers-Briggs Type Indicator (MBTI) Instrument." *CPP.* (2009) <http://www.CPP.com> Accessed 30. July 2011.

Hitchens, Michael, and Anders Drachen. "The Many Faces of Role-Playing Games." *International Journal of Role-Playing* 1 (2008): 3–21.

Hjørland, B., and H. Albrechtsen. "Toward a New Horizon in Information Science: Domain Analysis." *Journal of the American Society for Information Science* 46.6 (1995): 400–25.

Hodman, T., and M. Jacquard. "Leisure Activity Patterns and Marital Satisfaction." *Journal of Family Issues* 50 (1988): 59–77.

Hoerschelmann, Olaf. *Rules of the Game.* Albany: State University Press of New York, 2006.

Holstein, James A., and Jaber F. Gubrium. *The Self We Live By: Narrative Identity in a Postmodern World.* Oxford: Oxford University Press, 2000.

Holter, Matthijs. "Stop Saying Immersion." Jesper Donnis, Morten Gade and Line Thorup, eds. *Lifelike.* Frederiksberg, Denmark: Projektgruppen KP07, 2007: 18–22.

Homans, Peter. *Jung in Context: Modernity and the Making of a Psychology.* Chicago: University of Chicago Press, 1995.

Hook, Nathan. "Larp of a Thousand Faces: Applying Mythic Structure to Larp." Elge Larsson, ed. *Playing Reality.* Knutpunkt 2010. Stockholm, Sweden: Interacting Arts, 2010.

Hopeametsä, Heidi. "24 Hours in a Bomb Shelter: Player, Character, and Immersion in Ground Zero." Jaakko Stenros and Markus Montola, eds. *Playground Worlds.* Helsinki, Finland: Ropecon ry, 2008: 187–98.

Huizinga, Johan. *Homo Ludens: A Study of Play Element in Culture.* Boston: Beacon Press, 1955.

Hume, David. *The Natural History of Religion.* New York: Macmillan, 1992.

Hunt, S.J. "But We're Men Aren't We! Living History as a Site of Masculine Identity Construction." *Men and Masculinities* 10 (2008): 460–83.

Hyde, Louis. *Trickster Makes This World.* New York: North Point Press, 1999.

Jameson, Fredric. *Postmodernism; or, The Cultural Logic of Late Capitalism.* Durham: Duke University Press, 1991.

Jenkins, Henry. *Convergence Culture: Where Old and New Media Collide.* New York: New York University Press, 2008.

_____. *Textual Poachers: Television Fans and Participatory Culture.* Studies in Culture and Communication. New York: Routledge, 1992.

Jenkins, Richard. *Social Identity: Key Ideas.* London: Routledge, 2008.

Jung, Carl G., and M.-L. von Franz, eds. *Liber Novus: The Red Book.* Sonu Shamdasani, ed. Mark Kyburz and John Peck, trans. New York: W. W. Norton, 2009.

_____, and _____. *Man and His Symbols.* London, UK: Dell Publishing, 1964.

_____. *The Portable Jung.* Joseph Campbell, ed. R. F. C. Hull, trans. New York: Penguin Books, 1976.

Juul, Jesper. *Half-Real: Video Games Between Real Rules and Fictional Worlds.* Cambridge, MA: MIT Press, 2005.

Kahneman, Daniel. "Objective Happiness." Daniel Kahneman, Ed Diener, and Norbert Schwarz, eds. *Well-Being: The Foundations of Hedonic Psychology.* New York: Russel Sage, 1999: 3–25.

Kellermann, Peter F. *Focus on Psychodrama: The Therapeutic Aspects of Psychodrama.* London: Jessica Kingsley, 1992.

Kiecolt, K. Jill. "Self Change in Social Movements." Sheldon Stryker, Timothy J. Owens and Robert W. White, eds. *Self, Identity and Social Movements.* Minneapolis: University of Minnesota Press, 2000: 110–131.

Kilborn, Richard. *Staging the Real: Factual TV Programming in the Age of* Big Brother. Manchester: Manchester University Press, 2003.

Kim, John H. "Immersive Story." Markus Montola and Jaakko Stenros, eds. *Beyond Role and Play.* Helsinki, Finland: Ropecon ry, 2004: 31–38.

_____. "Simulationism Revisited." *The Forge Forums Read-Only Archive.* (2003) <http://indie-rpgs.com/archive/index.php?topic=9104.0> Accessed August 1 2011.

_____. "Who Are Role-Players?" (2008) <http://darkshire.net/jhkim/rpg/whatis/demographics.html> Accessed 8 August 2011.

Kimmel, M. "Consuming Manhood." L. Goldstein, ed. *The Male Body: Features, Destinies, Exposures.* Ann Arbor: University of Michigan Press, 1994: 12–43.

_____. *Manhood in America: A Cultural History.* New York: Free Press, 1996.

Kingsepp, Eva. "Immersive Historicity in World War II Digital Games." *HUMAN IT* 8.2 (2006): 60–89.

Kirby, Stacia. "Gen Con Indy 2011 Shatters All Previous Attendance Records." *Gen Con. Gen Con, LLC.* <http://www.gencon.com> Accessed 11 August 2011.

Kornberger, Martin, et al. "The Others of Hierarchy: Rhizomatics of Organising." Martin Fuglsang and Bent Meier Sørensen, eds. *Deleuze and the Social.* Edinburgh: Edinburgh University Press, 2006.

Kracauer, Siegfried. *Theory of Film: The Redemption of Physical Reality.* New York: Oxford University Press, 1960.

Kuhn, Thomas. *The Structure of Scientific Revolutions.* Chicago: University of Chicago Press, 1996.

Lacan, Jacques. *The Language of the Self: The Function of Language in Psychoanalysis.* Baltimore, MD: Johns Hopkins University Press, 1968.

Lahti, Martti. "As We Become Machines: Corporealized Pleasures in Video Games." Bernard Perron, ed. *The Video Game Reader.* New York: Psychology Press, 2003.

Lalancette Marie-France, and Lionel Standing. "Asch Fails Again." *Social Behaviour and Personality* 18.1 (1990): 7–12.

Lamont, Michele. *The Dignity of Working Men: Morality and the Boundaries of Race, Class, and Immigration.* Cambridge, MA: Harvard University Press, 2000.

_____, and Virag Molnar. "The Study of Boundaries in the Social Sciences." *Annual Review of Sociology* 28 (2002): 167–195.

Lappi, Ari-Pekka. "Contra-Moral of Play: From Ethics of Gaming Toward Ethics of Playing." Elge Larsson, ed. *Playing Reality.* Stockholm: Interacting Arts, 2010.

_____. "Playing Beyond Facts: Immersion as a Transformation of Everydayness." *Lifelike.* Jesper Donnis, Morten Gade and Line Thorup, eds. Frederiksberg, Denmark: Projektgruppen KP07, 2007: 74–79.

Laurendeau, J., and N. Sharara. "Women Could Be Every Bit as Good as Guys: Reproductive and Resistant Agency in Two 'Action' Sports." *Journal of Sport and Social Issues* 32 (2008): 24–47.

Lawler, Steph. *Identity: Sociological Perspectives.* Malden, MA: Polity Press, 2008.

Lehman, Ben. "CA Classification and Game Systems." *The Forge Forums Read-Only Archive.* (2004) <http://indie-rpgs.com/archive/index.php?topic=12002.0>. Accessed 1 August 2011.

Lehrich, Christopher I. "Ritual Discourse in Role-playing Games." *The Forge Forums Read-Only Archive.* (Oct. 2005) Web. Accessed 1 Apr. 2011.

Leppälahti, Merja. "About the Community of Role-Players." Markus Montola and Jaakko Stenros, eds. *Beyond Role and Play.* Helsinki, Finland: Ropecon ry, 2004: 289–96.

Levi-Strauss, Claude. *Structural Anthropology.* Claire Jacobson and Brooke Grundfest Schoepf, trans. Garden City, NY: Anchor Books, 1967.

Lindenfeld, David. "Jungian Archetypes and the Discourse of History." *Rethinking History* 13.2 (June 2009): 217–234.

Littleton, Cynthia. "Eye Is Standing Behind Its 'Kid.'" *Daily Variety* (24 August 2007).

Loponen, Mika, and Markus Montola. "A Semiotic View on Diegesis Construction."

Markus Montola and Jaakko Stenros, eds. *Beyond Role and Play*. Helsinki, Finland: Ropecon ry, 2004: 39–52.

Lortz, Stephen L. "Role-Playing." *Different Worlds* 1 (1979): 36–41.

Lukka, Lauri. "The Dual-Faceted Role." Thomas Duus Henriksen, et al., eds. *Think Larp*. Copenhagen, Denmark: Rollespilsakademiet, 2011: 152–71.

MacCallum-Stewart, Esther and Justin Parsler. "Illusory Agency in Vampire: The Masquerade — Bloodlines." *Dichtung Digital*. (2007) <http://dichtung-digital.mewi.unibas.ch/2007/Stewart%26Parsler/maccallumstewart_parsler.htm> Accessed 11 October 2011.

MacKay, Daniel. *The Fantasy Role-Playing Game: A New Performing Art*. Jefferson, NC: McFarland, 2001.

Malaby, Thomas. "Beyond Play: A New Approach to Games." *Games and Culture* 2.2 (2007): 95–115.

Marcuse, Herbert. "Repressive Tolerance." Robert Paul Wolff, Barrington Moore, Jr., and Herbert Marcuse, eds. *A Critique of Pure Tolerance*. Boston: Beacon Press, 1969: 95–137.

Martinez, Michelle, and Tyler Manolovitz. "Incest, Sexual Violence, and Rape in Video Games." *Videogame Cultures & the Future of Interactive Entertainment*. Conference (10–12 July 2009). Oxford, UK.

Masters, Kim. "*Kid Nation* Raises Controversy Ahead of Air." *NPR Morning Edition*. (3 August 2007) <http://www.npr.org/templates/story/story.php?storyId=12476751>. Accessed 1 September 2011.

"Mayor [*sic*] Glitch When Merging." *GetSatisfaction.com*. (31 Aug. 2009) Web. Accessed 30 March 2010.

McFarland, Sam, and Thomas Carnahan. "A Situation's First Powers Are Attracting Volunteers and Selecting Participants: A Reply to Haney and Zimbardo." *Personality and Social Psychology Bulletin* 35 (June 2009): 815–818.

McGonigal, Jane. *Reality Is Broken: Why Games Make Us Better and How They Can Change the World*. New York: Penguin Press, 2011.

_____. "This Might Be a Game: Ubiquitous Play and Performance at the Turn of the Twenty-First Century." Doctoral Dissertation, University of California Berkeley, 2006.

_____. "Why *I Love Bees*: A Case Study in Collective Intelligence Gaming." Katie

Salen, ed. *The Ecology of Games: Connecting Youth, Games, and Learning*. Cambridge, MA: MIT Press, 2008.

Mead, George Herbert. *Mind, Self, and Society: From the Standpoint of a Social Behaviorist*. Chicago: University of Chicago Press, 1934.

Mello, Heather L. "Invoking the Avatar: Gaming Skills as Cultural and Out-of-Game Capital." J. Patrick Williams, Sean Q. Hendricks, and W. Keith Winkler, eds. *Gaming as Culture: Essays on Reality, Identity and Experience in Fantasy Games*. Jefferson, NC: McFarland, 2006: 175–95.

Meloy, Mike. "From *Kid Nation* to Caste Nation: Mobility, Privilege, and the Paradox of Class on Reality Television." *Americana: The Journal of American Popular Culture* 8.1 (Spring 2009) <http://www.americanpopularculture.com/ journal/articles/spring_2009/meloy.htm> Accessed 5 August 2011.

Melucci, Alberto. *Challenging Codes: Collective Action in the Information Age*. Cambridge: Cambridge University Press, 1996.

"Merging Multiple Accounts Money and Points Bug Is Ruining Spymaster." *GetSatisfaction.com*. (31 August 2009) Web. 4 April 2010.

Mignola, Mike. *Hellboy: Wake the Devil*. Milwaukee: Dark Horse Comics, 1996.

Milgram, Stanley. "Behavioral Study of Obedience." *Journal of Abnormal and Social Psychology* 67 (1963): 371–378.

_____. *Obedience to Authority: An Experimental View*. New York: Harper Perennial, 1983.

Mittel, Jason. "All in the Game: *The Wire*, Serial Storytelling, and Procedural Logic." Pat Harrigan and Noah Wardrip-Fruin, eds. *Third Person: Authoring and Exploring Vast Narratives*. Cambridge, MA: MIT Press, 2009: 429–438.

Montola, Markus. "The Invisible Rules of Role-Playing: The Social Framework of Role-Playing Process." *International Journal of Role-Playing* 1 (2008): 22–36.

_____. "The Positive Negative Experience in Extreme Role-Playing." *Proceedings of Nordic DiGRA 2010*. Stockholm, Sweden. <http://www.digra.org/dl/db/10343.56524.pdf>.

_____. (forthcoming). "Social Constructionism for Ludology." *Simulation & Gaming* 2012.

_____, Stenros, Jaakko, and Annika Waern, eds. *Pervasive Games: Theory and Design*. Burlington, MA: Morgan Kaufman, 2009.

Moravcsik, Julius. "Why Philosophy of Art in a Cross-Cultural Perspective?" *Journal of*

Aesthetics and Art Criticism 51 (1993): 425–436.

Morton, Brian. "Larps and Their Cousins Through the Ages." Jesper Donnis, Line Thorup, and Morten Gade, eds. *Lifelike.* Projektgruppen KP07, 2007. <http://www.liveforum.dk/kp07book/lifelike_web.pdf.>

Murphy, Sheila. *How Television Invented New Media.* New Brunswick, NJ: Rutgers University Press, 2010.

Murray, Janet Horowitz. *Hamlet on the Holodeck: The Future of Narrative in Cyberspace.* New York: Free Press, 1997.

Myers, Frederik W.H. "Glossary of Terms Used in Psychical Research." *Proceedings of the Society for Psychical Research* 12 (1897): 166–74.

Naples, Nancy. *Feminism and Method: Ethnography, Discourse Analysis, and Activist Research.* New York: Routledge, 2003.

Nephew, Michelle. "Playing with Identity." J. Patrick Williams, Sean Q. Hendricks, and W. Keith Winkler, eds. *Gaming as Culture: Essays on Reality, Identity and Experience in Fantasy Games.* Jefferson, NC: McFarland, 2006: 120–39.

Neto, Felix. "Conformity and Independence Revisited." *Social Behavior and Personality: An International Journal* 23.3 (1995): 217–222(6).

Neumann, Erich. *The Origins and History of Consciousness.* Princeton, NJ: Princeton University Press, 1970.

Nichols, Bill. "Reality TV and Social Perversion." Paul Marris and Sue Thornham, eds. *Media Studies: A Reader.* Edinburgh: Edinburgh University Press, 1996: 393–402.

Nicholson, Nigel, Steven Cole, and Thomas Rocklin. "Conformity in the Asch Situation: A Comparison Between Contemporary British and American University Students." *British Journal of Social Psychology* (1985).

Olson, Debbie Clare. "Babes in Bonanzaland: *Kid Nation*, Commodification, and the Death of Play." Julie Anne Taddeo and Ken Dvorak, eds. *The Tube Has Spoken: Reality TV and History.* Lexington: University of Kentucky Press, 2010: 171–194.

Orthner, D. K., and J. A. Mancini. "Leisure Impacts on Family Interactions and Cohesion." *Journal of Leisure Research* 22 (1990): 125–37.

Pearce, Celia. "Productive Play: Game Culture from the Bottom Up." *Games and Culture* 1.1 (2006): 17–24.

Pedersen, Bjarke. "Delirium: Insanity and Love Bleeding from Larp to Life." Jaakko Stenros and Markus Montola, eds. *Nordic Larp.* Stockholm: Fëa Livia, 2010.

Pelak, C.F. "Women's Collective Identity Formation in Sports: A Case Study of Women's Ice Hockey." *Gender and Society* 16 (2002): 93–114.

Perrin, Sean, and Charles Spencer. "The Asch Effect: A Child of Its Time?" *Bulletin of the British Psychological Society* (1980).

Peterson, Richard A., and D. Anand. "The Production of Culture Perspective." *Annual Review of Sociology* 30 (2011): 311–34.

Pinker, Steven. *How the Mind Works.* New York: Penguin Books, 1997.

_____. *The Language Instinct: How the Mind Creates Language.* New York: Harper Collins, 2007.

Pohjola, Mike. *The Manifesto of the Turku School.* (1999) <http://www2.uiah.fi/~mpohjola/turku/manifesto.html>. Accessed 1 August 2011.

_____. *The Turku Manifesto Turns Ten.* (2010). <http://mikepohjola2.wordpress.com/2010/02/23/the-turku-manifesto-turns-ten/> Accessed 1 August 2011.

Polletta, Francesca. "'It Was Like a Fever...': Narrative and Identity in Social Protest." *Social Problems* 45.2 (1998): 137–159.

_____, and James M. Jasper. "Collective Identity and Social Movements." *Annual Review of Sociology* 27 (2001): 283–305.

Poniewozik, James. "Why Reality TV Is Good for Us." *Time* (12 February 2003).

Poremba, Cindy. "Critical Potential on the Brink of the Magic Circle." *Proceedings of DiGRA 2007 Conference.* 2007.

Propp, Vladimir. *Morphology of the Folktale.* Lawrence Scott, trans. Austin: University of Texas Press, 1968.

Radford, Colin. "How Can We Be Moved by the Fate of Anna Karenina?" *Proceedings of the Aristotelian Society.* Supplemental Vol. 49 (1975): 67–80.

Raessens, Joost. "Playful Identities, or the Ludification of Culture." *Games and Culture* 1.1 (2006): 52–57.

Ramachandran, V.S., and William Hirstein. "The Science of Art: A Neurological Study of Aesthetic Experience." *Journal of Consciousness Studies* 6 (June/July 1999): 15–51.

Ranciere, Jacques. *The Future of the Image.* New York: Verso, 2007.

Reeves, Byron, and J. Leighton Read. *Games at Work: How Games and Virtual Worlds Are Changing the Way That People Work and*

Businesses Compete. Boston: Harvard Business School Publishing, 2009.

Rejack, Brian. "Toward a Virtual Reenactment of History: Video Games and the Recreation of the Past." *Rethinking History* 11.3 (2007): 411–25.

Rettberg, Scott. "Corporate Ideology in World of Warcraft." Hilde G. Corneliussen and Jill Walker Rettberg, eds. *Digital Culture, Play and Identity: A World of Warcraft Reader.* Cambridge, MA: MIT Press, 2008: 19–38.

Riley, David. "20 Percent of the U.S. Population, or 56.8 Million U.S. Consumers, Reports Having Played a Game on a Social Network." *NPD Group* (25 March 2011).

Roberts, Garyn G. "Introduction, Stories for the Millennium: Science Fiction and Fantasy as Contemporary Mythology." Garyn G. Roberts, ed. *The Prentice Hall Anthology of Science Fiction and Fantasy.* Upper Saddle River, NJ: Prentice Hall, 2003.

Robinson, Jenefer. *Deeper Than Reason: Emotion and Its Role in Literature, Music, and Art.* Oxford: Oxford University Press, 2005.

Rolston, Ken. "My Story Never Ends." Pat Harrigan and Noah Wardrip-Fruin, eds. *Third Person: Authoring and Exploring Vast Narratives.* Cambridge, MA: MIT Press, 2009: 119–130.

Rose, Frank. *The Art of Immersion: How the Digital Generation Is Remaking Hollywood.* New York: W.W. Norton, 2011.

Rushing, Janice Hocker, and Thomas S. Frentz. *Projecting the Shadow: The Cyborg Hero in American Film.* Chicago: University of Chicago Press, 1995.

Ryle, Gilbert. *The Concept of Mind.* Chicago: University of Chicago Press, 1949.

Salen, Katie, and Eric Zimmerman. *Rules of Play: Game Design Fundamentals.* Cambridge, MA: MIT Press, 2004.

Sartre, Jean-Paul. "Consciousness and the Other." Robert Denoon Cumming, ed. *The Philosophy of Jean-Paul Sartre.* New York: Random House, 1965.

Schechner, Richard. *Performance Theory.* New York: Routledge, 2003.

Schick, Laurie. "Breaking Frame in Role-Play Simulation: A Language Socialization Perspective." *Simulation & Gaming* 39.2 (2008): 184–97.

Schneider, Christian. "'Mauer-Shooter': Strafanzeige Gegen Entwickler Von '1378 Km'?" *Gamestar.De* (2010) <http://www.gamestar.de> Accessed 28 Jun 2011.

Schneider, Steven. "The Paradox of Fiction." *Internet Encyclopedia of Philosophy* (24 January 2002) <http://www.iep.utm.edu/fictpar>. Accessed 1 August 2011.

Shamdasani, Sonu. *"Liber Novus: The Red Book* by C.G. Jung." Carl Jung; Mark Kyburz and John Peck, trans. *Liber Novus: The Red Book.* New York: W. W. Norton, 2009.

Sheridan, Charles, and Richard King. "Obedience to Authority with an Authentic Victim." *Proceedings of the 80th Annual Convention of the American Psychological Association,* 1972.

Sherif, Muzafer. "A Study of Some Social Factors in Perception." *Archives of Psychology* 27.187 (1935).

Shorter, Bani. *An Image Darkly Forming: Women and Initiation.* London: Routledge and Kegan Paul, 1987.

Shuttleworth, Martyn. *Stanford Prison Experiment.* (2008) <http://experiment-resources.com> Accessed 20 November 2011.

Simkins, David W., and Constance Steinkuehler. "Critical Ethical Reasoning and Role-Play." *Games and Culture* 3.3-4 (2008): 333–355.

Slater, Mel, et al. "A Virtual Reprise of the Stanley Milgram Obedience Experiments." *PLoS One* 1.1 (2006) <http://doi:10.1371/journal.pone.0000039> Accessed 15 July 2011.

Smith, Charles F. *Games and Game Leadership.* New York: Dodd, Mead, 1934.

Smuts, Aaron. "The Paradox of Painful Art." *Journal of Aesthetic Education* 41.3 (Fall 2007): 59–76.

Snow, David A., and Doug McAdam. "Identity Work Processes in the Context of Social Movements: Clarifying the Identity/Movement Nexus." Sheldon Stryker, Timothy J. Owens and Robert W. White, eds. *Self, Identity and Social Movements.* Minneapolis: University of Minnesota Press, 2000: 41–67.

"So widerwärtig! Die Morde Am Todesstreifen Als Online-Spiel." *Bild* (28 Sept 2010).

Sobchack, Vivian. *Carnal Thoughts: Embodiment and Moving Image Culture.* Berkeley: University of California Press, 2004: 53–84.

Some, Malidoma Patrice. *Ritual: Power, Healing, and Community.* New York: Penguin Compass, 1997.

Spiegelman, Art. *Maus.* New York: Pantheon, 1986.

Stalp, M.C. "Negotiating Time and Space for

Serious Leisure: Quilting in the Modern U.S. Home." *Journal of Leisure Research* 8 (2006): 104–32.

Stam, Robert, Robert Burgoyne, and Sandy Flitterman-Lewis. *New Vocabularies in Film Semiotics.* New York: Routledge, 1992.

Stenros, Jaakko. "Nordic Larp. Theatre, Art and Game." Jaakko Stenros and Markus Montola, eds. *Nordic Larp.* Stockholm: Fëa Livia, 2010.

_____, and Markus Montola. *Nordic Larp.* Stockholm: Fëa Livia, 2010.

St. Pierre, Elizabeth A., and Wanda S. Pillow, eds. *Working the Ruins: Feminist Poststructural Theory and Methods in Education.* New York: Routledge, 2000.

Stryker, Sheldon. "Identity Competition: Key to Differential Social Movement Participation?" Sheldon Stryker, Timothy J. Owens and Robert W. White, eds. *Self, Identity and Social Movements.* Minneapolis: University of Minnesota Press, 2000: 21–40.

Suits, Bernard H. *The Grasshopper: Games, Life, and Utopia.* Toronto: University of Toronto Press, 1978.

"*Survivor* Recaps." CBS. <http://www.cbs.com/primetime/survivor/recaps/> Accessed 1 May 2011.

Swidler, Ann. "Culture in Action: Symbols and Strategies." *American Sociological Review* 51.2 (1986): 273–86.

_____. *Talk of Love: How Culture Matters.* Chicago: University of Chicago Press, 2001.

Tajfel, Henri. *Human Groups and Social Categories.* New York: Cambridge University Press, 1981.

Tamborini, Ron, and Paul Skalski. "The Role of Presence in the Experience of Electronic Games." Vorderer, Peter and Jennings Bryant, eds. *Playing Video Games: Motives, Responses, and Consequences.* Mahwah, NJ: Lawrence Erlbaum, 2006: 225–40.

Tavinor, Grant. *The Art of Videogames.* Malden, MA: Wiley-Blackwell, 2009.

Taylor, Paul A., and Jan LI. Harris. Theories of Mass Media: Then and Now. New York: Open University Press, 2008.

Tea, A.J.H., and B.P.H. Lee. "Reference and Blending in a Computer Role-Playing Game." *Journal of Pragmatics* 36 (2004): 1609–33.

Thomas, Douglas, and John Seely Brown. "Play of Imagination: Extending the Literary Mind." *Games and Culture* 2.2 (2007): 149–172.

Tomasello, Michael. Why We Cooperate. Cambridge, MA: MIT Press, 2009.

Torner, Evan. "The Theory and Practice of Larp in Non-Fiction Film." Thomas Duus Henriksen, et al., eds. *Think Larp: Academic Writings from KP2011.* Copenhagen, Denmark: Rollespilsakademiet, 2011: 104–123.

Tresca, Michael J. *The Evolution of Fantasy Role-Playing Games.* Jefferson, NC: McFarland, 2011.

Truffaut, Francois. "Une Certain Tendance Du Cinema Français." *Cahiers du Cinéma* 31. April (1954).

Turkington, Moyra. "Abandoning Immersion." *Sin Aesthetics.* (2006) <http://www.spaceanddeath.com/sin_aesthetics/2006/11/abandoning-immersion.html>. Accessed 1 August 2011.

_____. "Covering the Bases." *Sin Aesthetics.* (2006) <http://www.spaceanddeath.com/sin_aesthetics/2006/11/covering-bases.html>. Accessed August 1 2011.

Turner, Victor. *The Ritual Process: Structure and Anti-Structure.* New York: Aldine De Gruyter, 1995.

"Ucana's Alts and Puma Trying to Destroy Spymaster and Ruin the Fun for Others." *GetSatisfaction.com.* (2 September 2009). Web. Accessed 4 April 2010.

van Gennep, Arnold. *The Rites of Passage.* Trans. Monika Vizedom and Gabrielle Caffee. Chicago: University of Chicago Press, 1960.

Vernon, Mark. "What Would Carl Jung Make of 2011?" *BBC News Magazine* (6 June 2011). Web. Accessed 30 July 2011.

Vogler, Christopher. *The Writer's Journey: Mythic Structure for Writers.* Studio City, CA: Michael Wise Productions, 1998.

von Franz, M.-L. "The Process of Individuation." Carl G. Jung and M.-L. von Franz, eds. *Man and His Symbols.* London, UK: Dell Publishing, 1964.

Voorhees, Gerald, Joshua Call and Katie Whitlock, eds. *Dungeons, Dragons and Digital Denizens: Digital Role-Playing Games.* New York: Continuum, 2012.

Voth, Grant L. "The Continuing Importance of Myth." *Myth in Human History.* Course No. 2332. Audiobook. Purdue University, 2010.

_____. "Inanna and Dumuzi." *Myth in Human History.* Course No. 2332. Audiobook. Purdue University, 2010.

_____. "Myth and Meaning." *Myth in Human History.* Course No. 2332. Audiobook. Purdue University, 2010.

Voytilla, Stuart. *Myth and the Movies: Discov-*

ering the Mythic Structure of 50 Unforgettable Films. Studio City, CA: Michael Wise Productions, 1999.

Waern Annika. "I'm in Love with Someone That Doesn't Exist!! Bleed in the Context of a Computer Game." Stockholm University (2011) <http://www.mobilelifecentre.org/upload/publication/162/original/waern_final.pdf> Accessed 15 July 2011.

Waggoner, Zachary. My Avatar, My Self: Identity in Video Role-Playing Games. Jefferson, NC: McFarland, 2009.

Walton, Kendall. Mimesis as Make-Believe: On the Foundations of the Representational Arts. Cambridge, MA: Harvard University Press, 1990.

Wan, C. S., and W. B. Chiou. "Psychological Motives and Online Games Addiction: A Test of Flow Theory and Humanistic Needs Theory for Taiwanese Adolescents." Cyberpsychology & Behavior 9.3 (2006): 317–24.

Wang, C.K.J., et al. "Passion and Intrinsic Motivation in Digital Gaming." Cyberpsychology & Behavior 11.1 (2008): 39–45.

Waskul, Dennis D., and Matt Lust. "Role-Playing and Playing Roles: The Person, Player, and Persona in Fantasy Role-Playing." Symbolic Interaction 27.3 (2004): 333–56.

_____. "The Role-Playing Game and the Game of Role-Playing: The Ludic Self in Everyday Life." J. Patrick Williams, Sean Q. Hendricks, and W. Keith Winkler, eds. Gaming as Culture: Essays on Reality, Identity and Experience in Fantasy Games. Jefferson, NC: McFarland, 2006.

Webley, Paul. "A Partial and Non-Evaluative History of the Asch Effect." Exeter University <http://people.exeter.ac.uk/PWebley/psy1002/asch.html>. Accessed 20 November 2011.

Wenger, Etienne. Communities of Practice: Learning, Meaning, and Identity. New York: Cambridge University Press, 1998.

Westlund, Aksel. "The Storyteller's Manifesto." Markus Montola and Jaakko Stenros, eds. Beyond Role and Play. Helsinki, Finland: Ropecon ry, 2004: 249–57.

White, Bill. "Blurring the Boundaries: Structured Freeform in the Indie RPG Design Community." Amber Eagar, ed. Journeys to Another World: Companion to the 2010 Larp Summit at Wyrdcon. Costa Mesa, CA: LARP Alliance, 2010: 17–24.

Williams, Dmitri. "Why Study Games Now? Gamers Don't Bowl Alone." Games and Culture 1.1 (2006): 13–16.

Williams, J. Patrick, Sean Q. Hendricks, and W. Keith Winkler, eds. Gaming as Culture: Essays on Reality, Identity and Experience in Fantasy Games. Jefferson, NC: McFarland, 2006.

Williams, Linda. "Film Bodies: Gender, Genre, and Excess." Film Quarterly 44.4 (1991): 2–13.

Williams, Rhys H. "Social Movements and Culture." George Ritzer, ed. Blackwell Encyclopedia of Sociology. Malden, MA: Blackwell, 2007: 954–955.

Willis, Paul E. Common Culture: Symbolic Work at Play in the Everyday Cultures of the Young. Boulder, CO: Westview Press, 1990.

Winkler, W. Keith. "The Business and Culture of Gaming." J. Patrick Williams, Sean Q. Hendricks, and W. Keith Winkler, eds. Gaming as Culture: Essays on Reality, Identity and Experience in Fantasy Games. Jefferson, NC: McFarland, 2006.

Wolf, Mark J.P. The Medium of the Video Game. Austin: University of Texas Press, 2002.

"Working on Updates and Fixes." GetSatisfaction.com. (19 Oct. 2009) Web. Accessed 4 April 2010.

Wright, J. Talmadge, David G. Embrick, and András Lukács, eds. Utopic Dreams and Apocalyptic Fantasies: Critical Approaches to Researching Video Game Play. Lanham, MD: Lexington Books, 2010.

Wrigstad, Tobias. "The Nuts and Bolts of Jeepform." Markus Montola & Jaakko Stenros, eds. Playground Worlds. Ropecon, 2008. <http://www.ropecon.fi/pw>

Young, M. Joseph. Theory 101: System and the Shared Imagined Space. (2005) <http://ptgptb.org/0026/theory101-01.html>. Accessed 1 August 2011.

Zimbardo, Philip G. "A Simulation Study of the Psychology of Imprisonment Conducted at Stanford University." (1999) <http://www.prisonexp.org>. Accessed 20 November 2011.

_____. The Lucifer Effect. Understanding How Good People Turn Evil. New York: Random House, 2007.

_____, Christina Maslach, and Craig Haney. "Chapter 11: Reflections on the Stanford Prison Experiment: Genesis, Transformations, Consequences." (1999) <www.prisonexp.org/pdf/blass.pdf> Accessed 20 November 2011.

Žižek, Slavoj. Violence. New York: Picador, 2008.

Zunshine, Lisa. Why We Read Fiction? Theory

of Mind and the Novel. Columbus: Ohio State University Press, 2006.

Games, Images and Audiovisual Media

Advanced Dungeons and Dragons Players Handbook. E. Gary Gygax. Lake Geneva, WI: TSR, 1978.

Amber Diceless Role-Playing Game. Erick Wujcik. Phage Press, 1991.

American Idol. Created by Simon Fuller. Fox, 2002–present. Television.

Apocalypse World. Dev. Vincent Baker. Greenfield, MA: lumpley games, 2010.

Back to the Future. Dir. Robert Zemeckis. Universal Pictures, 1985. Film.

Battle Royale. Dir. Kinji Fukusaku. Toei, 2000. Film.

Bejeweled. Dev. PopCap Games, 2001. Video Game.

Brothers in Arms: Road to Hill 30. Dev. Gearbox Software. Ubisoft, 2005. Video Game.

Café World. Dev. Zynga, 2009. Video Game.

Call of Duty: Black Ops. Game Des. Corky Lehmukuhl, David Vonderhaar, Joe Chiang. Activision, 2010. Video Game.

Castle Wolfenstein. Game Des. Silas Warner. Muse Software, 1981. Video Game.

Clive Barker's Jericho. Game Des. Clive Barker, Joe Falke. Codemasters, 2007. Video Game.

Dead Snow. Dir. Tommy Wirkola. Euforia Film, 2009. Film.

Education for Death. Dir. Clyde Geronimi. RKO Radio Pictures, 1943. Film.

Enter the Void. Dir. Gaspar Noé. Fidélité Films, 2010. Film.

Epic Mickey. Game Des. Warren Spector. Disney Interactive Studios, Nintendo, 2010. Video Game.

Fargo. Dir. Joel and Ethan Coen. Polygram Filmed Entertainment, 1996. Film.

Farmville. Dev. Zynga, 2009. Video Game.

Fiasco. Jason Morningstar. Chapel Hill, NC: Bully Pulpit Games, 2009.

Full Metal Village. Dir. Sung-Hyung. Flying Moon Filmproduktion, 2006. Film.

He's Watching You. Glenn Grother. (1942) <http://www.propagandaposters.us/ poster 11.html> Accessed 22 November 2011.

Kid Nation. Forman, Thomas and Jack Cannon. CBS. Aired: 19 September–12 December 2007.

Half-Life 2: Death Match. Valve Corporation, 2004. Video Game.

Holocaust. Dir. Marvin Chomsky. Perf. Meryl Streep, Tom Bell. NBC. 1978. Television.

The Hunger Games. Dir. Gary Ross. Lionsgate, 2012. Film.

(Lil) Green Patch. Dev. David King and Ashish Dixit, 2008. Video Game.

Mafia Wars. Zynga, 2009. Video Game.

Medal of Honor: Underground. Dev. DreamWorks Interactive. Electronic Arts, 2000. Video Game.

Mortal Kombat 9. Dev. NetherRealm Studios. Time Warner, 2011. Video Game.

1378(km). Game Des. Jens M. Stober. eLorx, 2010. Video Game.

Raiders of the Lost Ark. Dir. Steven Spielberg. Perf. Harrison Ford, Karen Allen. Paramount Pictures, 1981.

Return to Castle Wolfenstein. Game Des. Richard Farrelly. Activision, 2001. Video Game.

Saving Private Ryan. Dir. Steven Spielberg. Perf. Tom Hanks, Matt Damon, Tom Sizemore. DreamWorks, 1998. Film.

Scenariebogen. 9 fremragende danske rollespilsscenarier 2006–2010. Frikard Ellemand, Morten Greis Petersen & Klaus Meier Olsen. Copenhagen: Rollespilsakademiet, 2011.

A Simple Plan. Dir. Sam Raimi. Paramount Pictures, 1998. Film.

The Sims. Will Wright. Maxis, 2000. Video Game.

Sorcerer. Ron Edwards. Chicago: Adept Press, 2001.

"The Soup Nazi." *Seinfeld.* NBC. 1995. Television.

Spymaster. Chris Ibad and Eston Bond, 2009. Video Game.

Super Columbine Massacre RPG! Danny Ledonne, 2005. Video Game.

Super Mario Bros. Dev. Nintendo, 1985. Video Game.

Survivor: The Australian Outback (2001): "Let's Make a Deal." *Survivor: The Australian Outback.* Episode 10. CBS. 5 April 2001; "Enough Is Enough." *Survivor: The Australian Outback.* Episode 12. CBS. 19 April 2001; "The Most Deserving." *Survivor: The Australian Outback.* Episode 14. CBS. 3 May 2001.

Survivor: Cook Islands (2006): "Plan Voodoo." *Survivor: Cook Islands.* Episode 6. CBS. 19 October 2006; "People that You Like Want to See You Suffer." *Survivor: Cook Islands.* Episode 9. CBS. 16 November 2006; "You're a Rat..." *Survivor: Cook Islands.* Episode 11. CBS. 30 November 2006.

Survivor: Gabon (2008): "He's a Snake, but

He's My Snake." *Survivor: Gabon.* Episode 6. CBS. 23 October 2008; "It All Depends on the Pin-up Girl." *Survivor: Gabon.* Episode 7. CBS. 30 October 2008; "Nothing Tastes Better Than 500 Dollars." *Survivor: Gabon.* Episode 10. CBS. 20 November 2008; "Say Goodbye to Gabon." *Survivor: Gabon.* Episode 13. CBS. 14 December 2008.

Survivor: Guatemala (2005): "Big Trek, Big Trouble, Big Surprise." *Survivor: Guatemala.* Episode 1. CBS. 15 September 2005; "Man Down." *Survivor: Guatemala.* Episode 2. CBS. 22 September 2005.

Survivor: Nicaragua (2010): "Young at Heart." *Survivor: Nicaragua.* Episode 1. CBS. 15 September 2010; "Fatigue Makes Cowards of Us All." *Survivor: Nicaragua.* Episode 2. CBS. 22 September 2010; "Glitter in their Eyes." *Survivor: Nicaragua.* Episode 3. CBS. 29 September 2010; "What Goes Around Comes Around." *Survivor: Nicaragua.* Episode 7. CBS. 27 October 2010; "Company Will Be Arriving Soon." *Survivor: Nicaragua.* Episode 8. CBS. 3 November 2010.

Survivor: Palau (2005): "Love Is in the Air, Rats Are Everywhere." *Survivor: Palau.* Episode 2. CBS. 24 February 2005.

Survivor: Panama Exile Island (2006): "Crazy Fights, Snake Dinners." *Survivor: Panama Exile Island* Episode 3. CBS. 16 February 2006; "An Emerging Plan." *Survivor: Panama Exile Island* Episode 7. CBS. 30 March 2006; "The Power of the Idol." *Survivor: Panama Exile Island.* Episode 8. CBS. 6 April 2006; "Fight for Your Life or Eat."

Survivor: Panama Exile Island. Episode 9. CBS. 13 April 2006.

Survivor: Pearl Islands (2003): "To Quit or Not to Quit." *Survivor: Pearl Islands.* Episode 2. CBS. 25 September 2003; "United We Stand, Divided We ?" *Survivor: Pearl Islands.* Episode 3. CBS. 2 October 2003; "What the...? Part One.." *Survivor: Pearl Islands.* Episode 7. CBS. 30 October 2003; "The Great Lie." *Survivor: Pearl Islands.* Episode 11. CBS. 26 November 2003; "Flames and Endurance." *Survivor: Pearl Islands.* Episode 14. CBS. 14 December 2003; "Reunion." *Survivor: Pearl Islands.* Episode 15. CBS. 14 December 2003.

Survivor: Samoa (2009): "The Puppet Master." *Survivor: Samoa.* Episode 1. CBS. 17 September 2009; "All Hell Breaks Loose." *Survivor: Samoa.* Episode 8. CBS. 5 November 2009; "The Game Ain't Over." *Survivor: Samoa.* Episode 14. CBS. 20 December 2009.

Survivor: Tocantins (2009): "The Martyr Approach." *Survivor: Tocantins.* Episode 12. CBS. 14 May 2009.

Traveller. Marc Miller. Mongoose, 1977.

Vampire: The Masquerade. Graeme Davis, Tom Dowd, Mark Rein-Hagen, Lisa Stevens, and Stewart Wieck, 2nd Ed. Stone Mountain, GA: White Wolf, 1992.

Wolfenstein. Dev. Raven Software. Activision, 2009. Video Game.

Wolfenstein 3D. Dev. id Software. Apogee Software, 1992. Video Game.

World of Warcraft. Dev. Blizzard Entertainment, 2004. Video Game.

About the Contributors

Emily Care **Boss** is a writer, game designer and forester living in western Massachusetts and has independently published games since 2005. Her game *Under My Skin* won the Player's Choice Otto award at Fastaval in Denmark. She has been published in *Playground Worlds* and *Push: Volume 1 New Thinking About Roleplaying*. Her games can be found at Black & Green Games (blackgreengames.com).

Sarah Lynne **Bowman** received her Ph.D. from the University of Texas at Dallas in 2008 and is an adjunct professor at Ashford University and Richland College. She published *The Functions of Role-Playing Games: How Participants Create Community, Solve Problems and Explore Identity* (McFarland 2010). Her research focuses upon understanding social conflict within role-playing communities and applying Jungian theory to character enactment and narrative creation.

Erik **Dulick** is a recent graduate of Juniata College, where he received a B.S. in business and organizational administration. After graduating, he relocated to the Boston area and is pursuing post-graduate work combining his interests in business and music.

Todd Nicholas **Fuist** is a Ph.D. candidate in sociology at Loyola University, Chicago. His work is on religious communities that have messages and projects which revolve around social justice. His other academic interests include gaming and gamer culture, social movements, media, and identity.

J. Tuomas **Harviainen** is a Finnish chief librarian, game studies researcher and designer, who specializes in live-action role-playing. His mini-larps have been run in at least 14 countries, used as training tools in schools and universities, and been translated into seven languages. He is finishing a doctoral dissertation at the University of Tampere, Finland, on role-playing games as information systems, and is an editor at the *International Journal of Role-Playing*.

M.-Niclas **Heckner** is pursuing a joint doctoral degree between the Department of Screen Arts and Cultures and the Department of Germanic Languages and Literatures at the University of Michigan, Ann Arbor. He received an M.A. in English and German from the University of Freiburg. His interests lie in the reappropriation of historical iconography by popular and mass culture (e.g., the swastika).

Jussi **Holopainen** is a Finnish game scholar whose main research focus has been on design and player experience principles for games of all kinds. He has long worked at the Nokia Research Center in Tampere. His publications include *Patterns in Game Design* coauthored with Staffan Björk and numerous conference and journal papers as well as various book chapters.

Nathan **Hook** is a master's degree student studying psychology research methods with The Open University. He is using an ethnographic approach to study identity construction by recreational role-players and emotional bleed from fictive play experiences. He lives in Bristol, United Kingdom; his website is www.nathanhook. netii.net

Katherine Castiello **Jones** is a Ph.D. candidate in sociology (researching three American groups promoting abstinence until marriage) at the University of Massachusetts Amherst, from which she has a graduate certificate in advanced feminist studies. Her article "The Possibilities Are Endless: Creating New Worlds in an All-Woman Game" is in the August 2010 *RPGirl* zine. Her research interests include culture, gender and sexualities.

Markus **Montola** is a doctoral candidate in the School of Information Sciences at the University of Tampere, Finland. He is an author of *Pervasive Games: Theory and Design* (2009), and an editor of three books on larp; *Nordic Larp* (2010), *Playground Worlds* (2008) and *Beyond Role and Play* (2004). He is writing a doctoral dissertation on the various forms of role-playing and pervasive gaming.

Eric **Newsom** is a Ph.D. candidate in the Department of Language, Literature and Communication at Rensselaer Polytechnic Institute. His research interests include creative communities and new media production and his dissertation focuses on how recent forms of digital storytelling draw on practices of oral tradition.

Evan **Torner** is a Ph.D. candidate in German and film studies at the University of Massachusetts Amherst. He is finishing his dissertation on representations of race and the global South in East German genre cinema. He has written on modernist film, German science-fiction literature and live-action role-playing, and is the official translator of the Filmmuseum Potsdam's permanent exhibit "100 Years of Babelsberg."

William J. **White** is an associate professor of communication arts and sciences at Penn State Altoona, where he teaches speech communication and mass media courses. He received a Ph.D. from Rutgers University in communication, information and library studies. His research interests include communication theory and the rhetoric of science and science fiction. He is the designer of the small-press tabletop RPG *Ganakagok*.

Index